NO GLOSSING C

Gary Edwards is the author of two football-related memoirs, *Paint It White: Following Leeds Everywhere* and *Leeds United: The Second Coat*, and is a columnist for the club's match-day programmes. *Paint It White* was recently made into a stage play and, after a sold-out three-week run in Leeds, it will be touring nationwide in autumn 2011.

NO GLOSSING OVER IT

HOW FOOTBALL CHEATED LEEDS UNITED

GARY EDWARDS

MAINSTREAM
PUBLISHING

EDINBURGH AND LONDON

First published in Great Britain in 2011 by

MAINSTREAM PUBLISHING COMPANY

(EDINBURGH) LTD

7 Albany Street

Edinburgh EH1 3UG

ISBN 9781845967826

A catalogue record for this book is available from the British Library

Printed in Great Britain by

CPI Mackays, Chatham ME5 8TD

1 3 5 7 9 10 8 6 4 2

To Vicky, Ste and Charlie, and to Wub

Each Dog Has Its Day

Time slides by like grains of sand
And each contains a thousand tears
And each grain holds a thousand dreams
And each grain holds a thousand fears
That multiply throughout the years

But Lady Luck is just a whore
Who lazes languid in her bed
Who turns each card to seal our fate
Who lets strange thoughts creep through our heads
Whilst all the time we've been misled

Truth is scarce when times are lean
And we've been starved for decades past
And we've been dragged right through the mire
And we've been cheated, left aghast
A two-horse race where we came last

The names all conjure memories
Like Paris, Tinkler, Sunderland
Like Cardiff, Wembley, Munich too
Like Christos Michas, AC Milan
Let's not forget Kitabdjian

But LEEDS UNITED sing the fans
As old school ties still bar our way
As honours boards don't bear our name
As dodgy refs are led astray
Remember, each dog has its day

Gary Kaye, poet and folk singer

Acknowledgements

Duncan Revie is fiercely protective and rightly proud of his dad's reputation. When I contacted him regarding this book, he was understandably guarded in his response. As we chatted and I told him the rough outline of the book, I mentioned my contempt for many journalists (and referees) who openly hate Leeds United, in particular Richard Stott and more recently Patrick Collins of the *Mail on Sunday*. My forceful defence of Leeds struck a chord and Duncan interrupted me. 'Gary,' he said, 'you can have anything you want.' I am grateful for all his input, and to his staff at Soccerex, in particular Gina Mazzarelli, Duncan's PA, for keeping me in contact with an extremely busy man. Special thanks go also to Dave 'Junior' Cocker, the great Les Cocker's son, whose recollections, insights and memories were invaluable.

I would like to thank Tony Peart for his priceless assistance – a massive contribution. Once again, Neil Jeffries' guidance was pivotal. Many thanks to all the referees who responded to my requests with some absolutely brilliant stories. Of course, I'm indebted to the many members of Don Revie's legendary team who have generously contributed and to the coach driver of those 'crown jewels', Jim Lister. Huge thanks also to Gary Kaye, Rob Endeacott, David Peace, Paul Dews, Phil Hay, Paul Robinson, Steve Riding, Andrew Varley, Jeff Verrill, Alan Osborne, Sandra King, Trevor Cusack, Andy Starmore, Mick Hewitt, Mike Stoddart, Roger Furnandiz, Dick Skellington, Hamish Boyle, Glynn Snodin, Rod Johnson, Nigel Davey, Mike O'Grady, Peter Lorimer, Duncan McKenzie, John Sheridan, Steve Riding, Richard Sutcliffe, Brendan Ormsby, Jim Cadman, Graham Ibbeson, Stu Wheatman and Damian Taylor, and a special mention to Eddie Gray.

Contents

Foreword

This is a must-read book that investigates the many injustices suffered by Leeds United over the past 40-odd years. It also examines the adverse publicity suffered by our manager Don Revie, which continues to this day, and asks if it is really a true reflection of a very misunderstood man.

Some people would say that Leeds fans are paranoid, but what is said in this book is totally justified. Over the years, victories in European finals and crucial league and cup games have been snatched from Leeds as a result of controversial decisions, and it's all recounted here. Leeds United have a phenomenal network of fans worldwide, and I strongly believe that these travesties suffered by Leeds United are one of the reasons for the loyalty of their support.

The author is a lifelong Leeds fan and, as you read the book, you will witness his unswerving passion for the club. Whether you agree with him or not, he and other Leeds fans are in no way looking for sympathy from outside the club; they just want a chance to put the record straight on a few things.

Don Revie built this club up from nothing. He had a vision, which many, including some of the players, mocked at the time, of turning Leeds United into one of the best teams in Europe. You will read how he achieved that – 100 per cent – and about why all the players who ever worked for 'the Gaffer' will tell you without hesitation that he was the greatest manager they ever played for.

Enjoy the read.

Eddie Gray

1. An Unfair Game

At just after 7 a.m. on Saturday, 29 April 1967, I climbed aboard a battered old sky-blue Ford Transit minibus. At 11 years old, I was easily the youngest passenger amongst my dad and 11 other blokes, most of them smoking heavily, coughing, spluttering, belching and farting. I remember hearing the birds singing and watching a pale sun just starting to poke its head above the horizon, and as I looked at the driver I noticed he was wearing spectacles with the thickest lenses you would ever see. He wheezed as he leaned over the steering wheel and wiped his windscreen. I secretly prayed that the sun wouldn't come out just yet, as I was sure that its rays shining through those thick lenses would burn his eyes out in an instant. Not that it would have made much difference; I quickly found out that a bat had better eyesight than Mr Toes, and we spent more time on the pavements than on the road.

Even at that tender age, I knew the importance of the football match we were travelling to: it was the FA Cup semi-final at Villa Park between Leeds United and Chelsea. On the bus that morning with Dad and me was Mr Jim King, who used to follow Leeds home and away. Mr King had moved down to Leeds from the Durham area in the 1950s, seeking work down the Yorkshire mines, and he had quickly adopted Leeds United as his team. His two sons were Leeds fans, too. The elder, Melvyn, later accompanied me on many trips around the country. The younger son, Malcolm, began life as a Man City fan, purely because of a TV programme called *The Dustbinmen*. It featured a character called Winston who was a fanatical City fan and wore a denim jacket with the names of all the City players written on it in white paint. It only took a few months to persuade Malcolm that his loyalty should be placed elsewhere, namely just six miles away down at Elland Road. Sadly, in 1991, days before Malcolm and I were due to fly to Tokyo to watch Leeds United in an exhibition game, he was killed down the local mine, aged just 31.

In the aisle of the minibus there were a couple of wooden crates full of bottles of Worthington E, which were quickly handed out as we began what was then the long journey south to Birmingham. I was handed an apple.

My apple was reduced to a small, wrinkled and brown core lying in the ashtray in the back of the seat in front of me by the time we finally arrived at Villa Park. Rosettes were very popular at the time, and there were hundreds for sale around the ground. Mr King was a giant of a man who hardly ever showed any emotion at all, so I was thrilled when he bought me a 'Leeds United for the Cup' rosette and pinned it to my jacket. He never said a word, but there was just the slightest hint of a smile on his face. And it had saved my dad a shilling.

A while later, with just under a minute left to play, that smile of Mr King's turned to sheer delight as Peter Lorimer fired home from 25 yards to equalise for Leeds United.

Leeds had fallen behind earlier to a Tony Hateley header, but after a Terry Cooper effort had been ruled marginally offside Leeds threw everyone forward in the closing stages. Bobby Tambling pulled back Norman Hunter as he surged forward, and Johnny Giles placed the ball down for the free kick about a yard in from the touchline and close to the edge of the penalty area. Chelsea's defensive wall was not quite ten yards from the ball, but referee Ken Burns clearly signalled for the kick to be taken. Giles rolled the ball inside to Lorimer, who dispatched a blazing shot past the outstretched arms of Chelsea keeper Peter Bonetti and into the top right-hand corner of the goal.

Mr King picked me up and literally launched me up into the air. Leeds fans all around us went mad. Then there was total confusion as Ken Burns signalled for the kick to be retaken. The Leeds players couldn't believe it, and neither, it seemed, could the Chelsea players. Apparently, Burns had disallowed the goal because the Chelsea wall was not ten yards back.

Later that night, the BBC's Kenneth Wolstenholme said on *Match of the Day* of Lorimer's 'goal', 'He's disallowed it. He's disallowed it. He's disallowed it. He has disallowed it . . . And I think you would have to look at the rulebook backwards to find a reason why.'

Leeds defender Paul Reaney, speaking about the incident on an episode of Sky Sports' *Time of Our Lives* in 2009, said:

> In those days, the referee would come into the dressing-rooms before the game. He'd have five minutes with each team just to tell us what he would allow and what he wouldn't. That particular day, the ref, Ken Burns, said, 'If you want to take a quick free kick, just take it and get on with it.' And that's why we were so disgusted about what happened – because that's exactly what he told us we could do. There was only a minute to go. The game was dead and buried, really. But the Chelsea wall would not go back – as we wouldn't have. We'd have wasted time just as they were doing.
>
> So . . . we took our free kick, on Ken Burns' say-so, when they were less than ten yards away – Johnny Giles passed the ball and Peter scored. We argued with Burns, but he made us retake it. And still they wouldn't go back, and this time we didn't score. Who knows what would have happened if we'd have equalised?

In support of Reaney's comments, TV footage of the game clearly shows Burns whistling and gesturing for the free kick to be taken.

Behind the goal, the Leeds fans were still going berserk, and I looked at Mr King. The biggest veins I have ever seen were protruding from his forehead and neck as he seethed at the referee, waving one of his almighty fists in anger. I honestly thought his head was going to explode.

In his book *A Football Man*, Johnny Giles, who squared the ball to Peter Lorimer, said:

> The referee Ken Burns disallowed [the goal], claiming that he did not give the signal for the kick to be taken as the Chelsea defenders were not standing ten yards from the ball. Yet it is clear from television pictures that several seconds had elapsed between the time the referee awarded the kick and the moment I took it, and that the Chelsea players themselves seemed to think they'd had enough time, because none of them appealed to the ref when the goal was scored, and a couple of them had their heads in their hands in grief.

Recently, I wrote to Ken Burns at his home in Stourbridge. After initially agreeing to contribute his side of the story of that day at Villa Park, he suddenly broke off communications.

This dreadful incident certainly wasn't been the last time that Leeds were dealt a bad hand by the authorities, and it wasn't the first time, either. For that, you would have to go back to 1919.

On 9 November 1912, right-back Charlie Copeland made his debut for United's predecessors Leeds City. Their opponents that day were Glossop, who were easily disposed of 4–0. Copeland went on to make 44 appearances for City before the club came to an abrupt end in July 1919.

During the First World War, it was commonplace for teams up and down the country to pay 'guest players' to appear in their line-up. Leeds City were no exception, and amongst their guests were the great Charlie Buchan from Sunderland and Fanny Walden of Tottenham Hotspur, both England internationals. Although technically against FA rules, payments to guest players were widespread.

Leeds City were a fine side and it was during this period that they established a club record by beating Nottingham Forest 8–0, on 29 November 1913 in front of 14,000 at Elland Road.

By the start of the 1919–20 season, Charlie Copeland was in dispute with the club. Backed by his solicitor, James Bromley, a former Leeds City director, Copeland claimed that the club owed him money after they had allegedly offered him a pay rise. City refused his demands, stating that no further payments would be made until he became a first-team regular. Copeland knew about the payments to wartime guest players and threatened to expose the club to the Football League unless they met his demands. City refused, and in July 1919 Copeland apparently carried out his threat, although years later he would deny passing on the information.

A joint inquiry held by the Football League and the Football Association demanded to see City's records. It is unclear to this day why, but City refused to produce their books and, after a second request and a further refusal by City, the club was expelled from the Football League and disbanded.

There were many theories as to why City refused to hand over their records. One was that they wanted to protect the guest players involved or indeed to protect themselves. Many years after the event, however,

League chairman John McKenna went on record as saying that he had much sympathy with Leeds City and added, 'Perhaps others have escaped being found guilty of malpractice, but if they are found out now we shall not stand on ceremony or sentiment.' No other team was ever charged with similar activities.

Port Vale swiftly moved into the place vacated by City, but only a few short hours after an auction to sell off Leeds City lock, stock and barrel, moves were being made to build a new team in Leeds. More than 1,000 diehard fans from the Leeds United Supporters Club held a meeting at Salem Hall out of which Leeds United Football Club was founded. The club was elected to the Football League on 31 May 1920. Newly formed Leeds United may have thought they had shaken off the ghost of Leeds City and all its controversy, but this was to be only the beginning. Indeed, controversial decisions were to dog Leeds throughout the glory years of Don Revie and beyond, as we shall see.

2. The Middle Man

In mid-April 1971, almost two years after their first league title, United were on course to lift the championship trophy once again. With only four games remaining, a home fixture against lowly West Bromwich Albion appeared to pose no threat to United's title hopes.

Peter Lorimer says, 'I had a slight strain, and the Gaffer [Don Revie] decided to rest me and Paul Madeley for the game, which, to be honest, should have been a foregone conclusion.'

At around midday on 17 April, Ray Tinkler would have left his home in Boston, Lincolnshire, and driven north up the A1. Tinkler was to referee at Elland Road that afternoon.

Around an hour later, my dad, I and around eight or nine mates clambered into my dad's 18-cwt Thames Dormobile. Leeds scarves hung from every window. As we drove away from 28 The Drive, Kippax, we sang at the top of our voices: 'We're gonna win the league! We're gonna win the league! And now you're gonna believe us, now you're gonna believe us, now you're gonna believe us! We're gonna win the league!' Around this time, Tinkler would have been driving along the A63, less than a mile from Kippax, and on towards Leeds via the A64.

During this period, Dad and I had season tickets for the West Stand. When we arrived at the ground, the rest of the lads went into the boys' pen in the Lowfields Road Stand and we went to take up our seats in the opposite stand. Just below us, Tinkler would have been changing into his authoritative black uniform and would soon begin briefing his linesmen.

Then, in front of a crowd of just under 37,000, Tinkler blew his whistle and Leeds kicked off, starting brightly and going very close to scoring on a couple of occasions. Mick Jones had one effort kicked off the line and Allan Clarke hit the bar.

Surely it was only a matter of time until Leeds broke down the resilient Albion defence? Even when the visitors went a shock goal up, there seemed to be no danger of Leeds losing this game. In those days, whenever the opposition scored against Leeds, especially at Elland Road, it only seemed to spur United on, and usually within minutes the scoreline had been reversed. But today was going to be different.

In the second half, Norman Hunter lost the ball on the halfway line. It fell to Tony Brown, who charged upfield, but his teammate Colin Suggett was in an offside position yards in front of play. The linesman on the Lowfields Road side, Bill Troupe, immediately raised his flag. Everyone on the pitch stopped. Then, to the bewilderment of the crowd, Tinkler waved play on and, almost apologetically, Brown continued on his run. As he entered the Leeds area, he passed to Jeff Astle, who was also offside. Astle, looking more surprised than anyone else in the ground, took full advantage of a further 'play on' from the referee and slotted the ball past Gary Sprake.

The crowd literally couldn't believe it, and the noise of the booing and hissing was at a level I had never witnessed before in my life. Amidst all this, Tinkler remained calm; he brushed his thinning hair across his head with his fingers and walked towards the centre spot in readiness for the restart as if nothing had happened. He ignored the linesman's flag, which was still up in the air, and then several people ran onto the pitch. Johnny Giles recalled in *A Football Man* that the people who invaded the pitch weren't hooligans. 'There were a lot of middle-aged, middle-class men involved, ordinary respectable people who had been driven mad by this blatant injustice.'

Incidentally, the situation was so intense that one of those arrested for invading the pitch was Dave Cocker, son of Leeds' trainer Les Cocker. 'I got a right bollocking off Dad and Don for that!' says Dave.

The next to enter the field was the linesman Bill Troupe, who presumably wanted to tell Mr Tinkler he had got his decision wrong. Troupe later said, 'It was clearly offside, twice. I put my flag up and would do so again.' Mr Troupe intercepted a large missile thrown from the crowd with his head. 'Sorry, mate. That was obviously meant for Tinkler,' said Les Cocker as he tended to the official's injuries.

Don Revie, in a large overcoat and thick leather gloves, with a blanket over his arm, followed the linesman onto the pitch. As Troupe,

Revie and most of the Leeds players protested to Tinkler, supporters were being led away by police. Tinkler waved everyone away. That evening on BBC's *Match of the Day*, commentator Barry Davies watched Revie shaking his head and walking off the field and told the millions of viewers, 'Just look at Don Revie, a sickened man. Look at him looking up at the heavens in disgust.'

With the score standing at 2–0, the crowd were stunned into disbelief. Then, with only two minutes left on the clock, Clarke pulled one back. But when the final whistle blew, the score remained 2–1 to West Brom. Even the Albion players looked embarrassed as they left the field.

Many years later, appearing on *Fantasy Football League* with Frank Skinner and David Baddiel, Jeff Astle laughed as he said, 'Of course it was offside. Everyone could see that. Well, almost everyone!' During one of his one-man comedy shows in Leeds, comedian and lifelong West Brom fan Frank Skinner's opening line was, 'It wasn't offside, you know.' He then started laughing. Even though the match had happened more than 30 years ago, most of the audience knew what Frank was on about. Luckily for him, the people of Leeds were in a forgiving mood that evening.

Johnny Giles, speaking on the BBC video *Leeds United: The Glory Years 1965–1975*, commented:

> What hadn't been highlighted on the television was that it was a vital game for us, because we were going neck and neck with Arsenal for the league title, and it was a home game we were expected to win. Also, just prior to that decision, Eddie Gray pulled the ball back for Mick Jones to score. The goal was promptly disallowed for offside, even though the ball had been pulled back and Jones was behind the ball and with a defender in front of him.

As the *Match of the Day* audience watched the goal being disallowed, Barry Davies commented, 'Leeds will go mad. And they have every right to go mad!' Outside the ground after the game, thousands of irate Leeds fans filled the West Stand car park hoping to get a glimpse or a piece of Ray Tinkler. Two hours later, he still hadn't come out of the stadium, and the crowd was eventually dispersed by mounted police. Tinkler never refereed Leeds again.

Peter Lorimer: 'As I wasn't playing that day, I was at home waiting for the results like everyone else. As the television teleprinter revealed the score from Elland Road, I couldn't believe my eyes. Then the national news came on and the main story of the day was the events at Elland Road.'

Leeds went on to win their three remaining games, including one against Arsenal, but lost the league by one point. They had a better goal average than Arsenal, so a win or a draw that day against West Brom would have secured Leeds' second league-title success.

Leeds' full-back that day, Paul Reaney, said some time later:

> That single decision cost us the league that year. I've come to the conclusion that, today, professional players should be able to meet with refs and see what they have to put up with and refs should come to us and see what we practise. We were deliberately playing the offside trap and I was the last man, so I know Jeff Astle was two yards offside. Tony Brown was, too, and he was still offside even though I was chasing him; I never caught him. But Brown played a forward pass from which Jeff scored. As soon as Jeff went forward, the linesman put his flag up. But the referee said play on. Astle scored, they won 2–1 and we lost the league by one point. When you get decisions like that, you think, 'These decisions cost you a full season of work.' And when you've been runners-up five times and won it twice, you do get to thinking, 'Wouldn't it have been better if we'd won four?' or whatever. But if you think about that, you could go mad.

Tinkler would later claim that Suggett, although fully ten yards offside, was not interfering with play. That would be true in today's game, but back then it was deemed offside – end of story.

Despite countless phone calls, letters and emails to his office, Ray Tinkler refuses point-blank to speak with me about that Saturday afternoon back in 1971. But in an article in *The Guardian* in 2009, he blamed Bill Troupe for not putting his flag down:

> My linesman raised his flag straight away but I waved him down – the ball never went anywhere near Suggett. He saw my signal, but the problem was he didn't move. He should have lowered his

flag and tried to keep up with play. Because he didn't move, several Leeds players wrongly assumed that play had stopped.

I was known for always playing advantage, that was the way I refereed. This was no different.

Although Ray Tinkler was never put in charge of a Leeds United game again, he did have further contact with a Leeds United player. The last game Tinkler ever refereed was between Oldham and West Brom. It was the final game of the season and West Brom needed to win to ensure promotion to the First Division. West Brom's player-manager was Johnny Giles. They scored midway through the first half with a goal, ironically, by Tony Brown, who had scored that goal at Elland Road in 1971. After 90 minutes, the score remained at 1–0. The game carried on for what seemed an age, and Oldham were awarded several corners.

It was a tense time for Johnny Giles and his team. The minutes ticked away, and Giles could remain quiet no longer. 'I remember you from Leeds . . . are you going to do us again?' he said to Tinkler.

'I remember you too.'

Tinkler blew for full-time with the final score at 1–0. Tony Brown, Johnny Giles and Ray Tinkler had all been involved in the same match for the first time since that day back in 1971, this time with a favourable outcome for Giles. 'So maybe there is some poetic justice out there,' says Giles.

3. Doubting Thomas

Don Revie's right-hand man and Leeds' trainer was the brilliant Les Cocker. Les was a legend amongst the Leeds faithful and was famous throughout the footballing world for his hunched-up shoulders and characteristic sprint onto the field to tend to his injured flock. As he ran, he would cling on to his kitbag as if for dear life. I recently met up with Les's son, Dave 'Junior' Cocker. 'Dad died of a heart attack on 4 October 1979 at 11 a.m., during a training session with Doncaster Rovers,' said Dave. 'Billy Bremner, who was manager of Rovers at the time, ushered all the players into the supporters club next door while he drove to Harworth Colliery to collect my brother Stephen, who was down the pit at the time. He then drove to Leeds with Stephen, intending to meet up with myself, my younger brother Ian and my mum to tell us personally, as he was worried that the press would get hold of the story first.

'Meanwhile, a policeman called in at the Doncaster club and then immediately rang a Sheffield radio station and got paid £20 for his news. Word then got out and by the time Billy and our Stephen arrived in Leeds the news was all over the radio and television. The *Yorkshire Post* had even put billboards up announcing the news. I heard about it before Billy and Stephen arrived. Mum and Ian weren't at home and while we were searching for them in Billy's car we heard Jack Charlton on the car radio giving an interview about Dad's death. We made a formal complaint to Doncaster police, but nothing came of it.'

Two of the Doncaster players in the supporters club that day were Ian and Glynn Snodin, who both, of course, ended up playing at Leeds United a few years later.

Dave Cocker, it has to be said, wears his heart on his sleeve and is very passionate, to this day, about Leeds United Football Club.

However, his passion has landed him in hot water from time to time. One Saturday in 1970, 19-year-old Dave was sat behind the dugout at Elland Road, having just witnessed what he describes as a 'deplorable performance' by the referee that particular afternoon, Clive Thomas. Dave managed to slip unnoticed down the players' tunnel and confronted Thomas as he left the field. Dave was on the verge of thumping the referee when Allan Clarke luckily pulled him away at the last minute. Thomas was convinced that Dave was a player and tried to book him. Dave told him where to go and, still convinced he was a player, Thomas called Les Cocker and Don Revie out of the changing-room to identify him. Cocker and Revie both denied knowing him, so Thomas had him arrested by the police.

Dave says, 'The local bobby was Eric Brailsford, who was also a part-time physio at Elland Road. He went through the motions of "arresting" me and disappeared with me down the tunnel beneath the West Stand and the Kop. He then told me to go to the players' lounge, out of the way.'

Dave had a couple of pints until Revie and Cocker arrived. 'What happened?' they asked. 'I told them,' says Dave, 'and they told me to be more careful in future.' With his tongue firmly in his cheek, Dave adds, 'They fully understood why I was in the tunnel and knew that that was where 40,000 Leeds fans wished they could have been.'

Eric Brailsford was quite a character, a giant of a man. When the new police motorbikes came out in the late '60s and early '70s, they were something of a novelty. Known as 'Noddy bikes', they had huge, brightly coloured fender-type things, from which those police bikes seen today developed. It was highly amusing to the Leeds players when Eric would arrived at Elland Road during the week just to watch the team train. He would turn into the West Stand car park on his Noddy bike and the players would fall about laughing at this bear of a man sat atop what looked for all the world like a kid's toy bike. That said, the players and Don Revie loved Eric. He was always made welcome and on a couple of occasions was even allowed to massage the players, which was usually Don's personal job.

It would be fair to say that referee Clive Thomas attracted controversy from the start of his career. I read his autobiography *By the Book* with great interest. He recounts how, towards the end of one of his very early games in his hometown Rhondda League, between Blaenrhondda and Ystrad Athletic at Blaencwm, he sent off a Blaenrhondda player. His name was John Jones, and he was also the local boxer. This was a tight-knit community and, because of his huge frame and presence, no one had ever dared send Jones off before. Afterwards, Thomas, remembering the long walk under a dark bridge to an isolated bus stop, and feeling sure he would be followed by irate fans and players alike, told the club's secretary, 'If anyone lays a hand on me, you'll never see another ball kicked in Blaenrhondda because I'll report you to the Football Association of Wales!'

As a referee, Thomas could sometimes come across as arrogant, and he admitted that he enjoyed publicity. He loved being on television and radio, calling himself an entertainer and a performer. A good referee to me is one you don't notice – the 'invisible ref', in charge of a game that has flowed so well that no one can remember him being there. Admittedly, that is getting harder these days, with all the media coverage worldwide, but you get my point.

Thomas even received fan mail, mostly from women, 'presumably,' he wrote, 'on the basis that they appreciate my hairy legs'. He always started a game with a little kick of his leg and a wave of his arm as he blew the whistle. As a spectator, I got the impression that Thomas liked attention and some of his statements showed a condescending attitude towards less glamorous fixtures. He once said of taking charge of a game between Aldershot and Doncaster Rovers in 1973 that he thought he and his linesmen were 'above this particular fixture', and he referred mockingly to such places as Spotland, Rochdale, Gresty Road, Crewe and the Shay in Halifax as 'exotic palm-fringed resorts'.

Thomas could be high-handed on occasion. During one particular game between Plymouth and Reading in 1980, he sent Lawrie Sanchez off for a foul. On noticing that Sanchez had not gone down the tunnel but had sat on the bench alongside his manager and other players, Thomas went over and ordered Sanchez to the dressing-room. An FA spokesman was quoted afterwards as saying, 'A sending-off from the field of play does not mean the player has to go to the dressing-room. He is entitled to sit on the bench and only if he makes a nuisance of himself is the referee allowed to order him to the dressing-room.' Thomas admitted that the spokesman was correct but said, 'My view is still that the very presence of Sanchez constituted a nuisance.'

After a 1983 Milk Cup tie between West Brom and Aston Villa during which Thomas had booked seven players and had sent off West Brom's Gary Owen, he arrived in the dressing-room to find that there was no cup of tea waiting for him, or any sandwiches. In his autobiography, Thomas said, 'It is traditional that referees and linesmen receive at least a cup of tea.' Yes, a tradition – but not a condition. However, this did not stop the referee threatening to report West Brom to the Football League. Now I'd love to have seen that report.

Thomas didn't seem to like being the linesman, either. During an international game between Holland and Sweden in 1974, he threw down his flag in frustration in the dressing-room at half-time because the Canadian referee, Werner Winsemann, had overruled him twice.

When the Football Association of Wales recommended two of their referees for the 1974 World Cup in West Germany, Thomas was surprised to discover that he wasn't one of them. John Gow and Iorrie Jones were the two referees suggested to FIFA. 'They were not bad referees,' said Thomas, 'though in my opinion unlikely to reach the very top.' As it turned out, the three referees who were eventually chosen were Jack Taylor from England, Bob Davidson from Scotland and Clive Thomas from Wales.

On the flight to Stuttgart for his first game, between Argentina and Poland, Thomas travelled with his linesmen, a German, Rudolf Scheurer, and Bob Davidson. Thomas commented later that Davidson hadn't spoken more than a couple of words to him throughout the flight. He assumed that this was because the Scotsman was jealous and upset at not being the referee himself. Thomas himself had his own ambitions for the tournament: 'With Jack Taylor taking the relatively easy Bulgaria–Uruguay match, I knew that a good game would help me towards my goal: a place in the final.' Before the Argentina game, two Argentinian players missed the national anthem because Thomas had sent them back to the dressing-room to change their studs.

In 1976, during the European Championship in Yugoslavia, Thomas was the centre of a controversy that would feature in a documentary on Dutch TV in 2008. The game in question was the semi-final between Czechoslovakia and Holland. In extra time, Thomas failed to notice a very heavy challenge on Johan Cruyff by Antonín Panenka. As Cruyff lay crumpled in a heap, Zdenek Nehoda went on to score the winning goal for the Czechs. The Dutch were absolutely furious, so much so that Willem van Hanegem refused to play on. Thomas gave him a red card and his marching orders. Appearing on the documentary, an episode of Dutch TV programme *Andere Tijden Sport*, Thomas said that he had made a mistake by not noticing the foul. This was 32 years later.

One of Clive Thomas's most famous controversial decisions came during the 1978 World Cup in Argentina. With Brazil and Sweden standing level at 1–1 and the game slipping into injury time, Brazil were awarded a corner. The kick was taken but after the ball had travelled ten yards Thomas blew for full-time. Meantime, Brazil's Zico was in mid-air, coiling himself to meet the ball perfectly. Thomas had already turned away and was heading towards the tunnel when the ball hit the back of the net. Pandemonium and confusion ensued, but the goal did not stand. Jack Taylor told British reporters back home that Thomas had made the wrong decision. At the same time as the interview was taking place, Thomas was being led away to the airport under armed police guard.

Throughout his career, Thomas constantly fought with the Football Association of Wales, the Football Association and the Football League. Whenever he didn't agree with a decision by the authorities, he would bombard them with letters and telephone calls, resulting in countless meetings in various association offices and often at the Great Western Hotel at London's Paddington Station.

In 1978, the *News of the World* asked Thomas for his views on British referees. Beneath the heading, 'Thomas Blows the Whistle on Refs', he wrote:

> It is time we got off our backsides and did something to improve ourselves, instead of waffling. Once, British referees were widely recognised as the best in the world. I would question very much whether that is the case now.

The article infuriated the president of the Association of Football Referees and Linesmen, and he called for the Football Association of Wales to charge Thomas with bringing the game into disrepute. The name of that president was Mr Ray Tinkler.

Clive Thomas was the referee when Liverpool met Everton in the

1977 FA Cup semi-final. He disallowed a seemingly perfect goal by Everton, with even Liverpool players resigned to the fact that it was a goal. Toffees fans never forgot that decision. Everton fan Michael Berry, from Otley, recalled an encounter with Clive Thomas in an article for the *Observer Sport Monthly* magazine in 2005. Many years after the fateful match, Berry was in London for an away game. Having lost his friends, he was walking alone in the city centre. Several times in the course of an hour, he came across 'a familiar figure' in a suit, who, eyeing his Everton scarf, hurried away. Berry remembered:

> As I tried to hail [a taxi] I spotted the same man again, about to get into a cab. I ran over to ask if we could share and the moment he saw me he turned on his heels.
>
> 'What did you do to him?' asked the driver.
>
> 'It's that ref Clive Thomas. He must be wary of Everton fans since the FA Cup semi-final.' The truth was I didn't care about the decision. I just wanted to speak to him. At least he helped me get a taxi . . .

Thomas also made enemies of fans of Ipswich Town. After beating Leeds over four games in the 1975 FA Cup, Ipswich met West Ham in the semi-final. Bryan Hamilton scored what looked to be the equaliser late on, only for Thomas to disallow it for offside, even though a better-placed linesman hadn't flagged it.

Thomas didn't like Ipswich, particularly their manager, Bobby Robson. 'He could not stand, Robson, and wasn't keen on his captain Mick Mills either. He claimed he didn't like Mills because of the way he looked at him whenever he gave a decision against him. Ipswich's central defensive partnership of Terry Butcher and Russell Osman weren't very good either, according to Thomas, who claimed that neither ought to have played for England. 'Butcher,' said Thomas in *By the Book*, 'appears to have no particular skills other than to ensure that no one passes him. I would certainly have sent him off for one tackle during the [1982] World Cup in Spain.'

Thomas also gave his opinion of Revie's Leeds in *By the Book*:

> Many say that [Don Revie's] Leeds team of the '70s was the most professional we have ever seen in Britain. It depends on what you

mean by professional. Each time I refereed Leeds United I experienced hostility, disobedience and dissent from players and from staff... During matches the players would shout comments on your performance and then claim they were talking about their colleagues. I had more trouble with that side than with any other twenty teams added together.

Billy Bremner was a player who would never admit that he had committed an offence. It took him a few seasons to accept that he could not control me. He might have been a small man but he had an awful lot to say and was no doubt the right sergeant-major to take charge of the infantry from the commanding officer, Revie, whose sole concern seemed to be to win matches – or, rather, not to lose them.

After a game against Arsenal at Arsenal on 2 December 1972, Allan Clarke protested that he should not have been cautioned by Thomas and also accused Thomas of kicking him. The referee was dumbfounded and denied the allegation, which was subsequently heard by an FA commission. Thomas said in his autobiography, 'I was absolutely flabbergasted when the accusation was made. Even though Clarke made his claim in his written defence I never seriously thought he would use it.'

Thomas was further shocked when the chairman at the hearing pointed out that it was not the FA's responsibility to decide on the issue of the alleged kick but only to judge whether the caution had been deserved. Thomas wanted the opportunity to dispute the allegation, but the FA refused, saying that the Football League could be notified if required, and no further action was taken.

A claim was made to the Football League, backed by virtually every member of the Leeds playing and training staff. The League secretary at the time was Alan Hardaker, who regularly clashed with Don Revie and his Leeds team. Hardaker found himself in a bit of a quandary. There was no video evidence to back either Leeds or Thomas, and according to a man who would later become secretary himself, Graham Kelly, writing in *The Independent* in 2001:

Hardaker wasn't ever inclined to seek advice, much less accept any. But he had to decide who to believe, Revie, whom he loathed with a vengeance ... or the ebullient Thomas ... Hardaker, who had once memorably said publicly that he wouldn't hang a dog on the word of an ex-professional footballer, summarily threw out Revie's complaint, on the grounds that the authority of the referee was paramount.

Hardaker may have disliked Leeds and Revie, but, according to Kelly, he wasn't particularly keen on Clive Thomas either. He wrote:

> When he began to adopt the role of a B-list celebrity ... Hardaker, rapidly reaching the limit of his small stock of patience, gave orders that Thomas should be sent on a mid-winter tour of the less salubrious clubs.

Eventually, according to Thomas's book, Leeds United secretary Keith Archer wrote to him unreservedly withdrawing the accusation.

Not long after the 'kicking' incident, Thomas took charge of a game at Elland Road. As the teams stood in the tunnel before the match, Thomas said to Clarke, 'Hello, Allan, I hope I'm not going to have any trouble with you today.'

'Hello, Mr Thomas,' replied Clarke. 'No, you'll have no trouble from me, sir.'

'Good,' said Thomas, 'because if I thought you were going to be trouble, I'd book you now, but I can't book you for what you may be thinking.'

'Oh, that's good, Mr Thomas, because I think you're a bastard,' replied Clarke as he walked out onto the pitch bouncing the ball.

Thomas still held a grudge towards Clarke many years later, and this is made clear in a statement he made in his book about a match in 1983, when the former Leeds player was manager of Scunthorpe United:

> Sadly, but because it is only human nature, I am now suspicious of Allan Clarke as a manager and, therefore, of his players. Indeed during a match between Plymouth Argyle and his Scunthorpe United ... I had to caution three of his United players in as many minutes, for a lack of discipline.
>
> Even before his playing career was over I was refereeing at

Elland Road for a match between Leeds and Liverpool. With about 30 seconds left, Tommy Smith fouled Allan Clarke far out on the touchline, level with the Liverpool penalty area. Knowing Clarke as I did, I was not watching the ball as Terry Cooper took the kick, and as I had guessed, with the ball about ten yards away Clarke tapped Smith on the ankles in retaliation for the foul. Jack Charlton nodded the ball into the Liverpool net, but I awarded a free kick for Clarke's sly infringement. There was predictable uproar.

There are a couple of points worthy of note here. Anyone in the game knew of the animosity that existed between Clarke and Smith. Also, Smith upended Clarke on several occasions during this particular encounter, but without retribution from the referee. And let's be clear about this – don't you think that Thomas's obvious bias against Allan Clarke could have had a bearing on this?

Let's stay with Tommy Smith for a moment. Whilst playing for Liverpool in a league game at Maine Road, Thomas sent Smith off for arguing (second offence). At the subsequent disciplinary hearing, Smith was given a two-match ban. Liverpool manager Bill Shankly appealed over the suspension. Thomas wrote:

> Shankly was a wily old bird. The appeal had lasted over three months by the time the ban was confirmed, but Shankly had achieved his aim. Tommy Smith managed to play in a European Cup final whilst the appeal meandered on.

Well done to Shanks, but it does beg the question what would Thomas have said if the same situation had occurred at Leeds United with Don Revie making the appeal on behalf of his 'sergeant officer'?

I contacted Clive Thomas by letter at his home, courtesy of some great help in locating him from the Porthcawl Tourist Information Centre. I finally received a letter from Mr Thomas, but after a couple more letters he presumably felt unable to cooperate any further and I didn't receive any more correspondence from him.

4. Mr Pickwick

During the 1960s and '70s, there was one referee who stood out from the rest: Roger Kirkpatrick. A real character, he was flamboyant, admittedly, but in a good way. He was affectionately nicknamed 'Mr Pickwick' because of his small, stout frame and bald head surrounded by light grey locks of hair, his face framed by his trademark large grey sideburns. He liked a laugh and a joke, but above all he was a first-class referee.

I remember an incident when Everton were the visitors to Elland Road in the late '60s. One particular decision angered an Everton fan so much that he leapt over the wall and headed straight for Mr Kirkpatrick. As two police officers attempted to head the fan off, Kirkpatrick waved them away and welcomed the Everton fan by immediately putting his arm around him. He then proceeded to explain to the shocked and stunned Everton fan, with much pointing and waving of his arms, just why he had given his decision. After a few minutes of lecturing, the portly official escorted the totally bewildered Everton fan back over the wall and, amidst huge cheers from both sets of supporters, restarted the game.

Big Jack Charlton could be called a bit of a fan of Kirkpatrick. During one encounter at Elland Road, Big Jack kneed Denis Law in the lower back. Law was rolling around in agony and complained to Kirkpatrick, who simply leant over Law and said, 'Come on, Denis, you deserved that. Now get up and stop bloody moaning.'

To be honest, Big Jack was a bit of a hard man and, as if to confirm this, Les Cocker told his son Dave a story about an incident after the infamous England v. Argentina game at Wembley in the 1966 World Cup quarter-final. After the bad-tempered game, the Argentina players were so incensed at losing that they tried bursting into the England dressing-room. There was mayhem outside the dressing-room as they shouted and banged on the locked door. Big Jack said, 'Let the fuckers in – they can only get in one at a time, and I will have 'em!' Manager Alf Ramsey politely denied Jack's request.

Incidentally, it was this vicious encounter with Argentina that inspired the red card. Former World Cup referee Ken Aston was a member of FIFA's Referees' Committee and was chief of referees during the 1966 World Cup. In that quarter-final at Wembley, German referee Rudolf Kreitlein sent off Argentina's Antonio Rattín. Rattín had attempted to intervene with the referee, but Kreitlein didn't speak anything but German and, judging by Rattín's animated manner alone, sent him off for 'violence of the tongue'. Rattín, unable to understand why he had been sent off, refused to leave the field. Mr Aston intervened at the touchline and, in his limited Spanish, eventually persuaded Rattín to leave.

Whilst driving home after leaving Wembley, Mr Aston had to stop at three consecutive traffic lights as they went from amber to red. It occurred to him that it might avoid a lot of unnecessary confusion in football, especially international football, if a card system was introduced. Using a yellow card for a caution and then a red for a dismissal might make communication a lot easier. He put his idea to his committee, and for the 1970 World Cup in Mexico the card system was introduced. Amazingly, though, the red card was not used until the following World Cup, in West Germany in 1974. Australia's Ray Richards was the unfortunate first recipient.

Blackburn's David Wagstaffe became the first English player to be given the red card when the Football League introduced the system in 1976. With predictable uncertainty, the League withdrew the card system in January 1981 after the Professional Footballers' Association (PFA) complained that there were too many red cards being bandied about. When the referees reverted to the old system of pointing a player to the dressing-room, within a season the figure of sending-offs had more than doubled. After pressure from FIFA, the cards were reintroduced for the 1987–88 season. It is blatantly apparent that whatever system our referees have at their disposal, the sendings-off continue to rise every season.

Since, of the referees of the '70s, Roger Kirkpatrick stuck out in my memory as one of the biggest characters, I decided to get in touch with him and ask him about his memories of Leeds. He emailed back:

> I have been asked for my views and comments about my time as a referee and my connection with Don Revie. This will be a pleasure, as I have only happy memories of a dedicated young

35

player with outstanding talent, who progressed to become an equally extraordinary manager of Leeds United and a well-respected international manager.

The first time I met Don was at the training ground of Leicester City. He was, as I have previously stated, a very dedicated young man, and he and a few other players would return in the afternoon for extra training. He always had a word with me, asking various questions about the laws of the game and the matches which I had refereed. He then went on to greater things in his career.

My next memory of him was when he was the manager at Leeds United, the first club in the English league at that time to take on a major sponsorship for kit (Admiral). I can recall an incident involving Don and Leeds and their sponsor.

I was invited to referee the third -round of the FA Cup at Molineux – Wolverhampton v. Leeds. This was at the time that Leeds were still undefeated in the league. This match was being played in January in the time of Ted Heath's Tory government, with the power restrictions and the three-day working week. The kick-off was arranged for 1.30. These were very cold, damp, misty, dark days.

During this period, I was designing new referees' outfits to put a new image on the referees and get away from the long trousers and blazer look, which had followed the referees through the centuries. This time a very well-known Leicester sports company, who since have become known internationally and worldwide as Admiral, decided they would design a kit for this occasion, with a white stripe down the inside of my sleeve and down the side of my body. Bearing in mind there would be no floodlights because of the restrictions, this would be an excellent way that I could be seen to be doing my job.

When the day of the match eventually arrived, I ran out onto the pitch in my new uniform and was immediately the cause of some derision from the crowd, but dear Don Revie gave his approval of my outfit and said that it was obvious that I had approached this match with common sense and the design was great. Unfortunately this remark was overheard by the manager of Wolves, Bill McGarry, and his coach, Sam Chung. This was to cause embarrassment to me later.

The match started with Wolves having the best of play. This was the main feature on BBC television's *Match of the Day* and everything had gone well until the last three minutes. The only problem I had up to this time was that I had to caution Gordon McQueen for a tackle from behind. In the remaining period of play, Leeds were losing 2–1 and it looked as though they would be defeated for the first time that season.

Then suddenly there was a breakaway from Leeds and a cross was made over to the Wolves goalmouth area, and Powell of Wolves deliberately pushed Billy Bremner in the back (and to the ground). Whilst admitting that Bremner made a meal out of the situation, I awarded a penalty to Leeds, which they scored from, making it 2–2. You can imagine the home crowd's reaction.

The replay was arranged for the following Wednesday at Elland Road and there was certainly a lot of tension in the air. Before the game, Don came into my dressing-room and we just yarned about anything and wished each other all the best.

The match was a typical cup tie, end-to-end play. Leeds had scored a goal and the pressure was on Wolves. Then a shot from a Wolves player on its way to goal struck the arm of Mick Jones, who was in a defending position. I did not award a penalty as in my opinion the ball had struck the arm and not the other way round.

Leeds won the tie.

Following the game, Bill McGarry placed an official complaint about me being biased towards Leeds United and having personal and business interests.

Statement from McGarry: 'How can this referee be unbiased when I have been informed that he is the managing director of Admiral, who happen to be the sponsors of Leeds United?'

Just goes to show how you can get things wrong when overhearing a private conversation [such as the one] I had with Don Revie. The managing director of Admiral at that time was Bert Patrick and not Kirkpatrick.

After that day, I kept in contact with Don and I always supported him through the good and sometimes bad days. He will always be remembered by me as a true gentleman of football and will remain in the annals of football for ever.

During one conversation with Roger, I asked if he remembered the story about escorting the Everton fan from the Elland Road pitch. Of course he did, he said. 'But,' he told me, 'it was Leeds against Tottenham, not Everton. It was a Spurs fan who I put back in the crowd.' I stood corrected.

Rod Johnson played for Leeds United between 1962 and 1968; recently I told him that I'd been in dialogue with Roger Kirkpatrick. Rod laughed. 'Ah, Mr Pickwick,' he said. 'What a character. He certainly was one of the best referees I saw, without a doubt. When I left Leeds United, I went to Rotherham United. We played a game at Bristol Rovers – it will have been around 1969–70-ish – and Roger was the referee. During the game, Roger gave a bounce-up [a drop-ball]. It had been a bad-tempered match and tensions were running high. I faced up to the other lad and Roger dropped the ball between us. Then, for some unknown reason, Roger jumped between us and tried to retrieve the ball. It was too late, my studs had already sprung into action and I caught Roger on his upper thigh, leaving a trail of fresh blood trickling down his leg. Roger looked at me and then dropped to the floor, and passed out. One of the linesmen took over in the middle and a fan was plucked from the crowd to run the line. Meanwhile, Roger was whisked away by ambulance to Bristol General Infirmary.'

Jim Finney was another well-known face in the middle. Appointed to the Football League referees list in 1959, Finney, a Freemason, went on to become one of the world's top referees during the 1960s and early '70s. When I spoke to him, he said this of Leeds United: 'Leeds United under Don Revie were a very professional and much misunderstood team. They were without doubt the finest club side in Europe, if not the world, during their ten-year domination of English football.'

As well as being on the FIFA referees list, Finney took charge of the 1962 FA Cup final between Tottenham Hotspur and Burnley, after which Spurs captain Danny Blanchflower presented Finney with the match ball. Blanchflower broke with the tradition at the time of keeping the match ball himself to acknowledge a top-class display by the referee. Finney ran the line for the first-ever European Nations Cup final, in Paris in 1960, assisting referee Ken Aston. In 1963,

Finney refereed an international at Hampden Park between Scotland and Austria. This game became so volatile that Finney abandoned it with 11 minutes remaining. 'I felt that I had to abandon the match or somebody would have been seriously hurt,' he said afterwards.

Finney was selected as one of the English referees for the 1966 World Cup. During the quarter-final between West Germany and Uruguay at Hillsborough, he allowed German defender Karl-Heinz Schnellinger to claw the ball out of the top corner of the net with his hand, preventing the Uruguayans taking the lead. He then controversially sent off Uruguay's Horacio Troche and Héctor Silva in the second half, and the Germans won quite comfortably.

This was the same day as the controversial match at Wembley in which Rudolf Kreitlein sent off Rattín for Argentina against England. At the time, the two matches in which South American teams were defeated in part as a result of controversial decisions led to suggestions of partiality against European referees. Rattín's display that afternoon was scandalous, however. Refusing to leave the pitch, he insulted the Queen by sitting on the red carpet. The bruising match prompted England manager Alf Ramsey to comment, 'Our best football will come against the right type of opposition – a team who come to play football and not act as animals.'

However, some sympathy must be felt for the South Americans over the appointment of the referees for the 1966 World Cup. As mentioned earlier, Kreitlein spoke no Spanish, so could not have understood what Rattín had said to him. The South Americans were quick to point to the fact a German referee had been in charge of the England game, while the referee for the West Germans' quarter-final was English.

The circumstances of the draw for referees did nothing to stop the South Americans muttering about conspiracy, either. This rather dubious situation strengthened talk of conspiracy. Delegates from the countries involved, including Uruguay and Argentina, arrived at the stipulated time to witness the draw, but found that it had already taken place, leading a Dutch referee to declare, 'FIFA is controlled by three people – Sir, Stanley, Rouse.'

After officiating at the 1971 League Cup final at Wembley between Tottenham Hotspur and Aston Villa, Jim Finney was appointed referee for the European Cup final of the same year, also at Wembley.

Before the match could take place, however, a road accident ended his career, and Jack Taylor was the man who replaced him.

A very experienced referee, Jack Taylor also took charge of the 1974 World Cup final in West Germany between Holland and the host nation. He gave a penalty to Holland with less than two minutes gone. Twenty-five minutes later, he awarded West Germany a penalty when Holland's Wim Jansen appeared to trip the German midfielder Bernd Hölzenbein. The television replay later suggested that there had been no trip for the German penalty. Years later, Taylor told the press:

> The first penalty wasn't difficult to call. All I remember is thinking it was a 100 per cent correct decision. As the ball went on the spot the whole stadium went quiet. Beckenbauer, the German skipper, came to me and said, 'Taylor, you're an Englishman.' The kick went in and there was complete euphoria . . . What really does annoy me is the suggestion that I gave [the second penalty] to even things up. It was a trip or an attempted trip and the laws of the game are that's a penalty.

In a career spanning 33 years as a referee, Taylor took charge of more than 1,000 games, including over 100 internationals, and was inducted into the FIFA Hall of Fame in Barcelona in 1999. He went on to become a coach to referees in South Africa and Saudi Arabia.

Taylor says of Leeds United, 'They were a beautifully balanced side. If they had played in another country and you put different coloured shirts on them and blacked their faces, I would still know that it was Leeds United. Don Revie was personally charming. I had all the time in the world for him. He was never anything other than honest and frank.'

Jack Taylor was sometimes a guest in the Revie household. 'Often we would go out for a meal, me, Don and Elsie. And before you ask, not once was the impending game ever mentioned. He was such a courteous man and a thoroughly dedicated professional.'

It comes as no surprise, when you consider the standard of refereeing at many of Leeds' matches, that Don Revie occasionally requested that Jack Taylor take charge of his side's games. Unsurprisingly, the Football League, and in particular the then secretary Alan Hardaker, frowned upon such requests, but Taylor says, 'Revie always looked at every angle. I don't blame him; he had a job to do. His knowledge was so good. He knew referees inside out. He was the ultimate tactician.'

A former butcher from Wolverhampton, Taylor is still a referees' assessor today. Don Revie would have liked that.

Taylor also shared something else with Don Revie – their mutual admiration of the late, great comedian Eric Morecambe. Eric was a regular guest of Don's at Elland Road, and Jack also has great memories of him. He tells the story of a time when, during Morecambe's tenure as chairman of Luton Town, he was refereeing at Kenilworth Road, was hit by a penny thrown from the crowd and had to be taken off the pitch to have stitches. Morecambe came to check if he was OK and make sure he wasn't going to report Luton Town. When Taylor told him he was fine and didn't intend to report the club, Morecambe said, 'Good. Now can I have my penny back?'

5. A Winter's Tale or Two

There have been some pretty bizarre goings-on with FA referees over the years.

Given his name, Mike Reed could quite easily be mistaken for a comedian, but he was a referee. He celebrated the coming of the millennium with an extraordinary performance at Anfield. Leeds were the visitors, and when Liverpool scored through a Patrik Berger long-range effort Leeds fans were amazed to witness Reed punch the air in delight. He called a radio phone-in to explain his action, saying:

> I did punch the air, but I wasn't doing it in celebration of the goal but in triumph, as I had allowed Liverpool to play on after they could have been awarded a free kick . . . The referee does love to see the ball in the back of the net after he has waved play on, because it proves he was right.

Reed declined my invitation to elaborate further.

David Elleray didn't exactly endear himself to Leeds fans, either. Elleray was a housemaster at Harrow School, where he had also been a geography teacher. Well, I personally don't think that geography was his strong point. During a certain fixture at Elland Road in the mid-'90s, against Leeds' arch-rivals from Old Trafford, he was miles away from the action when he awarded a penalty to the visitors, and television replays clearly showed that a foul by Leeds' Brian Deane had happened three or four yards outside the penalty area.

Despite the occasional blip, Elleray was an extremely well-respected referee, so much so that shortly before he retired from football in 2003, he was asked to watch a video of the notoriously violent Leeds v. Chelsea 1970 FA Cup final replay at Old Trafford for a TV programme and explain how, if he had been the referee that evening, he would have reacted. It wasn't a game for faint hearts, either on or off the pitch.

In the first final at Wembley, Eddie Gray had completely destroyed Chelsea full-back David Webb. Gray went on to receive the Man of the Match award, but Chelsea somehow hung on to draw 2–2. In the replay, Chelsea shifted Webb to the centre, moving hard man Ron Harris to mark Gray. In the very early stages of the game, Harris challenged Gray with what can only be described as a kung fu-type kick, leaving the Leeds winger underpowered for the rest of the game. A total bloodbath ensued. Jack Charlton head-butted Peter Osgood, and Eddie McCreadie almost beheaded Billy Bremner with a preposterously high challenge.

Remarkably, only one player was booked. After watching the video recording and making notes, Elleray said that if he had been the referee that night, he would have produced at least six red and twenty yellow cards.

Elleray was no stranger to Elland Road. He recalled refereeing an FA Cup fourth-round replay in which Leeds lost to Oxford United. Elleray says:

> I remember walking off at the end with Leeds captain Gordon Strachan and he commented that the young players did not have the hunger they had in his day. He said that they got things too easily and by the time they were 20 years old, they already had a flashy car, a house and thought they had arrived. In his day, he was still cleaning the pro's boots and living in lodgings.
>
> His trenchant views were frequently heard when he managed Coventry City and then later Southampton. I have to say that we didn't get on that well over the years, and at half-time once at Derby he burst into my dressing-room like a human tornado, firing accusations at me. I was so irritated that I leant against the door and refused to let him out until I had my say. He then went to the press and told them that I had locked him in. This incident didn't help our relationship any and once when a linesman was injured at Leicester, and I, as fourth official, had to take over, Strachan put his head in his hands and said, 'I didn't think it could get any worse but your fucking appearance proves me wrong!'

Another game Elleray recalls, and with good reason, was a Premier League game at Elland Road when Newcastle United were the visitors. In an email, he told me:

> I had a shirt on which in the tunnel did not seem to clash with the Newcastle United shirts. But in the first 15 minutes, several Newcastle players passed the ball to me, and Leeds players tried to mark me, thinking I was a Newcastle player. I did not have another ref's shirt, so I went across to the home dugout and borrowed a plain-blue training top from Leeds United. As I restarted the game, I realised that my top had the Leeds United crest on it. I spent the next five minutes running around with my hand over the badge as the Newcastle fans chanted that Leeds had 12 men. To show it was not true I gave a yellow card to a Leeds player. At the first opportunity I took the top off and turned it inside out, but not before it had been captured by the photographers!
>
> I once did a feisty affair at Elland Road, against Leicester City. I produced seven yellow cards. At one point Lee Bowyer and Robbie Savage clashed. They were both very unpopular at the time and I called them over and said, 'If I have any more trouble from you two, I will send you both off and become the most popular person in English football!'
>
> 'Why?' they asked.
>
> 'Because you are the most hated players in England!' I replied.
>
> They were so shocked they said nothing and I had no more trouble from them for the rest of the game.

When Elleray was a kid, he wrote to lots of managers asking for their players' advice on refereeing. Don Revie was the only one to reply. Ironically, Elleray ended up giving Leeds more yellow cards than any other club. In his book *The Man in the Middle*, he reflected:

> Perhaps Mr Revie's influence had disappeared by the time I was a referee. I always enjoyed reffing Leeds but the crowds at Elland Road are quite hostile and they seem very adept at winding up their own players, which makes them quite aggressive.

Elleray was the fourth official for a Leeds game at West Ham in 1999. Rob Harris, the referee, sent off three West Ham players as the home team was beaten by Leeds. On his way home, Harris was in his car near the ground, waiting for the lights to change, when he was almost attacked by fans of the losing team. After that, the Premier League introduced a new policy whereby all officials were to be taken to matches and home again by people carrier.

In 2000, Harris was suspended for two months in the wake of an FA Cup match between Tranmere Rovers and Sunderland. In injury time, the referee ordered off a Tranmere player just as a substitution was being made, and somehow the Rovers ended up playing on with a full complement of players. Neither Harris nor his fellow officials noticed.

The following year, Graham Barber was the appointed referee for a crucial game at Elland Road against Manchester United. Leeds had relentlessly pounded the visitors' goalmouth throughout the first half when, just before the interval, Leeds' Ian Harte challenged Fabien Barthez in the air. The keeper won the ball and Harte crashed to the ground. Barthez then immediately stamped on Harte and the referee awarded a penalty to Leeds. Barthez was the last defender, yet he stayed on the field with a caution. He then saved the penalty. In the second half, during a Leeds attack, defender Wes Brown, with no one within three yards of him, put through his own goal, only for Barber to disallow it for offside. These incidents were recorded on TV. The result, a 1–1 draw, denied Leeds the last available league position for qualification for the Champions League. The consequences of this result were catastrophic, to say the least, and it could be argued that it was the catalyst for the dreadful downward spiral that the club suffered in the years to come.

George Courtney was another referee who made an impression on Leeds fans. Nearing the end of an FA Cup tie at Barnsley in the early '90s, Leeds were 1–0 up. With time running out, Barnsley threw everyone forward and a desperate shot was going hopelessly wide when the Barnsley right-winger jumped up (mainly to stop the ball going over the stand) and attempted to catch the ball. In doing so, he palmed the ball down and it fell, unbelievably, into the path of the striker who'd hit the original effort and who then unleashed an unstoppable shot into the top corner of the Leeds net. Initially, the Leeds defence did not react, believing that a free kick in their favour would be given. But Courtney had given the goal. Leeds were furious with the decision but had to wait until the replay at Elland Road a week later to go past Barnsley (4–0) and into the next round.

George Courtney still visits Elland Road as a referees' assessor. Despite originally agreeing to meet with me as his guest at Elland Road to discuss his Leeds memories, nothing was forthcoming and he declined my invitation to elaborate further on that Barnsley 'goal' in the dying seconds at Oakwell, other than to say, 'That Barnsley v. Leeds game was no laughing matter (at the time).'

He added, 'European travel has meant I have been away from home constantly for several weeks. I must apologise therefore for failing to respond to your request, deserving of at least a yellow card! Congratulations on Leeds' promotion. Hopefully they will consolidate their newfound position. I am sorry to disappoint you in not giving information on past experiences. I cannot remember past yesterday!'

One of the linesmen for that Barnsley–Leeds replay was Jeff Winter. When I emailed him about it, he replied:

> I always enjoyed reffing at Elland Road. There was always a good atmosphere, if somewhat hostile for both visitors and officials. One of my first memories was running the line in an FA Cup replay against Barnsley. The first game at Oakwell had ended in controversy with a George Courtney decision costing Leeds the game. As we entered the field, the home fans turned on George big style. He turned to speak to his assistants, who should have been right behind him, but we were both about ten yards further behind him. When he queried our position, I suggested that as he had caused the abuse, he could take it himself.
>
> It was not long before it was my turn, though. During the game, Gordon Strachan, not for the last time, queried a decision of mine over a throw-in. The camera panned onto Gordon, whose face was distorted with rage, coming out with a fine choice of expletives. Then it panned onto me holding my flag and indicating that the ball had gone out for a throw-in. I was asked for years what Gordon had said to me. To be honest, I hadn't got a clue. Firstly because I would not have understood him anyway and secondly because he was 40 yards away! Just goes to show how TV camera shots can deceive.

Winter unashamedly admits to having a sense of self-importance. This was what he said in his autobiography, *Who's the B****d in the Black?*, about his final game as a league referee:

> In the end I played a little bit extra, waiting until play was at the Kop end, before sounding the final shrill blast – a bit like the Last Post. The fans behind the goal burst into spontaneous applause. It was longer and louder than normal, even for a big home win. Did they know it was my final visit? Was the applause for me? They are such knowledgeable football people, that it would not surprise me.

Sadly for Jeff, a more plausible explanation for the extra applause was that Liverpool had beaten Blackburn Rovers 4–0 and in doing so had pipped Newcastle United to fourth place and taken the final UEFA Champions League place for the following season.

In October 2003, Winter caused massive controversy at Anfield when Leeds were the visitors. Jeff wasn't the most popular referee with Leeds fans and they had been giving him some stick on that afternoon. He gave a free kick to Liverpool, Danny Murphy knocked it low into the six-yard box and Leeds keeper Paul Robinson went for it but fumbled the ball. There were three Liverpool players clearly offside and one of them, Steven Gerrard, stabbed the ball home. The linesman's flag immediately went up, but Winter gave the goal.

A few days later, I wrote to Winter:

> Dear Mr Winter,
> I feel I must register my complaint at the way you handled the recent Liverpool/Leeds fixture at Anfield. Almost the entire Liverpool attack was offside when they went in front 2–1. For you to claim that they were not interfering with play was bad enough, but to then say that 'the benefit of doubt has to go to the attackers' was quite bewildering. I would also like to ask you whether if either David Batty or Alan Smith had committed the two-footed lunge carried out by Steven Gerrard you wouldn't have sent either of them off instantly?

I didn't receive a reply at the time, but Winter did agree to contribute to this book, and in doing so, he does touch on that offside goal, albeit briefly. He wrote:

> My credit rating with Leeds fans fell after I sent both [Danny] Mills and [Lee] Bowyer off in a game against Arsenal at Highbury.
>
> I usually didn't have a problem with Lee. He could rant a bit but usually took as good as he gave with me. Danny Mills was a different kettle of fish, after the Arsenal game; mind you, I don't think he was keen on me before then either. His body language just showed that he had absolutely no respect for me at all. Still, you can't win them all. Nigel Martyn was always a gentleman. Even now when you speak to him you think, he's too nice to have been a footballer. Paul Robinson was sound as well. I always enjoyed reffing Ian Harte and Gary Kelly, both were good craic and easy to get on with. Lucas Radebe was also great . . .
>
> David Batty was not always the easiest to manage, but he was an absolute angel in comparison to Alan Smith, who was an angel off the pitch, but once over the white line he was an absolute nightmare. Smith was probably the most foul-mouthed footballer I have ever come across. But take that aggression out of him and he would not be the same player.
>
> You had a few good managers, although David O'Leary is probably the most patronising, condescending manager I have ever met. Reidy [Peter Reid] and I enjoyed a love–hate relationship, which probably turned to be more hate than love after I allowed an 'offside' goal at Anfield.

I would have thought that there are very few Leeds-supporting referees, but I suppose Roger Milford comes pretty close. He told me:

> I was employed for many years with a company based in Leeds and when I was at head office I often went onto the terrace to watch some home games as a spectator – incognito, of course. One of my colleagues at the office was a Leeds fanatic and often went with me to a game and spoke to me every week about the club and football in general, so I suppose I was an unofficial Leeds fan!
>
> I can remember reffing Leeds at Chelsea on 14 September

1991, and I still have a photograph on my desk of Carl Shutt scoring the only goal of the game for Leeds. I also did the 1987 FA Cup semi-final against Coventry City at Hillsborough. Unfortunately for Leeds, Coventry won and went on to win the cup. After the game, Leeds' manager at the time, Billy Bremner, came into my dressing-room and congratulated me on a very fine and fair performance. No, he really did mean it and he never hit me! I also did the last game of the season in 1992, against Norwich at Elland Road, when Leeds were crowned champions.

Gordon Strachan once gave me a present of a golf glove. Perhaps he was telling me to take up golf instead.

I have no bad memories of Leeds United – that must be a first for a referee – and I always enjoyed the rapport that went on – nothing, of course, that can be printed!

Gordon Kew was another highly respected referee, but I think that this match report he sent to the Football League in 1976 is brilliant. It concerned a game between Sheffield Wednesday and York City:

> I have to report that this match was disrupted when within a few minutes of the start a naked male spectator ran two-thirds the length of the pitch and kicked the ball away from where it had been placed for a free kick. As he was in midfield, I grabbed him, covering his strategic point with a white handkerchief, and ushered him off the pitch, handing him over to the police.

Jon Moss is a head teacher in a West Yorkshire primary school and is an extremely competent referee who was appointed to the National List of Referees in 2005. Jon looks remarkably like the comedian Lee Mack. This is in no way a criticism of his ability as a referee. I think the best way to introduce him is via Robbie Savage. In his *Daily Mirror* column in 2010, Savage said this:

> Earlier in the campaign, he gave Adam Johnson, then with Middlesbrough, a penalty against us. I thought he'd made a mistake and said so. The ref put both hands up to the sides of his head in a look of mock agony, said, 'I got it wrong, wow,' in a sarcastic voice and trotted off happily.

I thought that was a bit weird, but even more bizarre was his reaction on Saturday when we got a free kick and Ipswich broke the wall before the kick was taken and blocked the ball away easily.

I caught up with Moss to complain and said, 'That was never ten yards.' He replied, 'No, it was more like four. Fell for that one, didn't you? Na-na-na-na-na,' and ran off again.

In an interview featured on the Football League's website, former Premier League ref Paul Taylor recalls his first game, at Priestfield Stadium, Gillingham. As he left the stadium, a young lad, aged about seven, ran up to Taylor and asked for his autograph and gave him a scrap of paper.

'I'm not a player. I was the referee,' said Taylor.

'I know, Mr Taylor. Can I have your autograph?'

So he wrote, 'To Kevin, best wishes, Paul Taylor, Gillingham v. Darlington, 1989.'

'I had an ego the size of a small planet,' remembered Taylor. 'The lad must have been nearly eight by the time I'd finished and given it back to him.'

Then, when the ref gave the kid his piece of paper, the young lad said, 'Thanks . . . and my dad says you were bloody rubbish,' before running off down the street.

It probably won't surprise anyone connected with football to discover that the referee is biased. In 2006, research undertaken by Dr Peter Dawson revealed that the man in black is more likely to give a yellow or red card to the away team than the home team. Dawson reported:

> Even after the importance of the game and the size of the crowd are taken into account, our research has found that referees penalise the away side. Our study also backs up the theory that referees are very inconsistent. Some officials are more likely to discipline some players than others, while the underdogs are punished more than the top sides. We hope that our findings will be used by football authorities to improve the game. The decisions made by the referees can have important financial consequences for the individuals and the clubs. I hope the evidence will lead to

a debate about what positive action the authorities might take to ensure fairer refereeing of matches.

One official, who must remain anonymous for obvious reasons, is most definitely a Leeds United fan. He told me:

> Many years ago, I was appointed to run the line at a game between Oldham Athletic and Brentford. It was early in the year and a hard frost had set in. I needed to be there for half past twelve, so I left in plenty of time to get there from my home. I arrived in time to find the referee looking at the pitch. It was hard in patches and he asked me what I thought of it. I took one look at my watch and worked out that if I left in the next 20 minutes, I'd have enough time to get to Elland Road for a Leeds game. I stamped my foot on the hardest patch of grass I could find and said, 'Nah, it's not playable this, ref.' He agreed and I quickly grabbed my bag, got my expenses and in just over half an hour I was in the Peacock pub on Elland Road, having a pint before heading off to the Kop in time for the kick-off.

Of course, referees are only human and can't be in two places at the same time; this is one of the reasons many people are in support of TV replays displayed on a large screen, similar to those used in cricket and rugby and in Major League Soccer in America. That way, the referee can call for a replay if he's not 100 per cent sure on a vital decision.

However, during the 2010 FA Cup final between Chelsea and Portsmouth, the referee, Chris Foy, didn't in fact need TV replays to assist him. Just before half-time he made the ITV commentary team of Clive Tyldesley and former Leeds defender Jim Beglin look not a little foolish. Portsmouth keeper David James tipped a screaming free kick from Didier Drogba onto the bar and the ball bounced down onto the goal line before being scrambled away for a corner.

As he watched the replay, Beglin said, 'That was in. It looked in straight away to me. Just . . . I think.'

Then Tyldesley said somewhat smugly, 'Yes, and it's only a corner. And just how long did it take us – television, the dreaded television – to prove that it was a goal? Fifteen seconds?'

Then, as they both watched the replay again, Beglin said, 'What a hit this is. Is it in? I think so. David James does get a hand to it, but is it in? Is it? Oh, it's inconclusive. Maybe the whole of the ball hasn't crossed the line. Maybe I jumped the gun a bit there.'

Tyldesley then responded, with a little embarrassed chuckle, 'Well, maybe it's taken 30 seconds to prove that it might have been a goal – either way, why on earth do we not use the technology?'

Well, on this occasion there was no need. And there wasn't a single word from either of them pointing out that the referee and his assistant had actually got it spot-on.

But before we embark on a fanfare for the referee, there have also been some pretty dubious decisions given by the man in black, green, red, yellow, whatever, and perhaps the most notorious have taken place on the international stage. The USSR played Belgium during the 1986 Mexico World Cup and were expected to ease through without much difficulty. The thrilling match went to extra time, but the Soviets quite clearly should have won in normal time. Swedish referee Erik Fredriksson allowed the Belgians to equalise twice through offside goals; the second one, by Jan Ceulemans, was easily an incredible five yards offside.

Tunisian referee Ali Bin Nasser is famous for allowing the notorious 'Hand of God' goal during that same 1986 World Cup. For the quarter-final between Argentina and England, 114,580 people crammed into the Estadio Azteca and every single one of them would have seen the deliberate handball by Diego Maradona that took his side through to the semi-final. Everyone, that is, except for Ali Bin Nasser.

As England keeper Peter Shilton came out to deal with a poor clearance from Steve Hodge, Maradona challenged Shilton in the air and punched the ball into the back of Shilton's net. At first, none of the England players, apart from Shilton, reacted, because the handball was so blatant that a free kick looked certain to be given. But Bin Nasser, amazingly, awarded the goal, and all hell was let loose. Nothing was said about Nasser by the authorities, and, even more incredibly, FIFA awarded the cheating Argentinian – who later confessed to having been a drug addict – the Golden Ball for the player of the tournament.

After the game, Maradona was unrepentant, claiming that the goal had been scored 'a little with the head of Maradona [it never came close to his head] and a little with the hand of God'. All the people in Britain who helped vote his second goal from that match the FIFA Goal of the Century should be thoroughly ashamed of themselves. Maradona is a cheat and a disgrace to football.

Many years later, Maradona said that the win was revenge for the Falklands War between England and Argentina four years earlier. Supposedly, that wasn't the first time that resentments stemming from war had influenced events in world football. During the 1966 World Cup final between West Germany and England, England were awarded a Geoff Hurst goal that appeared to bounce down from the crossbar onto the line and not over it. The Swiss referee, Gottfried Dienst, was undecided and went to consult his linesman, Azerbaijani Tofik Bakhramov. The goal was awarded and England won the final 4–2. Improvements in technology have since indicated that the ball may not have crossed the line.

According to one apocryphal story, when asked on his deathbed whether Hurst's goal had been in, linesman Bakhramov replied, 'Stalingrad,' referring to the infamous battle in which the Nazis killed or wounded more than two million Soviets – the bloodiest in the history of warfare.

There was no warfare involved in the 2002 Japan/South Korea World Cup, not in the military sense at any rate. The Ecuadorian official Byron Moreno angered the whole Italian nation with some bizarre refereeing. In the game between Italy and co-hosts South Korea, Francesco Totti was sent off for diving. Television footage suggested that he had simply slipped. After that, Moreno awarded a dubious penalty when he said that Christian Panucci had pulled back a Korean attacker. Ahn Jung-Hwan ultimately scored the winner to eliminate the sore Italians.

It wasn't just Byron Moreno who seemed to obstruct the Italians' path to glory. They had already been on the receiving end of some debatable decisions during their final two group games. Against Mexico (referee Carlos Simon, Brazil) and Croatia (referee Graham Poll, England), Italy were denied four perfectly good goals and just made it through to the second round to meet South Korea.

It wasn't just Italy who suffered from poor refereeing decisions against South Korea. In their final group game, Portugal played the Koreans and it has to be said that some strange decisions by the

Argentinian referee Ángel Sánchez helped to enable the co-hosts to reach the final stages.

Of South Korea's good fortune, Gary Lineker wrote on his BBC blog:

> South Korea's amazing World Cup run was one of the great things to come out of this tournament . . . It's true to say that they enjoyed more than their fair share of good luck with key refereeing decisions against Portugal, Italy and Spain, but the fact is that a team with no World Cup finals victories prior to 2002 went as far as the semi-finals . . . and that is a phenomenal achievement.

Lineker finished his comments by adding, worryingly, 'South Korea's example should be the platform for the whole of Asian football to build on.'

6. Grass Routes

Virtually every top-class referee, including David Elleray, Mike Riley and Dermot Gallagher, started his career in the Sunday leagues. 'It's a passport to paradise,' Peter Willis of the Referees' Association told *F. C.* magazine. 'For the modern ref, the world is his oyster. After the 1995 FA Cup final won by Everton, Dermot Gallagher flew out to referee a game in Brazil on the Monday.'

A 12-hour course run by the county FAs is all it takes to qualify initially. Then the referees step up the pyramid system, starting at grade three and working their way up to grade one. Refs are marked by the teams and by the county FA assessors and promoted only on the basis of their ability. 'I tell them they're in competition with each other. They can be promoted, but if their markings go down they can also be relegated,' said Willis.

David Ager was a licensed instructor of referees in the 1990s and the author of *The Soccer Referee's Manual*: 'The basic rule is to remain firm and in control, but to show the player respect. Don't bawl him out, wave your arms around, order him around, touch him or lecture him. You do it formally and say, "I'm cautioning you for ungentlemanly conduct; if you repeat the offence, you may be sent off." A moral lecture is always a bit disastrous.'

In 1996, Dave Braddish, 39, was a referee in the Sunday Sportsman's League in London. Once on Chelsea's books, Dave had to stop playing due to an injury sustained when he was 23. Dave told *F.C.*:

> I do the refereeing to keep involved. You're putting something back into the game, which is very satisfying. I don't get too much abuse as I'm not a small fella and I tend to give it back, which helps. Personality is the secret of being a good ref. You don't bend laws but you use them to your advantage. Sometimes you have

players doing things off the ball. You know it's going on but you can't see it. So you get them on technicalities later and make sure they're out of the game and don't get away with it.

I try to use a sense of humour, and if that doesn't work I go back to what the book says. A bloke called me a cunt once and technically I could have sent him off. I said to him quietly, 'You just missed an open goal – who's the cunt?' The player and the captain both heard it and he calmed down and turned to me and said, 'I get your point.' It's man-management. Good refs say that Law 18 is common sense.

Braddish has used his sense of humour to defuse potential flare-ups:

Once I booked a keeper and he said his name was Spam-Head. I said, 'Right, Mr Spam-Head, you've got the showers all to yourself now.' All his teammates cracked up laughing as they realised what an idiot he was.

It takes an unusual combination of events to defeat an indefatigable ref such as Braddish:

I had a situation where the keeper had come out and brought down the forward. An ambulance was on the pitch, then an air ambulance landed! I said, 'That's enough,' and postponed the game. The thing was, I'd been paid before the game. That was the best result of my career.

Some say that players are becoming more abusive towards referees, although what exactly constitutes abuse can be open to debate. In 1994, Nick Loughlin of the White Horse pub side in Hartlepool had his three-week suspension cut to a fortnight by a Durham FA appeal court. He used a dictionary to support his argument that 'bollocks' was not a swear word but an expression of disbelief.

Clearly, abuse does exist. Halifax referees went on strike during Christmas of 1993 when a referee was knocked unconscious after cautioning a player. It was the sixth attack on a Halifax referee in four seasons. But surely Wayne Kirkham experienced the ultimate referee's nightmare. It occurred in the early '90s during a game in the

Nottinghamshire Combination League. The Old Rose pub side were playing against Hucknall Chequers. After Kirkham sent off a third Old Rose player, an aggrieved individual clambered into his van and drove it onto the pitch, straight at Kirkham, who had to dive out of the path of the van and then be shielded by the Chequers players. The driver was subsequently charged with attempted grievous bodily harm.

In 2009, the *Sunday Mirror*'s Michael Calvin reported on the problem:

> Eric [Mann] is a 69-year-old grandfather, a referee in the Cheshire & Manchester Sunday League for 36 years. He carries a baby's dummy, which he offers players booked for dissent. It didn't lighten the mood of the thug who grabbed his head, and kneed him in the jaw, when he sent him off . . .
>
> On any given Sunday, Accident & Emergency departments are littered with football's hidden victims. Youth Cup finals . . . have been disrupted recently by mass brawls between parents. An eight-year-old boy in Huddersfield punched a referee in the stomach . . . In Liverpool, a 40-year-old referee was attacked in the street by 10 players from an Under-14 team.

Thousands of amateur referees give up the game each year because of hassle and intimidation, and unfortunately assaults against referees and linesmen in the amateur game are on the increase. Figures released in March 2011 by the Football Association showed that violent attacks had increased by more than 25 per cent during 2010. By February 2011, there had been 330 such assaults compared with 260 at the same point in the previous season.

To take one example, in January 2011 part-time referee Peter Suter, a 53-year-old bus driver from Doncaster, was attacked and head-butted by a player after a six-a-side match. Mr Suter suffered terrible injuries and was hospitalised. The offending player was arrested and cautioned but could not be banned from playing because the incident took place at an unaffiliated fixture. Mr Suter commented:

> I have been a ref for 37 years and the respect towards officials is definitely getting worse. Players are learning bad habits and a lack

of respect from watching high-level football on TV. For some of them, having a go at the ref is part of the game.

A refereeing development officer for Kent FA, John Newson, told the *Sunday Express*:

> Players think it is OK to go out on the lash on Saturday nights and then turn up with a bad head on a Sunday morning and take out their frustrations on the ref . . . I don't think we should stop Sunday morning matches . . . There will always be hotheads and lunatics, but serious assaults are still rare.

The rise in assaults took place despite the FA's Respect campaign, launched at the start of the 2008–09 season in an attempt to address poor behaviour on and off the pitch. However, during the same period, recruitment of referees was on the rise, with referee numbers up 7.4 per cent year on year since the campaign's launch.

Many people believe that ex-players should become referees as they 'know the game'. But football pundit and former player and manager Chris Kamara, who is heavily involved in teaching kids about the Respect campaign, believes that the call from the FA for retired players to take up the whistle will not be heeded until they are spared the 'humiliation' of starting at the bottom. Kamara recently told the *Sunday Express*:

> The thing that causes the problems is the training. Players come from the top-flight clubs and if they want to be referees, they've got to start on park pitches. I wouldn't be up for it and I'm sure a lot of players feel the same way. The money's not there and they would feel humiliated. They've spent the whole of their careers being refereed by the best officials. They understand the game, they know how players think and react. There should be a fast-track system that takes these players to a level where they can be coached by a top referee.

Kamara also urged officials to make themselves more accountable by explaining their decisions:

I know how it feels when decisions go against you. They can cost you your job, so it's very difficult to keep your calm. The problem is that referees aren't forced to explain a decision, either in public or private. If a referee came out – or went to see a manager – straight after a game and explained himself, it might stop the manager saying something he'd later regret. Even if a ref has got it wrong, he should try to explain why he made the decision. That's what we all want to hear.

For those who are starting out as amateur refs, former instructor David Ager has some advice. He told *F.C.* magazine:

> There are two unofficial rules among amateur referees. The first is, don't ref games between policemen. Disciplined and controlled as they may be on the street, on the pitch they're bloody lethal. I'll always remember one police game I reffed where one side had only nine players. A car full of officers had got lost. I was almost tempted to suggest that they should have asked a policeman for the way, but their manager was a big bloke. The second rule is, don't ever handle matches between referees. They're obviously murderous, as every single decision is disputed and discussed.

During my own 25 years in amateur football I encountered many bad referees but also quite a number of good ones. A friend of mine for many years, Mike Stoddart has been refereeing for more than 32 years. Perhaps surprisingly, he cites Leeds' notorious defeat in the 1973 European Cup-Winners' Cup final as the reason he took up refereeing. He told me:

> I was there on that fateful night, getting wet through, watching the lightning light up the sky as we played AC Milan. After that match and also the 1975 European Cup final defeat in Paris, I decided enough was enough and I was going to start refereeing, because certainly I couldn't do any worse than they did. After it was proved that the Greek referee had been bribed, the ECWC should have been awarded to Leeds United.
>
> I'm still reffing these days and it's bloody hard work. I've just

returned from an afternoon game in Yeadon where I had to send off four players and book two from the away team. They were disgraceful and showed little respect for my decisions, but I'll be out again tomorrow morning in the Wakefield league praying for an easier passage.

I didn't quite make it to a European final, but I did the line in two FA Cup finals and ran the line in Copenhagen in the UEFA Cup, as well as running the line in the Premiership and the Championship. Best of all was a goal I disallowed at Old Trafford that inadvertently helped Leeds United win the Division One league title back in 1992. The game in question was against Chelsea late in that season and I was running the line for referee Vic Callow. Halfway through the first half, I had cause to disallow a goal for Man United for a complicated offside. Vic gave the goal, but then ruled it out upon seeing my raised flag. The crowd went mad and began chanting, 'You Leeds bastard! You Leeds bastard!' I wanted the ground to open up and swallow me whole. Fancy putting in the match programme, 'Linesman with the yellow flag, M.J. Stoddart (Leeds).' How insensitive is that?

As we walked off the pitch at half-time, Alex Ferguson came storming up to me and said, 'I bet you've made Howard a very happy man tonight.'

Knowing full well that he was referring to Leeds manager Howard Wilkinson, I replied, 'Howard who?'

A very, very late goal from Mark Hughes earned them a point, but those two dropped points helped towards Leeds clinching the league title. Let me confirm, however, that television replays proved me right to disallow the goal.

Refereeing is certainly a hard job, but at least the game in Britain is clean and all the decisions I give – whether right or wrong – are, and were, honest.

Mike also ran the line at a Middlesbrough match in 1997 in which he was instrumental in getting Fabrizio Ravanelli sent off for persistent abuse.

Little did I know when I set out that day on my journey to the Riverside Stadium to line for the Premiership clash between

Middlesbrough and Sheffield Wednesday that this would be my Andy Warhol, 15-minutes-of-fame day.

As was usually the case, my partner, Gill, and I set off early so as to be able to 'see the sights' on the way. My philosophy is, if you're going to a place to officiate that you wouldn't normally visit, then you might as well explore the town centre and the countryside while you're there. I mean, who in their right mind would take a day trip to, say, Hartlepool or Rochdale? But let me tell you, they were well worth discovering. That particular day at Middlesbrough was a cold January day. We parked up near the centre and 'did the shops', one of Gill's favourite pastimes. At twelve, we would move the car to within striking distance of the ground to have a spot of lunch, which always consisted of cheese and pickle sandwiches, currant teacakes, cheese and onion crisps, a piece of Gill's favourite baking and an apple, all this washed down with a bottle of orange juice and lemonade. It never failed to get me through the match without food poisoning or a stomach upset.

Arriving at the ground two and a half hours before kick-off was the norm in those days. The referee that afternoon was Paul Durkin, and it was to be my last game with him as this was to be my last season, having reached the age of 44. One thing I always admired about Paul was his willingness to stand up and be counted, and this day he certainly didn't let me down. After an exciting, trouble-free first half and with the score tied at 2–2, the ball was passed through to that famous Italian striker Fabrizio Ravanelli, who slotted the ball home. Unfortunately for him, when the ball was played he was stood in an offside position and I had no hesitation in raising my flag. On realising that his goal had been disallowed, Ravanelli raced across to me. If I had not lowered my flag from its horizontally outstretched position, he would have impaled himself on it. I decided to adopt a passive stance as he came right up to me in my face. What did I say? Actually, nothing, except the one word of Italian I knew, 'basta', a word I had only learnt the previous day from a work colleague . . . it means 'enough' and he thought it might come in handy should a certain Italian gentleman need calming down.

The referee, seeing that there was a confrontation, approached at speed and promptly showed Ravanelli the yellow card and told him in no uncertain terms that 'enough was enough', so to speak. Play eventually continued but not before I had picked up a 50p piece that had landed at my foot ... One minute later, I was again flagging Ravanelli offside; he looked at me in disgust and then, in the very next attack, I had cause to flag him offside again. This time, he came racing over to me, gesturing threateningly with his fist. Paul Durkin, a man who, as I already said, didn't shirk his responsibilities, came over and immediately issued Ravanelli with his second yellow card and sent him from the field. The crowd was in uproar and it was the most intimidating atmosphere I have ever witnessed. 'Get out of this alive,' I thought to myself. Luckily the gods were shining down on us in the form of a wonder goal from that magical Brazilian, Juninho, which put Middlesbrough 3–2 up. With the final score at 4–2 and the supporters all talking about 'that goal', our police escort back to the car park wasn't required.

By this time, Gill was back in the car and not too pleased at having spent the past half-hour or so sat in the stand amongst people who were verbally abusing her 'much beloved'. We decided not to visit our usual restaurant in Middlesbrough in case of there being any trouble, so instead we drove a bit further on to a pub/restaurant at Preston Farm. As we entered the pub, I made a point of covering up the Premier League badge on my blazer in the hope that no one would notice us.

I ordered our drinks at the bar and the landlord took one look at me and said, 'It was you who got our man sent off this afternoon, wasn't it?' And before we could turn and run, he added, 'Nobody should have to put up with that sort of behaviour on a football field. These drinks are on me. You'll be all right here.' And we were. We ended up sitting next to a couple and their son who were Sheffield Wednesday supporters. During our meal, a young lad came over and asked politely for my autograph. It's a funny old world.

While it's obvious that there are cameras at every Premier League match, mostly filming for *Match of the Day*, I didn't realise that the Middlesbrough game had been shown live all across Europe. That evening, I tuned in to *Match of the Day* and was more than satisfied that the decisions I had made were the correct ones. The panel analysed the Ravanelli incidents and were also of the opinion that justice had been done. I always made a point of not getting the Sunday papers, so I was oblivious to what, if anything, had been said in the press.

At about 8.30 on the following Monday morning, I was surveying a busy junction in the west of Leeds for my employers, Leeds City Council. Cars were coming to a halt in the middle of the road, waiting to turn right just opposite where I was stood. Suddenly, a young man in a Mini shouts out through his open window, 'Are you a referee?', to which I replied, 'Yes.' On hearing this, he said, 'Is that you?', holding up a page from a newspaper, and there was I face to face with Ravanelli – the full length of the page. 'My God,' I replied, nodding, as he sped away laughing. Apparently, an Italian photographer, Paolo Minnoli, had taken the shot and it had been bought by the Mirror Group. A few days later, the photo editor, an ex-League referee, Tony Ward, kindly sent me an inscribed copy. It's surprising the number of people who can relate to that photo. I've been on holiday in Malta, Crete and Spain and been recognised from that shot. The incident also featured on 'What Happened Next?' on the BBC's *A Question of Sport* a couple of years later.

I'm often asked if this moment of notoriety has changed me in any way. Absolutely not. I'm still refereeing, 13 years after retiring from the Premier League, in local football, Saturdays and Sundays, just like I did in my first season back in 1976 – but the difference is the people who were causing me trouble back then were the likes of the author of this book! Only joking – he was a joy to referee ... for a goalie!

One referee who I thought was absolutely hopeless during my amateur days was a chap called Achmed Niyazi. There weren't many games when he didn't create havoc with inept and inadequate displays. In one game I played, he sent off three of our players and four of theirs before both teams walked off together. In the same game, he gave me my first and only booking of my career. I was a goalkeeper and I had kicked the ball out of my area only for it to hit Mr Niyazi full in the face, knocking his glasses off. I have to admit that I was upset at another horrendous decision he'd made and, in my frustration, had meant to kick the ball at him, but I didn't think for one minute that I'd hit my target from 20 yards! At a West Riding FA disciplinary hearing, both teams were cleared and all cautions and sendings-off were quashed. Shortly afterwards, Niyazi left the country and became a listed referee in the professional Cypriot league.

There is no doubt that the vast majority of referees are in it for the good of the game – and, along with the good intentions, a bit of first-aid knowledge doesn't go amiss, either. In 1994, a referee saved the life of his linesman. It was in the Doncaster and District Sunday Alliance League, during a game between Little Plough and Wincanton. In the final minutes, referee Rob Yates was alerted by some of the players to the fact that a linesman had gone down. 'I ran over and saw him lying on the ground,' said Yates. 'His face was a grey-blue colour and I saw that he'd swallowed his tongue. I released it with my index finger. He went into a fit, though, and swallowed his tongue again, so we had to repeat the procedure. I then put him into the recovery position for the arriving emergency services to take over.'

Another referee from Doncaster regularly took charge of games that I played in on cold and wet Sunday mornings. Roger Furnandiz started refereeing back in 1975. On any given Saturday, he would be in charge at Maine Road, Anfield or Highbury. The following day, he would take control of a game in the Castleford and District Sunday League.

During the 1980s, Roger was running the line at Elland Road when Spurs were the visitors. Paul Gascoigne played that day and every time Gazza, who had put on a bit of weight, came near Roger's touchline, the crowd threw Mars bars at him. 'It took a lot of willpower not to pick any up for later,' says Roger.

There is a manager, however, who would probably argue that it wouldn't have made much difference if Mr Furnandiz had, after all, picked up one or two of those Mars bars that day. Dave Jones was manager of Wolves in April 2002, when they lost 3–1 to Norwich City in the first leg of the First Division play-off semi-final. This was the penultimate game of Roger Furnandiz's 17-year career. Afterwards, Jones said, 'The referee was atrocious. I do not think he is physically fit enough to referee at this level. He was chugging around like an old tugboat. The referee did not cost us the game or anything, but at this level you have to be fit. He's not fit.'

Furnandiz was, quite understandably, not impressed when informed of Jones's remarks about his refereeing or indeed of his appearance. 'Dave is quite entitled to his opinion, of course,' said Roger. 'But if he wants to come and say that to me again, he could get himself into trouble. I refereed Wolves' game against Wimbledon two weeks ago and afterwards he wanted to kiss me!'

Furnandiz certainly left an impression on the Premier League. In 1998, he was in charge of the Sheffield United v. Bradford City fixture at Bramall Lane. With the score at 0–0 and the match heading towards half-time, Bradford defender Eddie Youds cleared the ball but only as far as Furnandiz, who was situated inside the Bradford half. The ball hit Furnandiz on the head and looped 30 yards back to the edge of the Bradford area, where an unmarked Sheffield defender had the easy task of putting the Blades ahead. United's manager at the time, Nigel Spackman, said, 'A chap behind me said it was the best pass of the day, and I have to agree with him.' Thirty-six-year-old Ian Rush was making his home debut for the Blades that day and commented, 'I just heard the referee shout, "Ouch!" I've seen some things in my career, but that's got to be up there with the best of them.' Bradford boss Paul Jewell said, 'I've never seen anything like it. You can call it weird, but to me it was just unlucky. The ref never even apologised, but we were so poor in the first half that we didn't deserve any luck.'

Just over a month later, Charlton Athletic were playing Swindon Town when Furnandiz caught Swindon's striker Iffy Onuora with a stray elbow, fracturing his jaw, minutes before Steve Jones put Charlton ahead. Swindon manager Steve McMahon wasn't happy with the official and said, 'He should never have been that close. He was doing a better man-marking job than Claudio Gentile! He should have sent himself off! I thought he had a terrible game. He denied us a clear penalty earlier, so you could say he hit us with two big blows.'

One boss who did praise Furnandiz was Graham Taylor. After a game in November 1998 between Watford and Bury, he told reporters, 'It was great credit to Roger Furnandiz that he did not succumb to the suggestions made from the Bury bench. I would not want to be a party to some of the shouts which came from their part of the touchline.' But Bury's boss at the time, Neil Warnock, claimed that video evidence proved that Bury ought to have been given at least two penalties in the first half, saying, 'Furnandiz is a good ref, but today he had a poor day at the office.'

Despite some of the aforementioned blips, I can vouch with some authority that Roger Furnandiz, who made his final league appearance in 2002, was a very good referee, on the amateur scene at least. After he retired, he became the referee development officer for the West Riding County Football Association.

Tony Peart is another dedicated amateur referee destined for the top. Tony has recently been upgraded from the grass roots of local football to leagues One and Two as well as the Championship. He is Leeds born and bred, and, of course, a staunch Leeds United fan. Tony ran the line in a pre-season friendly between York City and Leeds. Playing up front for Leeds was Jermaine Beckford, who had just refused to sign a new contract with the club. To his credit, Beckford performed well throughout those pre-season games and was subsequently taken off the transfer list. He scored a goal at this game in York, but Tony flagged him offside. Afterwards, Tony said to Beckford, 'If you'd have signed the new contract with Leeds, I'd have let your goal stand.' Of course, he was joking, adding that Beckford had indeed been offside.

Sky TV presenters Andy Gray and Richard Keys were sensationally sacked in January 2011 for making sexist remarks. At a Wolves–Liverpool fixture, Keys was heard to say about assistant referee Sian Massey, 'Somebody better get down there and explain offside to her.' Gray added, 'Women don't know the offside rule,' to which Keys replied, 'Course they don't. I can guarantee you there will be a big one today. Kenny [Dalglish, Liverpool manager] will go potty.' Later, he went on, 'The game's gone mad. See charming Karren Brady this morning complaining about sexism? Do me a favour, love.'

It would have been interesting to hear the comments of Gray and Keys had they attended one particular game in the Cheltenham League in April 1997, between Northleach Town and Smiths Athletic. The referee that day was Phil Pawsey. 'There were six minutes left, it was a very tense game and the home team needed a point to stay up when my wife appeared on the pitch. The players were saying, "Who's this fucking woman? She's run right across the field."'

Mrs Pawsey had locked herself out and as she had tickets for the theatre and was due there soon, her only option was to run over and get her husband's keys. By the time the situation had been remedied, the light had faded too much for play to continue and the game had to be abandoned, much to the obvious annoyance of hosts Northleach, who looked to have secured the point they needed to avoid relegation. For the record, Mrs Pawsey arrived at the theatre on time and Northleach won the rearranged fixture 4–0.

We can't leave the grass roots of amateur football without adding another amusing little story. During the 1999 season, Richmond St Mary's were playing Chessington Evangelical Church in the Southern Area Christian League. It was the week before Christmas. Just minutes from the end, the entire Richmond St Mary's team was shown the red card for the rather un-Christian behaviour of swearing like troopers. Marshall Baron, club secretary – and in his spare time an altar server at Richmond Parish Church – was among those to get his marching orders. 'It was a complete farce,' he said. 'I admit I said "Jesus Christ" and should have been sent off. I'm not saying we were angels, but we object to the fact that . . . we were punished and Chessington were not – there was swearing on both sides.' No exchanging of Christmas cards there, then.

Even linesmen get in on the act at times. Dick Skellington from Milton Keynes was lining at Bedford Town one night when the referee went over to him and told him that he had lost his dentures. Six front teeth on a plate had leapt from his mouth as he ran diagonally across the pitch. He asked Dick to keep an eye out for them and see if he could see them glistening in the lights. But neither he nor the other linesman could see the teeth in the mudbath of a pitch. Back in the dressing-room afterwards, an old man with a pitchfork came in with the teeth in bits. 'They were on the fucking penalty spot, Ernie,' he said to the ref. 'Sorry, I put me fork straight through them.' The referee was from the Football League and Dick said, 'Sometimes they would talk down to us linos when they middled the Southern League. We never saw this referee from Enfield again.'

On another occasion, Dick was lining for a referee called Graham Earl in a United Counties fixture at Kempston Hardwick. Dick told me:

> It was early in the season and Graham rang me to say he would
> pick me up half an hour earlier than we had previously arranged.

When we arrived at the ground, he said, 'Let's go and walk the pitch,' which was lush and verdant green. He then asked the groundsman to put the floodlights on, although it was still daylight, and he told me to wait down near the six-yard line and see what happened. The lights came on and Graham said, 'Look,' and all over the pitch mushrooms popped up, dozens of them. We scooped them all up in Graham's large bag. They were delicious. He said that if we ever got this fixture again we'd do it again – and we did. Two seasons later, we went and bagged another three kilos. 'Only happens in Kempston . . . famous for it,' Graham said.

7. Double Trouble

The season of 1971–72 saw Leeds powering their way towards achieving the coveted League and FA Cup double.

They reached their fifth FA Cup semi-final in seven years with an emphatic 3–0 victory over Birmingham City at Hillsborough that signalled Leeds' second visit to Wembley in three seasons.

This was no ordinary final. It was the FA Cup centenary final. A crowd of 100,000 packed into Wembley Stadium and the teams, Leeds United and Arsenal, emerged from the tunnel flanked by the flags of all the clubs that had lifted the trophy since 1872. Incidentally, the first-ever winners of the FA Cup, 100 years before, were Wanderers FC, a London team, in a bizarre contest. Because some of their opponents withdrew, and because at that time both teams progressed to the next round if there was a draw, Wanderers had only won one of their games, by the time they reached the semi-finals, where they played Queen's Park of Scotland in a match that ended 1–1. The Scots, however, withdrew from the competition because they could not afford to return to London for the replay.

At the end of a memorable centenary match, a diving header by Allan Clarke separated the two teams and it was Leeds captain Billy Bremner who received the FA Cup from Her Majesty the Queen. Unfortunately, however, Leeds were unable to celebrate their momentous victory in style, as they had a crucial league game to play only 48 hours later.

The day after the Wembley final, all the players and families, including all the reserves and juniors, boarded a chartered Pullman train back to Leeds. Dave Cocker was travelling with the reserves in their carriage and the first-team players were in another. The players who were with Dave persuaded him to ask Revie if they could have the FA Cup in their carriage for a while. Revie agreed and the British

Rail stewards duly filled the cup with champagne. Inevitably, things got a little out of hand and the champagne and beer were flowing freely. Dave recalls the juniors' centre-half getting a tad excited as the train passed slowly through his home town of Doncaster. Says Dave, 'At one stage, he was hanging out of the window with the cup in his hand!'

As the train arrived in Leeds, back gardens along the way all had huge banners in them welcoming the team and the fans home. 'The Leeds train must have been publicised,' adds Dave. As the team arrived back in the station, photographs were being taken by the press and public alike. But eagle-eyed fans would notice from any of the press pictures that the lid is missing from the cup. Dave can explain this: 'We were a bit tipsy and in the process the lid got "mislaid". We searched high and low for it, but, aided no doubt by the alcohol intake, we never found it. Before the players could join the parade to the Civic Hall for the reception, the train was searched thoroughly and the lid was eventually found under a seat. I got another major bollocking for that.'

In the end, Leeds missed out on the double, coming second in the league to Derby County. Derby had 58 points; Leeds had 57 but a far superior goal average. Even a point at Wolves on the Monday night would have ensured the double for United. Derby were so convinced that Leeds would gain the necessary result that immediately after their final league game they jetted off to Majorca. Not surprisingly, Leeds were jaded after the FA Cup final and felt it was unfair to expect them to play such a vital game only 48 hours later. Leeds asked the Football League to put the game back to the Wednesday in order to rest the players and attempt to get the injured fit again. The League said, 'By all means, but you'll have to play without your England internationals.' Preparations were under way for a forthcoming England game against West Germany in the European Championship and, although it had never happened before and hasn't since, all Leeds' England internationals were expected to attend. This would have meant Leeds facing Wolves without Paul Reaney, Terry Cooper, Jack Charlton, Norman Hunter, Paul Madeley and Allan Clarke. They were already without Mick Jones, who had been injured in the FA Cup final.

It's worth noting that only the month before the Football League had agreed to a request from Wolves to postpone all of their Easter league games to enable them to prepare for a UEFA Cup semi-final against Hungarian side Ferencváros. Once more, secretary Alan Hardaker will have taken great satisfaction in putting yet another obstacle between Leeds and further success.

Incidentally, in the previous season, on Easter Monday in 1970, Leeds had fielded a weakened side for a league fixture at Derby County. With the league title almost out of United's reach, Revie put all his resources into the European Cup and FA Cup (something that is a common occurrence these days).

One bizarre incident that I remember from that day is keeper David Harvey being booked for apparently taking his goal kicks off a small cushion-type pad to enable more height and distance.

In any case, the side at Derby that afternoon consisted mostly of reserve players, and the Football League fined Leeds £5,000, despite their having medical certificates proving each missing player was unfit. Yet, only two weeks later a flu epidemic hit the club, leaving several players unfit. Aware of the League's previous action against Leeds, Revie asked for a postponement of the Burnley game at Elland Road, but Leeds were told they must play the game. Billy Bremner, Peter Lorimer and Eddie Gray were the only first-teamers to play that day. For the record, Eddie Gray scored two superb goals that day, including his much televised wonder goal, where he beat seven players, including going around Albert Johanneson, who was lying injured on the pitch, before coolly dispatching a low shot past keeper Peter Mellor.

As a result of the disturbances that followed Leeds' match at Elland Road against West Brom, the team were made to play their first four home games of the '71–'72 season away from Elland Road. Leeds' 'home' run began like this: Leeds v. Wolves (at Huddersfield Town), drew 1–1; Leeds v. Spurs (at Hull City), drew 1–1; Leeds v. Newcastle (at Sheffield Wednesday), won 5–1; Leeds v. Crystal Palace (at Huddersfield Town), won 2–0. It can be strongly argued that the two points dropped against Wolves and Spurs would have been secured had the games been played at Elland Road.

For the crucial final game of the season, around 25,000 Leeds fans arrived at Molineux in anticipation of seeing United win the much-deserved league and cup double, and many thousands didn't get in. Before the game, Ladbrokes had Leeds at 2–5 on to win the league.

Derby were 7–2 against, with Liverpool at 6–1. I remember squashing into the South Bank and shouting myself hoarse as Leeds ran out onto the pitch. Not surprisingly, our team was tired. On top of that, half the team played having been given pain-killing injections, Eddie Gray had his shoulder heavily strapped and reserve midfielder Mick Bates was in at centre-forward (although it was Billy Bremner who dominated the attack). Despite all this, the general feeling amongst us was optimistic. The referee that night was Bill J. Gow from Swansea. Although Leeds fell behind just before half-time to a Frank Munro goal, they looked the stronger side – but once again the game was littered with controversy.

Bill Gow recently told the *Yorkshire Evening Post*:

> Whenever I refereed Leeds I knew I was in for a hard time from the first minute through to the final whistle. After a few games I became exasperated and decided to stamp my authority from the off. In one game against Arsenal I gave a throw-in to the Gunners. The next thing Billy Bremner was in my face contesting my decision. I blew the whistle, called him over and ordered him to take off his shirt. I gave him the whistle and said I was going to play for Leeds United and he was to be the referee. He and the rest of the players burst into hysterics and I never had a decision questioned again.

That was, of course, until this fateful night in Wolverhampton in 1972.

Wolves' keeper Phil Parkes brought down Allan Clarke in the penalty area. Full-back Bernard Shaw twice handled on the line from Clarke and Peter Lorimer, and on one occasion Frank Munro literally held the ball in his hands for a few seconds in the penalty area. But Mr Gow was having none of it. Norman Hunter said recently, 'When Munro caught the ball, everything went quiet. He could have taken the lace out!'

Disaster struck in the second half when, much against the run of play, Derek Dougan (who 48 hours previously had presented Allan Clarke with the Golden Boot award at the players' Wembley hotel) hit a second for Wolves. Minutes later, Bremner was bundled over in the six-yard box as Les Cocker screamed at the referee. Leeds continued to press and, inevitably, Bremner grabbed one for Leeds, but it wasn't to be United's night.

As if defeat wasn't bad enough, months after the game allegations were made by the *Sunday People* that three players from Wolves had been offered – and had declined – around £1,000 to throw the match. Even the CID was brought in to assist the Football Association in its investigations, all of which proved to be inconclusive. Five years later, however, the sister paper to the *Sunday People* revived the alleged scandal. The *Daily Mirror* ran what can only be called a smear campaign against Leeds United and they contacted former Leeds winger Mike O'Grady to testify to the bribery accusations. O'Grady had been transferred to Wolves three years earlier, but was on loan to Birmingham at the time of that game at Molineux. Although O'Grady had not played in the game, the *Mirror* claimed that he knew who the three players who had been offered bribes were. Dave Wagstaffe and Frank Munro had already claimed in the *Sunday People* that an attempt to bribe them had been made. According to the *Mirror*, O'Grady said that an offer had also been made to Bernard Shaw, who, like his teammates, had refused. However, O'Grady later denied any allegations attributed to him and refused to substantiate the paper's story.

Mike O'Grady told me:

> Richard Stott and Frank Palmer of the *Daily Mirror* offered me £40,000 to say that I was the 'go-between' who had arranged the 'bribe' to Wolves to throw the game. That amount of money was phenomenal in those days, but I refused because it simply wasn't true. Stott said that they would run the story anyway, with or without my collaboration. The fact is that it was Gary Sprake who had told the *Mirror* that I was the 'go-between'. Gary was down on his luck at the time, he obviously needed the money and wanted someone else to back up his story. The following year, the *News of the World* contacted me asking me to reconsider going with the 'story'; again I refused.

It is to his immense credit that O'Grady refused the *Mirror*'s advances, but Gary Sprake was different. He named former Leeds player the late Terry Hibbitt as another go-between. In 1978, Sprake accepted £7,500 from the *Daily Mirror* in exchange for information 'proving' that Don Revie and Billy Bremner had tried to bribe Wolves players.

To this day, Sprake is shunned by almost all of Don Revie's '60s and '70s squad for what they see as an obvious case of betrayal of a man who stood by his goalkeeper despite regular costly mistakes that undoubtedly lost United trophies. Sprake made horrific blunders in FA Cup semi-finals and final alike, but Don Revie stayed loyal to him, despite having a more than capable understudy in David Harvey. In fact, long after he left Leeds United, Revie admitted that he should have switched his keepers long before he did. Speaking to the *Yorkshire Evening Post* in 1981, Revie said:

> Gary was a terrific goalkeeper and helped us win some trophies, but unfortunately his mistakes cost us dear in many other contests. In hindsight, I should have had Harvey in goal long before I put him in for the 1972 FA Cup semi-final against Birmingham when we went on to win the FA Cup.

Gary Sprake was popular with the ladies, by his own admission. But this got him into trouble on more than one occasion. Don Revie went out on a limb to protect his goalkeeper countless times, but none more so than after an incident in 1971. The Leeds players, including Sprake, had gone to a nightclub in Leeds on the night that Arsenal clinched the league title at Tottenham with a 1–0 win. Had Arsenal failed to get a point, the title would have gone to Leeds, so the players decided to drown their sorrows. Sprake and three others left in a car late at night. In *Careless Hands*, a biography by Stuart Sprake and Tim Johnson, the former Leeds goalie says:

> There were a lot of girls in the club, so we invited everyone back to the Mecca DJ Pete Madeley's flat, and he and two girls jumped in my car. I lost control of my car and as I crashed off the road one of the girls flew from the back seat through the windscreen. She was very badly injured and needed over two dozen stitches in her face. As we were wandering around in the dark, one of my teammates pulled up and in a panic I jumped into his car and he took me home. Within minutes the police arrived and asked where I'd been that night. Foolishly I told them I had been at home. They said my car had been involved in an accident so could

they look in my garage. Obviously the car was not there so I told them that it must have been stolen. Just as they were about to take me in for questioning, the Boss arrived. He took the officers to one side and had a word with them. The next thing was they said they would report my car as stolen. I was fined for careless driving, but once again the Boss had saved me, this time possibly from serious charges.

None of Sprake's and the *Mirror*'s allegations were proven to be true, and Bremner and Revie were left with no case to answer. Later, the *Sunday People* had another try at claiming bribery attempts by Bremner, who subsequently sued the newspaper and received a then record settlement of £100,000. Wolves player Derek Dougan offered his support to Bremner at the hearing, saying that the claims were nonsense. Revie decided not to pursue the matter, but a few years down the line would fight the Football Association in court.

Peter Lorimer has commented in the *Yorkshire Evening Post*:

> The game in those days was awash with bribery allegations, and because of the intense dislike towards Leeds from the media, most were levelled at Leeds United. To 'get' at a team or fix a match, you could only probably approach a couple of players and not the entire team. You would also definitely have to have a word with the goalie.

That night at Molineux, Wolves keeper Phil Parkes had the game of his life. He caught, punched and tipped the ball away all night long. The only players who handled the ball better were Wolves defenders Bernard Shaw and Frank Munro.

8. The Dictator

'Alan Hardaker loathed Don Revie with a vengeance.'
Graham Kelly,
Hardaker's successor as Football League secretary

Alan Hardaker was the secretary of the Football League for some 20 years and during his tenure he was described as 'the League's most celebrated enforcer', 'the great dictator', 'football's Godfather', 'a cross between Cagney and Caligula', 'St Alan of St Annes' and even 'Lytham's answer to Idi Amin'. Despite these descriptions, in his autobiography, *Hardaker of the League*, he wrote that he was never 'anything more than a paid servant responsible at all times to the president and members of the League Management Committee'. Under this guise, Hardaker was to cross swords with Don Revie and Leeds United on a regular basis for many years.

Hardaker was born into a middle-class family in Hull, East Yorkshire, in 1912, roughly halfway between Hull FC rugby league club and Hull City AFC at 230 The Boulevard. His father, John, was heavily involved in politics. He was a staunch Liberal supporter and a big fan of rugby union before progressing to rugby league. Alan Hardaker disliked politics immensely and went on to choose football over rugby.

After turning out for a number of local amateur sides, he played briefly for Hull City, but in 1939 the Second World War changed the course of his life temporarily; while watching Yorkshire Cricket Club at Hull one afternoon, he discovered that recruiting had begun for the Humber Division of the Royal Navy Volunteer Regiment. By the time war broke out on 3 September, Hardaker was on board HMS *Calcutta*. He later served on HMS *Newcastle*, which patrolled off the coast of Iceland to prevent German vessels from getting back to their own ports or breaking out into the Atlantic. By 1942, he had progressed to lieutenant commander. The navy obviously instilled discipline and, some would say, stubbornness into Hardaker's make-up.

After the war, Hardaker became secretary to the mayor of Hull. One afternoon, he saw an advertisement in the *Daily Telegraph*:

> The Football League invites applications for a position of trust and responsibility in its administrative office. Applicants should possess executive ability and a thorough knowledge of modern office routine. Experience in Association Football affairs is desirable. Excellent prospects. Pension scheme.

After working in the League's offices for many years, Hardaker eventually replaced Fred Howarth as Football League secretary in 1957. In his rise to the top, Hardaker wasn't afraid to step on toes and was instrumental in getting rid of any 'dead wood'.

The Football League was already the oldest in the world but, despite constant battles with the media, fellow committee members and the Football Association, Hardaker slowly moulded the League into the shape he desired. He was often described as arrogant and high-handed, but he always maintained, at all costs, that things would be done his way or not at all. Of course there were discussions, but with only one possible outcome. As he put it in his autobiography:

> Some things happened later that would have happened whoever was secretary; but there were other things – innovations which I think were improvements, although I accept that not everybody agrees with me – which happened only because I made them happen.

Hardaker was set in his ways and didn't like change unless he had instigated it. One of the many examples of this was his objection to the European Cup. He and the Football League advised Chelsea, the first-ever British candidates for the European Cup as league champions in 1955, not to enter the competition. Chelsea were under no obligation to succumb to Hardaker's request – but did so anyway. Hardaker didn't welcome what he saw as foreign encroachment and the potential overshadowing of his competition. Indeed, he once told journalist Brian Glanville that he didn't much enjoy dealing with football on the Continent. 'Too many wogs and dagoes,' he said.

In the early 1960s, Hardaker and the League were locked in battle with the PFA over the maximum wage for footballers. The maximum wage as it stood was £20 a week and the PFA, led by chairman Jimmy Hill, a former Fulham footballer and part-time football pundit, were campaigning for 'no limit'. The PFA encouraged its members to strike if their demands were not met. The League had vainly suggested a £25 to £30 limit for two years, to see how things panned out, but this was one battle the League wasn't going to win and the maximum wage was eventually scrapped, the consequences of which are clearly in evidence today.

At one of the many meetings between the League and the PFA, the League's president, Joe Richards, said, 'For the good of the game, I suggest –' He was instantly interrupted by Jimmy Hill, who said, 'We're not interested in the good of the game. We're only here to talk about our members.'

During that period, Hardaker was shark fishing with a friend off the Cornish coast at Looe. Hardaker hauled in a 100-lb catch and as it landed in the boat, his friend gave the shark a clout. 'Hit it again,' said Hardaker. 'It looks like Jimmy Hill.'

In March 1972, Hardaker announced:

> Regrettably, there now seems to be a state of war between the League and the Football Association. It will be construed that the FA fired the first shots. It was certainly not the wish of the League Management Committee and can only do tremendous damage to the game.

The disagreement was over the size of the fee to be paid for the live screening of an important international at Wembley – but the reason for that particular row was irrelevant, really. 'Because,' Hardaker wrote in his autobiography, 'if we had not fallen out over this particular issue, it would have been another.' He went on:

> The League and the FA have been laying about each other for the best part of a century. It is a cold war of course. No triggers are

squeezed, no blood is ever drawn, but it is a war that has been spitting away ever since the Football Association's muddled attitude to professionalism back in the 1880s led to the birth of the Football League. The FA had good reason to regret and resent the prosperity of the League. It has regularly attempted to clip the wings and even assume control of the League: but that will never be, because we are fiercely proud of our independence. Most other leagues are directly controlled by their national associations, and in England too, the FA is the game's controlling body, responsible for such matters as law making, all international business, discipline and the amateur game. But although, broadly speaking, the Football League is only licensed by the FA to run its own competition, the League has acquired such strength and character down through the twentieth century that, once its rules have been approved by the FA, it now has a clearly defined right to look after its own destiny. Nothing is going to change that.

. . . Jealousy and squabbling for power at the top ruling end of football are now inseparable from the game as fleas are from dogs.

There was no love lost between Fred Howarth, the League secretary from 1933 to 1957, and Sir Stanley Rous, who was the FA's secretary from 1934 to 1961. Howarth had applied for the vacant FA's secretary's job, which eventually went to Rous, and the two men quite simply never got on after that. Inevitably the relationship between the League and the FA suffered.

Alan Hardaker was to fall out with Sir Stanley Rous himself. By Hardaker's own admission, he and Rous were never in danger of becoming close friends. Hardaker was deeply mistrustful of Rous, who he said 'ruled supreme'. Hardaker opposed Rous on several issues over the years, but he said, 'If Sir Stanley Rous had been a politician, he would very probably have become Prime Minister.'

Rous was a very powerful figure, moving up to take over as president of FIFA in 1961. Walter Winterbottom, England's manager and director of coaching at the time, was strongly tipped to succeed him as FA secretary. He was a Rous man, his flag-lieutenant, but somehow he fell between two stools. It was also in 1961 that a certain Don Revie was handed the reins as player-manager at Elland Road. And, although of course no one knew it at the time, he was destined to become England manager himself 13 years down the line.

A year earlier 'Hardaker's Baby' had been born. This was one of the many names given to the newly created Football League Cup, of which Hardaker was originally credited with being the founder. It was, however, none other than Sir Stanley Rous who in fact had suggested the idea, some 20 years earlier. In his autobiography, Hardaker relates that in 1940 there was a joint committee of the League and FA called the Post-War Reconstruction Committee, whose job it was to think of bright ideas to get football back on its feet again. One of the suggestions by Stanley Rous was that there should be a consolation cup for clubs knocked out in the early rounds of the FA Cup, but it proved impossible to organise for a variety of practical reasons. Many years later, during another quiet afternoon at the Football League, 'office boy' Hardaker was sifting through some old minutes, when he came across this very proposal by Rous. The seed had been planted.

Although originally called 'the small-time pretender' and 'a cardboard replica of the FA Cup', the League Cup steadily grew in status over the years. It gave a chance for Third Division clubs to enter the big stage and left established First Division sides open to criticism. Originally, the League Cup final was played over two legs, home and away, but in 1967 it was moved to the big stage: Wembley Stadium. The first of these finals was between West Bromwich Albion of the First Division and Queens Park Rangers of the Third Division. 'It was a magnificent match,' wrote Hardaker. 'The first half was not too promising, though, as West Brom looked much the better side and at half-time they led 2–0. Thankfully, QPR put their game together in the second half and staged a dramatic 3–2 victory.'

The second League Cup final to be played at Wembley, in 1968, was between First Division sides Leeds and Arsenal. Hardaker commented:

> I can only be grateful this wasn't the first final at Wembley. Their ambitions were so limited and their styles so similar that the game never got off the ground. They committed the worst crime of all in football. They were boring. If somebody had taken the ball from the pitch the players of Arsenal and Leeds would have been the last to notice.

It would perhaps have escaped Hardaker's notice, but this 1–0 victory provided Leeds with their first-ever major trophy. The match was played on 2 March and Leeds had already played 45 games that season, with a further 20 still to go. Understandably, they were a little leg-weary, and the team that played was injury-hit. Jack Charlton had back problems, Gary Sprake and Jimmy Lumsden both had knee strains, Johnny Giles played with the flu and centre-forward Mick Jones was cup-tied.

In the few seasons preceding this particular final, Leeds had lost two finals and two semi-finals and had been runners-up in the league twice. The pressure was on United to come good. And they did.

Arsenal were back at Wembley the following year against Third Division Swindon Town. The underdogs Swindon won 3–1 and Hardaker was ecstatic, recalling, 'Swindon's victory gave the League Cup yet another new and strong injection of romance.'

Three years later, in 1972, Leeds United faced Arsenal at Wembley once more, this time in the FA Cup final, resulting in another 1–0 victory for the Yorkshire side. Alan Hardaker declined the obligatory invitation to join the winners' contingent at the after-match banquet. One of the reasons could have been that Leeds United had been forced by Hardaker to play their final league game 48 hours after the final – a game that could and should have seen them complete the league and cup double. Another reason could have been that this was the FA Centenary Cup final, celebrating 100 years of the Football Association Cup – and not the Football League Cup.

However, such loyalties did not prevent the League secretary attending the following year's FA Cup winners' banquet. The victors in 1973 were Sunderland – who beat Leeds United. Against all odds, Sunderland created a miracle by beating Leeds 1–0, and Hardaker wasted no time in accepting the offer to attend the banquet. He said afterwards, 'One of the most enjoyable evenings of my life in football was spent at Sunderland's banquet after their memorable FA Cup final triumph over Leeds United in 1973.'

Of course, Alan Hardaker never made any secret of his dislike of Don Revie and his Leeds United team, although he did always maintain that he was trying to 'help them'. In *Hardaker of the League*, he remembered:

As secretary of the Football League, I found Don Revie, as manager of Leeds United, to be a pain in the neck. I had a job to do, he had one to do, and our duties and obligations as we saw them frequently collided head-on.

He praised Revie, after a fashion, writing:

> I think Don Revie has all the qualities and faults of the modern manager. He is a contradiction in so many ways. He is a great family man, an engaging personality, acutely aware of his responsibilities and enormously hard working. But I also know him, in a football sense, to be totally ruthless, selfish, devious and prepared to cut corners to get his own way. It is a rare combination of all these qualities which has made him into one of the game's outstanding managers.

In 1970, Leeds United were going for the treble of the league championship, the FA Cup and the European Cup, something that had never been done before. Jack Charlton said at the time, 'Leeds could have won all three trophies if only people had cooperated with us.'

In the league games, and because of the total amount of matches required of them, the Leeds team were under immense pressure. Fatigue, injuries and sheer exhaustion forced Revie to play squad players whenever possible, while still attempting to maintain a backbone of established players. It has to be mentioned at this stage, and more will be said about it later, that these so-called squad players would have walked into any other First Division side.

Hardaker, throughout this campaign, offered little or no assistance to Leeds United, claiming that the fixture pile-up was the fault of the club and in particular Don Revie. Prior to 1970, Revie had asked for assistance from Hardaker on a number of occasions only to be refused.

Hardaker wrote:

> There were times when Don Revie skirted round the truth. He once asked me, on a Wednesday, to postpone his club's league match the following Saturday because he had three players, so he

inferred, on the point of death. I refused the request categorically; and four days later these three players made a remarkable recovery and not only did all three players play, one of them scored two goals.

Because Hardaker doesn't specify which particular game this was, it's difficult to speculate about this, but suffice it to ask: why would Don Revie ask for a postponement if all his players were fit, as Hardaker seemed to think? Furthermore, I would suggest that Hardaker's usual refusal may even have contributed to these players putting in such fine performances in the match.

But there are another couple of vital points here. Towards the closing stages of the 1970 season, Revie once again asked for fixtures to be rearranged. Everton were closing in on the title, and Don Revie, because of other cup commitments, all but surrendered the championship to the Liverpool side. Before doing so, however, he actually asked for a postponement of the league game at home to Southampton on 28 March, because certain players were drained 'mentally and physically'. Revie's request was instantly refused. So a crowd of more than 38,000 saw a scratch Leeds United side entertain Southampton. Half of the side were first-team players and the other half squad players such as Rod Belfitt, Terry Hibbitt, Mick Bates, Nigel Davey and Jimmy Lumsden. Leeds were soundly beaten, 3–1.

On Easter Monday, two days later, Leeds had to travel to Derby County. There was no 'remarkable recovery' of players and the Leeds team included even more squad players: reserve keeper David Harvey was in goal; the full-backs were Nigel Davey and Paul Peterson (making his debut and only full first-team appearance); the half-back line consisted of another debutant, David Kennedy, flanked by Terry Yorath and Jimmy Lumsden. Up front were Chris Galvin, Mick Bates, Rod Belfitt, Terry Hibbitt and John Faulkner (the young centre-half Faulkner had caught Don Revie's eye while playing against Leeds for Sutton in the FA Cup third round a couple of months previously). Kennedy scored Leeds' goal in a 4–1 defeat and United were fined £5,000 by Hardaker's League for fielding a 'below-strength side'. Hardaker said at the time that 'the circumstances are considered unacceptable'.

Despite Alan Hardaker regularly rearranging fixtures at the request of clubs from the First Division downwards, Leeds United never had one single request for a postponement granted during their attempt to secure the first-ever treble of the league, the FA Cup and the European Cup. Hardaker continually blamed the fixture pile-up on Leeds' own success, and in a perverse way I suppose he was right, but he still steadfastly refused to give Leeds any leeway of any kind.

This was Leeds' incredible run-in to the end of season 1969–70: 7 March, Liverpool away (league); 14 March, Manchester United (FA Cup semi-final, Hillsborough); 21 March, Wolves away (league); 23 March, Manchester United (FA Cup semi-final first replay, Villa Park); 26 March, Manchester United (FA Cup semi-final second replay, Bolton); 28 March, Southampton home (league); 30 March, Derby County away (league); 1 April, Celtic home (European Cup semi-final); 2 April, West Ham away (league); 4 April, Burnley home (league); 11 April, Chelsea (FA Cup final, Wembley); 15 April, Celtic away (European Cup semi-final); 18 April, Manchester City away (league); 21 April, Ipswich Town away (league); 29 April, Chelsea (FA Cup final replay, Old Trafford).

In his autobiography *A Football Man*, Johnny Giles remembers:

> We said nothing about it at the time, but, towards the end, we were most certainly exhausted. In most years, you can win the FA Cup by playing six matches in total and we still had five matches to go after we reached the semi-final, with a fair bit of extra time on top of that. And when the European Cup semi-final was thrown into the mix, it meant that we had seven of these huge matches in a row with either glory at the end of it all, or devastation.

After finishing the 1969–70 season empty-handed and the following season also, Leeds beat Arsenal in the 1972 FA Cup centenary final and, as we have seen, needed just one point at Wolves in their final league game to win the coveted double. Leeds were forced to play that final league match just 48 hours after the Wembley game because Alan Hardaker felt unable, yet again, to comply with Don Revie's request for a rearrangement. Hardaker explained:

> Leeds were unusually hard-pressed, but they should not have had

to play two such important matches in little more than 48 hours if there had been an alternative. But as well as our duty to the League, we also had obligations to England and UEFA. England, at the time, were facing West Germany in the two legs of the European Championship quarter-finals, the first leg the week before the FA Cup final, the second leg ten days afterwards. The England players were required for five days before each game and, as usual, Leeds players figured prominently in Alf Ramsey's plans. To complicate matters Wolves were playing Tottenham over two legs of the UEFA Cup final at around the same time. The fault was not blindness on the part of the Management Committee, but the chronic lack of room for manoeuvre in our season, and for that the clubs are to blame.

So, according to Hardaker, Leeds' success was the reason why they were forced to play the most important fixture of the season hours after winning the FA Cup.

What Hardaker fails to elaborate on is that Alf Ramsey only called on two Leeds United players, Paul Madeley and Norman Hunter, for those two games against West Germany a week either side of the FA Cup final. And the first leg of the UEFA Cup final was played three days before the FA Cup final, while the second leg did not take place until eleven days after, so there clearly *was* room for manoeuvre, even if only for an extra day or two's rest. But it was apparently never Alan Hardaker's intention to allow that.

Hardaker admitted that he was called 'every name under the sun' after the Wolves fiasco. It was pointed out to him by one fan that his initials were the same as those of a certain German dictator. In *Hardaker of the League*, he reprinted this letter received from an irate Leeds fan a few days after the Wolves game:

> Sir, after a hard fought cup final on Saturday – which might indeed have gone into extra time – Leeds United failed two days after to win the League title. They were unsuccessful, but you and your vindictive and jealous-minded friends on the League Management Committee succeeded in your object. League Management? You couldn't manage a Paris urinal.

Hardaker reacted, somewhat condescendingly, by saying, 'I resisted the temptation to reply that I could still take a holiday at my own convenience.'

Quite understandably, Don Revie as Leeds United manager was reluctant to release his players for international duty if it interfered directly with club affairs. Hardaker would say, 'I wonder how Don Revie of Leeds would have reacted to the proposal by Don Revie of England?' But interestingly, when Revie was appointed manager of England in 1974 Hardaker took the complete opposite attitude from that which he had adopted with him at club level, and after a meeting between himself, Revie and FA secretary Ted Croker, he promised Revie, somewhat sarcastically, 'the same cooperation that he himself had given Alf Ramsey'.

When Don Revie was made England manager, Hardaker went so far as to tell the Football Association that they should have their heads examined. Clearly, the former Leeds manager was to receive no assistance of any kind from the League secretary – quite the opposite, in fact.

After a defeat by Holland at Wembley over Revie's England, Hardaker admitted that the Dutch played superbly. However, forty-eight hours later, Hardaker was accosted by two rather irate old ladies in Lytham St Annes; they weren't happy about the defeat and demanded to know what he was going to do about it. 'Good God, ladies,' Hardaker told them, 'I get blamed for everything. I'll tell you what I'll do – I'll give you Don Revie's address.'

9. The Italian Fix

A few months after the fiasco at Molineux, Leeds United kicked off the 1972–73 season with a crashing 4–0 defeat at Chelsea after keeper David Harvey was carried off injured and Peter Lorimer had to take over in goal. However, they then went on an eight-match unbeaten run before opening their first-ever campaign in the European Cup-Winners' Cup in Ankara, Turkey. Their league campaign ended with a 6–1 thrashing of Arsenal, and Leeds managed to finish third in the table.

In May, however, there was the little matter of an FA Cup final against Second Division Sunderland. Bob Stokoe was the Sunderland manager and another enemy of Don Revie. The two had clashed in April 1962, when Revie was manager of Leeds and Stokoe was player-manager at Bury. Fifteen years after the event, once again prompted by the *Daily Mirror*, Stokoe claimed Revie had offered him £500 to 'take it easy' before a Bury–Leeds clash. This allegation, originally an exclusive for them in 1975, has been regurgitated every now and again by the *Mirror*, but they have never once explained how Revie would have been able to pay the £500 way back in 1962. Five hundred quid would have been a phenomenal amount of cash to find. By Stokoe's own admission, there were no witnesses to the alleged bribe and, once again, despite the allegations against his name, Don Revie was left with no case to answer – yet the slurs continue to fester to this day.

Even before that, Revie and Stokoe did not get on, and when they met at Wembley in 1973 the rift between them had already become an almighty chasm. Leeds, of course, were overwhelming favourites to lift the cup for the second year running. The referee that day was Ken Burns, not a favourite of the Leeds fans after the Chelsea match in 1967. Although there is no evidence that Bob Stokoe tried to prejudice the referee that day, it is true that he told the London *Evening*

Standard, 'I want Mr Burns to make the decisions, not Mr Bremner,' and it is true that on the day Bremner hardly received a free kick in his favour. It's ancient history that Leeds underachieved and Sunderland gained an unexpected but momentous 1–0 victory. The Sunderland keeper that day was Jim Montgomery, whose stunning saves, particularly one from Peter Lorimer where he somehow managed to tip the ball onto the bar from Lorimer's close-range effort, were the ultimate reason the FA Cup ended up on Wearside.

While speaking with Montgomery in 2009, I asked about the relationship between Stokoe and Revie, but he politely said that he couldn't add any more to what was 'already in the pubic domain'. He did add, however, 'Don Revie described my save [at Wembley] as the best he'd ever seen, and said that that one save decided the match.' Montgomery then told me, 'I didn't know what all the fuss was about until I was shown it back on television replays.'

As disappointing as it was, Leeds United didn't have time to mourn the FA Cup final with the European Cup-Winners' Cup final in Greece 11 days later looming on the horizon. But, once again, controversy was to follow Leeds in a big way.

This was Leeds' first (and only) involvement in the ECWC. By April, they had progressed to the semi-final, where their opponents were Hajduk Split from Yugoslavia, who had beaten Wrexham and Hibernian en route. An even contest in front of more than 35,000 at Elland Road saw a solo effort from Allan Clarke give Leeds a valuable 1–0 first-leg lead. But, with Leeds looking to add to their advantage, Split defender Mario Boljat scythed Clarke down. Clarke immediately retaliated and was dismissed. Boljat escaped without even a booking.

Clarke has said:

> My marker had been kicking hell out of me all night and a few minutes after my goal, he crashed into me again and took my legs away. I had a rush of blood and kicked him where it hurts.

He is often asked who was the best or hardest defender he ever played against. 'I don't pay much attention to defenders,' he says, 'I usually let them worry about me, but Boljat was simply an animal.' UEFA decided to ban Clarke for two games instead of the usual one, ruling him out of the final. Unsurprisingly, there was no right of appeal.

Knowing full well that Hajduk Split were a formidable side at home, Leeds must have been pleased to manage to take their 1–0 lead with them to Yugoslavia for the second leg. Don Revie, knowing the lead was slender, told his players, 'The main thing is to be patient and wait for the breaks.'

I arrived in Split with a few mates the day before the match, travelling with a company called 4S Sports. As we left the airport, local fans banged on our coach windows. The Leeds team coach was just in front of us and the home fans banged on their bus and waved banners and blew horns at them. The Leeds players remained calm and expressionless. Our bus wasn't so calm. A big Leeds fan on the back seat banged on the window and shouted at them, 'Fuck off, yer foreign twats!'

Later that night, the Leeds players' hotel was besieged with local fans driving past outside sounding car horns and chanting songs in an effort to disrupt the team's sleep. This had become a common occurrence over the past eight years' consecutive appearances in European competition. One Leeds player trying to sleep that night was Terry Yorath. Back in Leeds, Christine, his wife, had just given birth to a daughter, Gabrielle. Yorath proclaimed recently, 'I attend quite a few after-dinner functions these days and I can hear people whispering between them, "You know who that is, don't you?" I blush a little, then I hear them say, "That's Gabby Logan's dad."'

On the pitch that night at the Kod Stare Plinare Stadium, Joe Jordan replaced Allan Clarke alongside Mick Jones. With the reliable midfield duo of Bremner and Giles (who had a last-minute goal ruled out because the referee, Frenchman Robert Héliès, blew for full-time at the precise moment the ball entered the net), Leeds were magnificent. Paul Madeley, settling in at centre-half in place of the injured Jack Charlton, played alongside the ever reliable Norman Hunter and Terry Yorath as Revie's men held Split to a 0–0 draw to book their place in the final, prompting the manager to announce: 'This was our best display since winning the Fairs Cup in Budapest in 1968.' Almost inevitably, though, Bremner had been booked and would miss the final against AC Milan in Greece.

Thessalonika airport is so close to the sea that, as I looked out of the plane window, it seemed as if we were going to be touching down in the water. In stark contrast to the welcome in Yugoslavia, the Greeks received us with open arms. As we passed through the airport and ventured outside, many locals, young and old, harassed us for our scarves, banners, hats – anything, in fact, that said 'Leeds United'. By now, the Greeks had adopted our favourite phrase and used it in abundance: 'Supa Leeds! Supa Leeds!' Rotherham United manager Jack Mansell, then in charge of a First Division side in Thessalonika, told reporters that most of the locals, including his players, were 'Leeds United daft'. He added, 'There was tremendous disappointment here when they lost the FA Cup final [against Sunderland] . . . three of my players actually cried.'

As we headed for the Kaftanzoglio Stadium, we had no idea what lay in store. This was to be one of the biggest injustices suffered by any club any time, anywhere in the world. Clarke and Bremner were ruled out and Jack Charlton was still injured, along with Eddie Gray and Johnny Giles. A hamstring strain had sidelined Giles and he was invited by the BBC to be their guest analyst for the evening. As has been widely reported, Giles discovered through the media that the ref had been 'got at'.

Peter Lorimer, writing in his autobiography *Peter Lorimer: Leeds and Scotland Hero*, takes up the story:

> It was wholly, indisputably and wretchedly bent . . . Before the game, John Giles, who, along with Bremner, Clarke and Gray, was injured and had to miss the final, had picked up on stories that the Italians had taken steps to ensure that they would win the trophy come what may and he relayed to our team: 'There's no way we can win.'

Christos Michas was a local referee. In those days, it was commonplace for an official from the country where a European final was to take place to officiate, and Michas, having reached the end of his career, was offered this prestigious occasion to bow out with. It turned out to be some bow.

For a start, although it was common for a referee to officiate in a final in his own country, it certainly wasn't common for that referee to arrive in his country on the same plane as one of the competing teams. Paul Reaney, who was captain that evening in the absence of Bremner, told Sky Sports' *Time of Our Lives*, 'We [the Leeds team] were in the airport when the AC Milan plane landed. We were watching them as they came through . . . Imagine our surprise when coming through with them was the referee, Christos Michas.'

As we took our seats in the stadium (I say 'seats'; they were actually just large concrete steps), it was raining so hard it almost hurt. There was no cover whatsoever in the ground and within seconds we were all soaked to the skin. However, our damp arses were nothing compared with events unfolding on the field. From the outset, Leeds were up against it and Michas made his intentions clear as early as the fourth minute. Paul Madeley took the ball cleanly from Milan striker Alberto Bigon and, as is quite clear from TV recordings of the game, made absolutely no contact with the striker, yet as he moved away with the ball, Michas blew for an indirect free kick to Milan. Luciano Chiarugi took the kick and, via the slightest touch from Leeds' Terry Yorath and the foot of the post, the ball slipped into the Leeds goal.

From then on, the game was littered with infuriating decisions, with all these incidents captured quite clearly by television footage. Commentator John Motson remarked in his assessment afterwards, 'AC Milan had scored first and seemed to have more than just luck on their side.'

As a shot from Joe Jordan bounced off a defender, Mick Jones entered the penalty area to latch on to the loose ball. He was immediately hacked down by Angelo Anquilletti and the referee, standing less than a yard away, waved play on. The crowd booed incessantly throughout, but Michas was clearly on a mission. Paul Reaney went racing towards the Milan goal and then unleashed a blistering shot that was blatantly handled on the line by defender Romeo Benetti and subsequently cleared.

Peter Lorimer remembers:

> I cut inside and as I pulled my leg back to shoot, it disappeared! I crashed to the floor. I was on the edge of their six-yard box and the referee just waved play on. By now we had simply given up appealing. It was almost every time we went in their box. We were denied anything.

Joe Jordan was pulled back on the edge of the area and, bizarrely, Michas gave the free kick to Milan. In the dying seconds of the game,

Rivera fouled Norman Hunter. It was just too much for Hunter and he snapped and retaliated, felling Rivera with one punch. Then another Milan player came running in and attacked Hunter and he too was knocked down with a 'left-half hook'. Hunter was sent off and the booing around the stadium was deafening.

When the match was over, Syd Owen, the Leeds coach, ran onto the pitch to tell his players not to swap shirts with their opponents. They didn't need any telling. An attempt to parade the trophy round the pitch after the match was abandoned as the Italians were pelted by the very irate Greeks in the crowd with everything that wasn't bolted down.

Even the *Daily Mirror* couldn't hide from the truth and had to accept that Leeds had been hard done by. Reporter Derek Wallis wrote afterwards, 'The catcalls, barracking and general disapproval continued as Milan took the trophy on a lap of honour. Rather it should be a lap of dishonour.'

When the Leeds players attended a post-match banquet in their honour, they were staggered to discover that also in attendance was Christos Michas. Don Revie was heard to say, 'How he has the nerve to sit and eat with us and smile, I'll never know. He should be ashamed of himself.'

A few days afterwards, UEFA banned Michas for life. AC Milan were suspended from European competition for four years. But, of course, there was never any talk of a replay or the cup being presented to Leeds. Also, on appeal Milan had their suspension cut.

Italian clubs, it has to be said, have a long tradition of flouting the rules and regulations. In recent years, along with Milan, Lazio, Fiorentina and Juventus have all been found guilty by the Italian Football Federation of fixing or attempting to fix results in games. Various penalties were given out, such as points deductions and relegation, but all were later overturned or at least reduced. AC Milan were suspended from playing in the Champions League and that too was reversed. Milan were also relegated back in 1980 in relation to a match-fixing scandal. AC Milan, it seems, was rife with corruption.

The Leeds players from 1973 still talk about that night in Thessalonika on 16 May. Paul Reaney has said: 'That ref got paid. He got banned for life. You can't do a right lot about that.' Mick Jones has commented:

The decisions that went against us were scandalous. We never stood a chance. The refereeing was appalling and the worst I'd ever experienced. The reception we received from the Greek supporters was incredible, but it didn't take away the disappointment we felt afterwards in the dressing-room. Their centre-half elbowed me, punched me in the back, spat in my face, and he even tried to gouge out my eyes . . . but the referee did nothing.

Allan Clarke, who had to watch it all from the bench, remembered, 'The refereeing was diabolical. We never stood a chance. The match should have been replayed at the very least.'

In August 2006, the Labour MEP for Yorkshire and Humberside, Richard Corbett, wrote to UEFA asking them to consider investigating the match and awarding the trophy to Leeds United if the evidence merited it. He told the readers of his blog:

This is not the first occasion Italian clubs have been involved in match fixing . . . and it instantly brought back memories of some deeply suspicious results English teams have suffered. The one which sticks out in my mind most is Leeds' defeat to AC Milan in the 1973 Cup-Winners' Cup final, where the referee, Christos Michas, performed so dubiously he was suspended for life!

UEFA can show they take any form of corruption in the game seriously by stripping clubs of trophies won thanks to match fixing. Such action would dramatically demonstrate a commitment to fair play and help restore faith in UEFA as a strong but fair governing body. And it is never too late to correct an injustice: if Milan did indeed bribe the referee in that match, then the winners' medals should belatedly be given to Peter Lorimer and his Leeds teammates.

Richard Corbett is actually from Merseyside and is a Liverpool fan, but his press officer, Luke Thorne, said: 'This is important to all football fans and not just fans of Leeds United.'

In April 2009, Corbett arranged an online petition to present to UEFA demanding an investigation into the 1973 final and that, should evidence that match was fixed be found, the trophy be awarded, albeit late, to its rightful owners, Leeds United. He was 'staggered' at the response, and although the petition was online for only a few days, it was signed by in excess of 12,000 people from around the world.

On the 36th anniversary of the final, 16 May 2009, Corbett delivered his petition to UEFA in Geneva. Before the meeting, Corbett told waiting journalists outside, 'I am amazed that so many people signed this petition in such a short time, but it is important, not just for Leeds United, that justice is seen to be done.' Also speaking to journalists there was the head of legal affairs for UEFA, Peter Limacher, who added, 'I too was staggered at the response to Richard Corbett's petition on behalf of Leeds United, particularly as it dates back to a game that took place so long ago.'

Unfortunately and, it has to be said, not unexpectedly, nothing was ever done by UEFA to remedy this blatant case of injustice. Corbett was told by UEFA that they would not be reinvestigating the case. Corbett blogged:

First, I had the following written response from UEFA:

'We have received your letter and the petition regarding the 1973 Cup-Winners' Cup final between Leeds United and AC Milan. This is obviously a subject that is of enormous importance to many people, and we acknowledge and thank each person who took the time to sign this petition. We of course understand the frustration involved, but our room for manoeuvre is constrained by UEFA's Disciplinary Regulations (Article 7), which clearly dictate the statute of limitations. In the case of a game that took place more than 35 years ago, we have long passed the legal time frame in which any action could have been taken.

'The fight against match-fixing is a high priority for UEFA and we can only look to the future to put a stop to it. From our perspective, if the results are fixed in advance then football has no further reason to exist. Because of this we are implementing, with all 53 national associations of UEFA, a new system that will monitor some 30,000 matches as from next season – and we are determined to root out the problem.'

Then, I followed this up by travelling to Geneva to meet a number of UEFA officials at their headquarters. I must say that their response was actually sympathetic, and they were very impressed by the number of signatures, but they feel constrained by the legal situation. I understand that a few years ago, they took action against Anderlecht when it was discovered, over ten years after the event, that they had bribed a referee in a European match (against Nottingham Forest). However, Anderlecht went to the courts and won against UEFA when the court ruled that the events had taken place too far back (and beyond their statute of limitations of, at that time, 10 years, which they had raised to 20 years, but the court ruled that they cannot raise it and then discipline a club after the original deadline had expired). The same would certainly happen again if they tried to re-open an event of more than 36 years ago. Even most criminal offences have a much shorter cut-off period. I got the impression that they would not be averse to taking on AC Milan (who, let us not forget, have a record of misdemeanours), but that they genuinely feel that their previous court defeat prevents them from doing so.

UEFA did explain to me at great length the measures they are now taking to try to prevent match-fixing (be it through referees or players) happening again. This includes, among other things, monitoring betting patterns, working with the police to infiltrate gangs, bringing in more severe penalties for those who get caught, trying (with difficulty) to regulate players' agents, and so on.

Small consolation for those of us who believe that the 1973 result should be reversed, but at least they are making serious efforts to stop such things happening again.

As well as the Leeds players from that night in Thessalonika, two European journalists threw their weight behind this brave campaign. Martin Banks, a former chief reporter for the *Birmingham Evening Mail* and now a journalist of 30 years' experience as an EU correspondent in Brussels, and David Charter, who is the Europe correspondent for *The Times* in Brussels, were both appalled at the inept display of Christos Michas that night of 16 May 1973. Charter contacted the Hellenic FA for their response, but they declined to comment. Charter told me, 'I would really like to know if the referee from that night is still alive!', while Martin Banks wrote:

Leeds United seem to occupy a special place in the hearts and minds of many, many people of all ages, hence their ability to draw support from all over the country and their enduring appeal – despite the many and bitter setbacks of recent years. It is, therefore, of little surprise to many of us that efforts to right a wrong dating back so many years should attract such endorsement.

10. The Lure of the Lira

During their countless forays into Europe, Leeds United encountered many Italian clubs. Indeed, on their very first European tie in 1965 in the old Inter-Cities Fairs Cup, the forerunner of the UEFA Cup and now the Europa League, United travelled to Torino, defending a slim 2–1 lead from the first leg at Elland Road.

Leeds arrived at the Stadio Comunale in Turin to find that the 'hard men' tag bestowed on them by a malicious media campaign had already reached the shores of Italy. Within seconds of the start, LucianoTeneggi felled Leeds striker Alan Peacock with a scything two-footed tackle that was totally ignored by the Dutch referee, Piet Roomer, who told Peacock to get up before giving a throw-in to Torino. Don Revie and Syd Owen had flown to Italy a week earlier to watch Torino and prepare a detailed dossier (these dossiers of Revie's would become famous during his time at Leeds) to take back to his players. Syd Owen was principally responsible for the development of the young players at the club and also acted as a valuable scout on the opposition. Despite all the preparation, though, Leeds were to be shocked by the intensity of the match.

The game was littered with horrendous tackles, but early in the second half a diabolical challenge by Fabrizio Poletti left Leeds' midfield general Bobby Collins with a broken thigh. The ball had been fully ten yards away. Quoted in John Giles' *A Football Man*, Paul Madeley says:

> We knew we were in for a battle, but none of us had experienced just how cynical foreign players could be. That tackle in Turin that broke Bobby's thigh and finished his career was one of the worst I have ever seen.

Billy Bremner was also incensed by the challenge on his teammate. He admitted later that he'd said to Poletti, 'I'll kill you for this!' The Italian never went near Bremner for the remainder of the contest. Bremner, also quoted in *A Football Man* says:

> That taught me something. I have never, since that day, gone onto the field with such feelings that I had that night. If I had come anywhere near that Italian in a challenge, I could not have been responsible for my actions. The foul was so unnecessary and vindictive. Bobby was nowhere near the ball.

The Leeds team that night in Turin learned a lesson about what lay ahead of them in the next decade. Losing Collins meant that United had to play the rest of the game with ten men (no substitutes were allowed back then). They gelled together, and with Jack Charlton and Norman Hunter performing remarkably in the heart of the defence, a 0–0 draw saw United through to the next round and eventually to the semi-final in their first-ever European campaign.

In the following season's Fairs Cup competition, United met more Italian opponents in the form of Bologna in the quarter-finals. This was the first season in European competitions that replays were scrapped. Instead, the tossing of a disc was introduced. This new system was required after Leeds drew with Bologna 1–1 on aggregate. Leeds trailed 1–0 after the first leg in Italy, but a Johnny Giles penalty squared the tie. Captain Billy Bremner called correctly as the disc came down and Leeds went through to the next round to face Kilmarnock.

Two seasons later, Leeds needed the disc again, but in quite different circumstances. They had been paired once more with Italian opposition, namely Naples, or as they are also known, Napoli. It is perhaps fitting that many years later Naples would have in their ranks quite possibly the biggest and most famous cheat of all time, Diego Maradona – but I digress.

Leeds arrived at the Stadio San Paolo carrying a 2–0 win with them from the first leg, courtesy of two headed goals from Jack Charlton. But Don Revie had concerns about Naples and their fans for the second leg – two years before, Burnley players and fans had had to be escorted away from the stadium by a police escort for their own protection – and had asked for two Fairs Cup official observers to attend the match. Revie's worries turned out to be well founded.

A crowd of fewer than 20,000 had turned up to the 90,000-capacity stadium as a protest at Naples' desperately poor start to the season. However, those supporters who did come certainly made their presence felt, even though they were separated from the pitch by police patrols and a huge, deep moat that was about eight feet wide. Fireworks whizzed across the pitch throughout the match and huge bonfires burned away all evening, scattered around the huge terraces. East German referee Rudi Glöckner seemed oblivious to the firework display going on around him and the missiles that were constantly thrown onto the pitch. Towards the end of the match, one of those missiles, a broken bottle, struck keeper Gary Sprake and he had to have five stitches in his hand, but only after he had run almost the full length of the pitch to attract Glöckner's attention.

Eight minutes into the game, Italian defender Mario Zurlini was booked for a shocking foul on Billy Bremner, which would have received a sending-off under any other circumstances. Minutes later, Bremner was again fouled and then, as he got up off the floor, Dino Panzanato punched him in the face. On the afternoon of the game, Les Cocker had been taken ill with a stomach complaint and was replaced on the touchline by the club's doctor and medical officer, Ian Adams. Dr Adams was certainly kept busy and was narrowly missed by a rocket as he tended to Paul Madeley, who was lying injured. Madeley had been unconscious for more than a minute, ignored by the referee. Substitute Peter Lorimer ran onto the pitch to replace Madeley but was pulled back by Naples keeper Dino Zoff, apparently for entering the field of play without permission. Minutes later, Lorimer too was fouled, again ignored by the referee. This time, Dr Adams had to drag Lorimer off the field by his boots so that he could treat him.

Naples inevitably scored after about quarter of an hour, through Claudio Sala, who was also involved in Naples' equaliser four minutes from time. Jack Charlton was adjudged to have brought Sala down on the edge of the penalty area, and captain Antonio Juliano converted the resulting spot kick to make it 2–2 on aggregate. Charlton hotly disputed that penalty: 'It was the worst penalty decision I have ever known in my life. I was determined not to touch their player but he took a dive and in any case we were outside of the box.'

Referee Glöckner, who had allowed two-footed tackles on United all evening, blew for full-time after 30 minutes' extra time and signalled for the disc that was to decide who would go through to the next round. Incidentally, Glöckner had only booked three players all night: Stelio Nardin and Zurlini of Naples and Mike O'Grady of Leeds. Apparently, though, it was discovered overnight that Mick Jones had been booked in the first minute, although he didn't know. But Leeds' players from that night insist that at least 20 names went into the referee's book. It was also later discovered that Nardin had in fact been booked twice, but there was no way that Glöckner was going to send anyone off, certainly not an Italian.

As the officials, including the two observers, gathered in the centre circle, the two captains came face to face. Juliano gave Bremner the right to call 'as a guest'. The red and white disc was tossed into the air and Bremner called red – and red it was. But the referee asked for a 'retake'. Bremner called correctly again and Glöckner, after a short deliberation, declared Leeds the winners, prompting a somersault from the Leeds captain, who was then joined by Don Revie and the rest of the players in celebration.

Afterwards, Revie was fuming and refused to talk to the Italian press. He told British journalists, 'Everything about this match was worse than I had expected. If this is how they treat their guests, then I hope we never have to play Naples again.'

Mike O'Grady told me, 'Normally after an away match on the Continent, we would go out on the town for a few beers, but after the game in Naples the police advised very strongly against us leaving the hotel, in case we were recognised.'

The second leg had been only Leeds' fourth defeat in four years in the Fairs Cup. And despite the presence of the two official match observers, no action was ever taken against Naples, for the hostile reception the visitors were given, or the referee, for his poor performance.

Leeds weren't the only English club to suffer at the hands of Italian clubs and Italian corruption.

The Stadio Comunale in Turin, where Leeds United had made their European debut in 1965, was the scene for yet another hostile encounter involving an English club in 1973. Juventus were playing hosts to Derby County, who were managed by one of Don Revie's adversaries, Brian Clough. This was the first leg of the European Cup semi-final and was taking place about one month before that fateful night for Leeds in Thessalonika.

The game started brightly enough, and although one or two decisions given by German referee Gerhard Schulenburg were slightly dubious, there was nothing untoward. However, at half-time, Clough's right-hand man, Peter Taylor, noticed that Juve's Helmut Haller, who was on the substitutes' bench for the first half, was walking off with the referee Schulenburg, deep in German conversation. There is no evidence that anything underhand was involved, but Taylor tried to intervene, fearing something was 'going on'. He was stopped by a group of Italian security men, apparently, according to Taylor, 'on Haller's instructions'. Taylor claimed that former Leeds and Juventus star John Charles was at the game and had warned him that Haller was 'in with the referee'. 'Nothing can be proved,' said Taylor, 'but I believe it was corrupt and dirty.'

During the second half, Derby's Archie Gemmill and Roy McFarland were both booked for no apparent reason and would both miss the second leg at Derby. After the game, which Juventus won 3–1, there was a bust-up in the tunnel, resulting in Brian Clough's infamous tirade hurled towards the Italians. Having disappeared into the dressing-room, alongside John Charles, he emerged to declare, 'No cheating bastards will I talk to! I will not talk to cheating bastards!' 'Bastardi Truffatori!' was the headline on one Italian front page the following morning.

Then a trail of events leading up to the second leg at the Baseball Ground showed yet again the sinister side of Italian football. The referee that night at Derby was to be Francisco Marques Lobo of Portugal, widely reputed to be an extremely honourable man. A Hungarian refugee called Dezso Solti, a notorious fixer, was enlisted by Juventus to travel to Lisbon to bribe Lobo to favour the Italians. Lobo refused and reported Juve to UEFA. Interestingly, Lobo never refereed another European game again.

I originally asked respected journalist Brian Glanville for his thoughts on the Leeds v. AC Milan final in Greece, but he came back with a lot more than I had bargained for. Referring to the Lobo/Solti incident, he said. As my colleague Keith Botsford and I uncovered for the *Sunday Times*, Juve were bang to rights.'

Dezso Solti had asked Lobo to meet him in Room 142 at the Ritz Hotel in Lisbon to discuss further the return match at Derby. Claiming to have close contacts with Dr Artemio Franchi, who was president of both the Italian Football Federation and UEFA, and was a man who could 'promote his career as an international referee', Solti then offered Lobo a car and $5,000. Fortunately, all this conversation was recorded on tape thanks to Lobo being an employee with the Portuguese telephone company. The situation was also secretly being followed by the Portuguese referees' association and then later the Portuguese Football Federation. As Glanville says, 'Juve [and Solti] were bang to rights', but all this evidence against Solti was to be of little use.

After hearing the tape UEFA secretary Hans Bangerter confirmed on the day before the second leg in Derby that Lobo would still be refereeing the game, which he did, and he performed impeccably. Sadly for Derby, the game ended 0–0 and Juventus progressed to the final.

In June 1973, UEFA's disciplinary sub-committee met to discuss the case at the Atlantis Hotel in Zurich. It turned out to be nothing short of farcical. Lobo said afterwards:

> There were nine persons present – I repeated my report, and was listened to politely and asked no questions. Then, when I had finished, Dr Franchi invited me into an adjoining room. We went in alone, without any other members of the committee, and there I was shown a group of gentlemen and asked by Franchi if I recognised any of them as the person who had offered me the bribe. No words were exchanged when I was in the room, nor could I put any questions. I quickly said that it was none of those present, and with that I was given permission to withdraw.

It turned out later that the men in the room had all been directors of Juventus and, even more surprisingly, the line-up did not include Dezso Solti. Lobo claims to have seen Solti elsewhere in the hotel, but the two were never brought face to face. Even stranger was the fact that Artemio Franchi later said that he wasn't at the meeting at all!

Lobo told Keith Botsford some time later:

> I am not a rich man. $5,000 and a car is four years' work for me. I
> could have taken the money and no one would have known. I'd be
> a richer man than today. But I didn't. I did my duty. And I didn't
> get to be on the World Cup list, which was the one thing I
> wanted. Why?

The outcome of this sordid affair was that UEFA ruled that there was
insufficient evidence to proceed, but Solti was punished with a one-
year suspension. UEFA added that they would circulate information
about Solti to its clubs warning them of him, but this was never done
because Franchi said that Solti might sue them.

Later, in July 1973, UEFA, sent Juventus a letter thanking them for
their cooperation and informing them that they had been completely
exonerated.

Artemio Franchi had quite obviously been involved in much of
what went on in Italian football. Brian Glanville says this of him: 'I
always found Franchi to be a man who preferred to be honest, but
given the nature of his own career in business and football, this was
always going to be difficult.'

The conspiracy theories about Franchi gathered momentum after
he died in a road accident. Many believed it was no accident when
Franchi, driving near Siena, was killed when he hit a lorry head-on.
Some said that Franchi was an excellent driver and therefore such a
thing could never have happened in normal circumstances.

It is true, however, that after Franchi's death on 12 August 1983
almost all of his dealings of the past were virtually ignored – in Italy,
at least.

In an obituary, the president of FIFA, Joao Havelange, paid this
homage:

> The FIFA and world football have lost a great leader, a dynamic
> and competent personality, a peerless tactician, a diplomat who
> could play the role of mediator to perfection. As for me, I have
> lost a dear, devoted and enthusiastic friend, an alert companion,
> both mischievous and witty, and a distinguished, respected and
> efficient collaborator . . . A wise and respected vice president of

our federation, he managed our finances with restraint and the referees with tact. His advice was much appreciated by the organising committee for the World Cup and his competence was recognised by all the major world sports organisations

High praise indeed. And there was another glowing tribute from the president of the IOC (the Italian Olympic Committee), Franco Carraro:

> Artemio Franchi had been in the world of football for almost 40 years, and he devoted his best qualities of intelligence and energy to this sport he deeply loved. During his career as a sports leader he performed numerous important tasks in Italian, European and world football organisations ... He was a distinguished diplomat who devoted his attention to, and knew in depth, all the problems of football. Together with Guilo Onesti he represented an important milestone in Italian sports. His ... premature departure is a great loss for world sports.

Even more praise, then, for Dr Franchi. However, I guarantee that there are still many football clubs in England and across Europe who endured the results of Franchi's 'diplomacy', 'mediation' and 'collaboration' and will hold a very different view.

We can't leave the subject of English teams' trials and tribulations in Italy without mentioning Liverpool's experience in 1965. Only three days after competing with Leeds at Wembley in the FA Cup final, Liverpool had to travel to the San Siro to play Inter Milan in the second leg of the European Cup semi-final. Liverpool had won the first leg 3–1 and were fully expected to progress to the final. However, the referee, Spaniard Ortiz de Mendibil, seemed to be reading from a different script. Inter scored three goals, two of which were highly suspect, one going straight in from a free kick taken by Mariolino Corso, although Mendibil had clearly signalled beforehand that the kick was to be indirect. Joaquin Peiro, a Spanish international, scored a goal even though he had kicked the ball out of keeper Tommy Lawrence's hands. Liverpool's Tommy Smith famously kicked Mendibil all the way back down the tunnel and into his dressing-room without any reaction whatsoever from the referee.

Liverpool made no official complaint, seemingly feeling it was futile, despite Bill Shankly, according to Glanville's *Chamions of Europe*, having been told by an Italian journalist after the first leg at Anfield, 'You will not be allowed to win.'

11. A Town Called Paris

Ever since the early days of the 1960s, when he began to build up his new, soon-to-become-legendary young Leeds United team, Don Revie's one big ambition had been for his side to win the European Cup. English clubs were originally delayed in entering the competition by the then secretary of the Football League, Alan Hardaker, who, as we have seen, persuaded new champions Chelsea not to enter the 1955–56 European Cup. In the end, Revie took his club to the semi-finals in Leeds' first-ever venture in the European Cup, in 1970, eventually losing out to Celtic.

By the time Leeds next entered the competition, in 1974, Revie had left to take up the position of manager of England. He looked on as 'his' team, now under the guidance of Jimmy Armfield, reached the final, to be played in Paris in May 1975. Revie was there that evening as a pundit for the BBC. It must have been strange for him to watch Leeds United march out onto the pitch at the Parc des Princes with another manager at the helm.

Leeds had begun this particular campaign against FC Zurich in September 1974, easing past the Swiss outfit 5–3 on aggregate. Hungarians Újpest Dózsa were their next opponents. Six years earlier, as a twelve-year-old, I had witnessed Leeds United given a lesson in football by Újpest in the quarter-finals of the 1968–69 Inter-Cities Fairs Cup. There had been a mix-up by the Hungarians over their kit and they ended up wearing white shirts loaned to them by their opponents, complete with the famous Leeds owl badge. United played in all blue, also with an owl on the shirt. Újpest looked invincible and produced 1–0, with a superb goal scored by Antal Dunai that had his teammate László Fazekas swinging from the crossbar in celebration. Even the usually dependable Johnny Giles failed to convert a penalty, producing a stupendous save by Hungary's national keeper, Olympic gold medal winner Antal Szentmihályi.

Leeds were in no mood to play second fiddle in '74 and ran out 5–1 winners on aggregate. In the next round, I watched Leeds dispose of the Belgian club Anderlecht with a 3–0 victory at Elland Road, remembered most for the fact that it was impossible to see the other end of the pitch due to thick fog. Fans cheering from the South Stand end kept Leeds fans in the opposite Gelderd End up to date with the progress and vice versa. A Billy Bremner goal in the second leg in Belgium saw Leeds reach the semi-final, where they would meet Spanish giants Barcelona, who had world-renowned players such as Johan Cruyff and Johan Neeskens in their ranks. Both of these Dutchmen were stars with Ajax, of course, before moving to Barcelona. And they were just two in a Barcelona side full of famous names.

A narrow 2–1 victory in the first leg at Elland Road left many Leeds supporters thinking that it wouldn't be enough to ensure passage to the final. This view was widely held by the players and fans of Barcelona, too. However, an early goal by Peter Lorimer at the impressive Nou Camp gave Leeds a 3–1 aggregate lead to silence the 110,000 crowd – except, of course, the Leeds contingent. An equaliser from the Spaniards ensured a tense second half for United, but they held firm and huge celebrations on the pitch marked their first-ever progression to the European Cup final. The important part played by Leeds keeper David Stewart, in for David Harvey, cannot be overlooked; he was absolutely outstanding.

Leeds had survived some extremely brutal challenges throughout the game. In particular, an elbow by centre-half Migueli on Joe Jordan left the Scot needing four stitches in his cheek, while Francisco Gallego was booked for a horrific foul on Billy Bremner and Juan Carlos Heredia kicked Terry Yorath constantly for 90 minutes. But the bruises quickly healed with the prospect of the European Cup final.

Bayern Munich were defending the European Cup that evening in Paris, and they went on to win it the following year, too, but even the staunchest of Bayern fans would have had to admit that the German side was easily outclassed that evening. Leeds, in contrast, were relatively inexperienced in the European Cup, having competed in it only once before, five years earlier.

As the two famous captains Billy Bremner and Franz Beckenbauer faced each other in the centre circle to exchange team pennants, German fans were vastly outnumbered by the hordes of Leeds supporters, and I truly felt very confident that Leeds would be parading the European Cup in front of us before long. Jimmy Armfield had made a couple of questionable decisions in team selection, seemingly allowing 'Don Revie's team' a crack at what would surely be their last chance of lifting their holy grail. Popular centre-forward Duncan McKenzie, who had been brought in during Brian Clough's brief reign as Leeds manager, was dropped for the final. McKenzie told me in December 2010 that he had been disappointed by Armfield's decision:

> I would have loved to have played in that European Cup final, and I honestly feel I would have made a difference, but Jimmy gave the team of Don Revie their chance, which I could fully understand. That said, it was hard to sit on the bench, but I thought I might have got on when they scored for their first goal. But the manager's indecision was always final!

As with the 1973 Cup-Winners' Cup final in Greece, a local referee was in charge, a Frenchman by the name of Michel Kitabdjian. Terry Yorath fouled the Bayern right-back Björn Andersson after just a few minutes and was lucky to escape with only a talking-to from the referee. Andersson was stretchered off and replaced by substitute Sepp Weiss. Three minutes later, Paul Reaney was booked for a foul on Weiss. As the game began to settle down, however, a couple of the referee's slightly dubious decisions went unnoticed in the buoyant atmosphere. Frank Gray appeared to have been fouled as he tried to send Paul Madeley on a run up front, and then when Bremner was clattered from behind by Beckenbauer just inside the box after neat footwork by Peter Lorimer had left the German player sprawled on the floor, mutters from the Leeds fans became louder.

Then it got worse. Clarke rounded the Bayern right-back, Bernd Dürnberger, and as he entered the six-yard box he was poleaxed by Beckenbauer. Allan Clarke said, 'It was obviously a penalty. He took my legs from under me. Then, amazingly, the referee only awarded a corner.' The Bayern captain had already escaped conceding a penalty when he'd blatantly handled the ball, perhaps accidentally, preventing

Peter Lorimer from getting in a strike. Jimmy Armfield said about the penalty claim on Clarke, 'I thought it was an obvious penalty.'

From the outset, Leeds had been by far the better side, and they completely dominated the first half, with Leeds keeper David Stewart called upon only once before half-time. Unfortunately, the second half was to be no better. Leeds continued to play well and, despite more bizarre refereeing, it seemed only a matter of time before they went ahead – and they did, in the 66th minute, when Lorimer smashed a terrific volley into the net.

Leeds fans had become accustomed to, shall we say, dubious referees by now, and everyone seemed to look at the referee before the celebrations began. There it was, the referee's clear signal that it was a goal. The Leeds players and fans alike went wild with ecstasy.

Television pictures and newspaper photographs clearly show Beckenbauer walking away from the goal looking very despondent indeed, while in the background Kitabdjian can be seen with arm outstretched pointing towards the centre for a restart. Then Beckenbauer ran over to the linesman on our left. After what seemed like a ten-minute debate between the linesman and the referee, the goal was astonishingly ruled offside. I have since watched TV footage of the game and the commentator, David Coleman, repeatedly says, 'I don't know what Beckenbauer is claiming, but it clearly is a goal.'

Speaking on Sky Sports in 1996, Bremner said:

> I was pushed offside, accidentally, by my own player, Joe Jordan, who was coming down after a challenge for a high ball with Roth, I think it was. I clambered out of the way as I could see Peter lining up for a shot. There was no way on earth I was interfering with play. And besides, the referee gave the goal initially and the linesman didn't flag for offside. It was Franz Beckenbauer who disallowed that goal, and who admitted that years later on television.

In his autobiography, Johnny Giles recalled, 'The referee seemed unable to make up his mind over Peter Lorimer's goal. He gave the goal in the first place then changed his mind. It was ridiculous.' Bobby Charlton has added his support, saying, 'It was definitely an injustice. There was nothing wrong with that goal.'

Alan Thompson of the *Daily Express* wrote:

> It was the moment of heartbreak for Leeds. It is still no score for
> Leeds, as Peter Lorimer, the man Bayern Munich feared the most,
> finds the net with a screaming right-foot volley. Yorkshiremen in
> the Parc des Princes Stadium and in a few million armchairs erupt.
> But their joy is extinguished after an agonising consultation
> between referee Kitabdjian and his linesman.
>
> Skipper Billy Bremner is ruled offside. TV pictures clearly
> show that Bremner is behind the Bayern defence. It shows he is
> clearly close to the line of the flight of the ball and therefore
> 'interfering' with play. But Bremner was knocked offside by the
> German defender whose header found Lorimer. He was
> powerless. That was the tragedy of the goal that got away.

Bayern went on to score two breakaway goals late on against a Leeds
side that was clearly stunned by what was happening around them.

Years later, Beckenbauer told the BBC, 'We were very lucky that
the referee disallowed the goal because of offside. Then we came back
into the game and scored two lucky goals and at the end we were the
winners, but . . . very, very lucky.'

Sadly, angry and frustrated Leeds supporters began to riot behind
the goal and ugly scenes became the centre of attention. Terry Yorath,
who had been substituted and replaced by Eddie Gray, went behind
the goal in an attempt to calm the fans down and prevent any further
trouble. 'I thought it was the best thing to do to try and quieten the
fans down,' he said. 'They were het up, so I did my best to calm them
down, but they were very angry indeed.' During the trouble, there
were confrontations with French police dressed in tracksuits and
being extremely provocative. Several Leeds fans were dragged over a
very high wall by these tracksuited officers, while heavily armed
gendarmes remained only a few feet away.

The rioting by the fans did not really surprise the Leeds camp.
Jimmy Armfield said in a statement afterwards, 'It's over-enthusiasm
really. They support from the heart and in European competition it
takes on a national flavour.' Bayern manager Dettmar Cramer said, 'I
was not shocked by the behaviour of the fans. This sort of thing is
prevalent these days in all forms of life.'

As Duncan McKenzie has commented, 'It says a lot for the referee when he needs a police escort from the pitch at the end of the game – especially an escort to protect him from the players!' The Leeds dressing-room was a sad and unhappy place afterwards. For over an hour, the Parc des Princes had been the playground of the footballing kings of Leeds. This was to be the last opportunity for glory for many of the team, and Paris finally became the graveyard of their dreams.

As a result of the unrest, Leeds were banned from European competition for four years. This was later reduced to two years after a personal intervention from Jimmy Armfield. UEFA awarded two marks out of a possible twenty to referee Kitabdjian but did nothing further.

Recently, after months of attempts, I finally tracked down the referee from that night in Paris. Michel Kitabdjian now lives in Nice, in the south of France. He speaks very little English and my French is only at a poor CSE level, but we did manage, with the aid of his daughter, to converse a little about that night in May 1975.

I have to confess, though, that I did not come absolutely clean at the beginning. I contacted Kitabdjian by claiming to be doing a project on top European referees from the 1970s. After going through the French FA, the German FA and finally FIFA, thanks to the French Football Federation, I made a breakthrough. I continued under the guise of a person interested in referees and, through broken English and broken French, Kitabdjian and I established a connection in early January 2007, and I received this email:

Dear Mr Edwards,
I have received a letter from the intermediere of the Federation Française de Football your message that I read with a lot of pleasures.

By the help of my girl I translate. I am still in soccer in the regional plan since 2002. [I understood this to mean he was now a local referee.]

To the moment I will reach your questions I will allow to present your views and wish you the sincere best for 2007.

I remain at your entire disposal for more complete pieces of information.

With my athletic feelings,
Michel Kitabdjian

I still look back on that evening in 1975 with pain, anguish and anger. And here I was, speaking to the man who caused all those feelings. But it was no good me coming out from the start and asking about the 1975 European Cup final, as I felt sure that would end things there and then. Instead, I concocted some basically irrelevant questions, such as his favourite colour, favourite food, favourite boyhood team and then – wham – question number seven: 'How on earth could you disallow Peter Lorimer's goal in the 1975 European Cup final?' I pointed out to Kitabdjian that he was clearly seen signalling the goal and that he had even returned to the centre spot. I didn't hear back from Kitabdjian for some weeks and I was convinced that I'd blown it. Then I received an email about the 'goal' by Lorimer:

> Cher Monsieur Edwards,
> Has declare M Kitabdjian. It is true I have whistles has retardment for I have no right away judges it to get up his flag because of my ecran forms by the players.
>   This is for that I am the will see to the center of the terrain to know if itself well offside. It has it for me confirms. I have done normal to refuse this goal.
>   Michel Kitabdjian

I couldn't be sure what he meant, but I decided to strike while the iron was hot and asked him about the blatant foul on Allan Clarke by Beckenbauer in the penalty area, as well as the one on Bremner. Mr Kitabdjian replied with a short email claiming he couldn't remember these particular incidents. I tried to jog his memory by forwarding him a picture of the Clarke penalty, but he never followed up.

Between these precious emails, I had a small number of telephone conversations with Mr Kitabdjian. One thing that he repeated in subsequent phone calls was that 'Leeds United were a very fine team and very unfortunate'. On another occasion, he told me that three Leeds players were offside when Lorimer scored. I questioned this, but he replied in French and there was no way I could understand what he was saying, except that he mentioned Beckenbauer's name twice. After a last brief telephone conversation, during which he told me that he 'admired Billy Bremner very much', I never heard from Kitabdjian again.

TOP: Leeds City in 1907, three years after their formation. Twelve years later, they were expelled from the League by the FA.

ABOVE: Salem Hall in Leeds. It was here that a group of supporters formed Leeds United Football Club only hours after the demise of Leeds City in 1919.

RIGHT: Billy Bremner was constantly homesick during his early days at Leeds and often returned home to Scotland. Here he is with his bag outside Elland Road – to stay. (Photo reproduced by arrangement with the Don Revie Tribute)

ABOVE: His pride and joy: Don Revie with his beloved Leeds United squad in 1967. (Photo reproduced by arrangement with the Don Revie Tribute)

BELOW: Despair as Leeds players protest to referee Ken Burns after he has disallowed what seemed to be a perfectly good goal against Chelsea in the semi-final at Villa Park in 1967.

LEFT: The Earl of Harewood, the Leeds president and former president of the FA, with Billy Bremner and the 1969 FA Charity Shield. (Photo reproduced by arrangement with the Don Revie Tribute)

BELOW: For this game in 1970, Leeds had to field a side consisting largely of reserves because of illness. They were fined £5,000 by the FA.

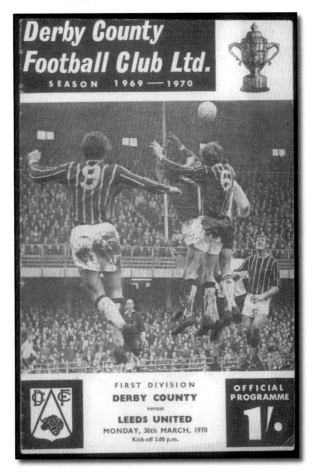

Derby County Football Club Ltd.

SEASON 1969 — 1970

FIRST DIVISION
DERBY COUNTY
versus
LEEDS UNITED
MONDAY, 30th MARCH, 1970
Kick-off 3.00 p.m.

OFFICIAL PROGRAMME

1/-

ABOVE: Leeds are front-page news as the club wins its first-ever league championship in 1969.

RIGHT: Don Revie with his wife, Elsie, at home with the 1972 FA Cup. (Photo reproduced by arrangement with the Don Revie Tribute)

TOP: Leeds groundsmen Ray Hardy (left) and John Reynolds (right) with Don Revie shortly before the European Cup-Winners' Cup final in 1973.

LEFT: The front page of a leading Greek newspaper the morning after the Cup-Winners' Cup final. Greeks all over the country were incensed by the refereeing of one of their fellow countrymen, who was banned for life following bribery allegations.

Leeds United applaud the fans and parade the 1974 league championship trophy.
(Courtesy of Varley Picture Agency)

ABOVE LEFT: Jim King, the gentle Leeds giant from Kippax
with whom I travelled to Villa Park in April 1967.

ABOVE RIGHT: Mike Stoddart stands up to the 'White Feather', Fabrizio Ravanelli.
(© Paolo Minnoli)

BELOW: David Elleray takes charge of an Elland Road clash between
Leeds and Newcastle United in a Leeds shirt. (© Action Images)

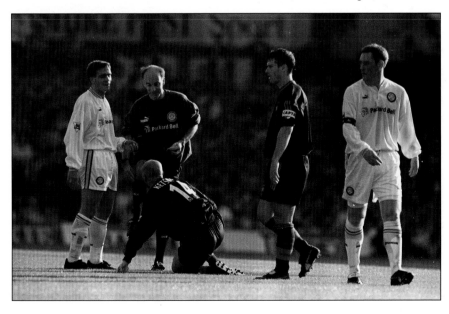

ABOVE: The author in Spain with the BBC's Harry Gration, discussing the bizarre banning of Lee Bowyer hours before the Champions League semi-final against Valencia in 2001.

BELOW LEFT: MEP Richard Corbett with just one box of many thousands of signatures after he petitioned to have the result of the 1973 European Cup-Winners' Cup final investigated by UEFA.

BELOW RIGHT: Award-winning sculptor Graham Ibbeson is to create a seven-foot bronze statue of Don Revie, which will be unveiled at Elland Road in the summer of 2012.

12. The Damned Truth

Another man and, coincidentally, another Yorkshireman, despised Don Revie just as much as, if not more than, Alan Hardaker. That man was Brian Clough.

Despite their well-publicised disagreements over the years, the two men were remarkably similar. Both were born in Middlesbrough, with Revie being eight years older than Clough, and both were talented players as well as becoming very successful managers. Both went on to receive the OBE. Revie has a street and a stand at Elland Road named after him. Clough has several roads named after him, as well as two statues in Nottingham and one in Middlesbrough. Plans are now well under way for a long-overdue statue of Don Revie to be erected.

The film *The Damned United* dramatises Clough's hatred of Revie as beginning on 3 January 1967. He had recently left Hartlepool United to become manager of up-and-coming Second Division side Derby County, taking his assistant from Hartlepool, Peter Taylor, with him. Leeds were sitting at the top of the First Division, and were to play Derby at the Baseball Ground on 3 January. In the film, Clough prepares to lay the red carpet out for his star guests. He scrubs the shower walls and baths and neatly lays out towels for the VIP visitors, complete with oranges and an ashtray each. He also sets out a bottle of the finest wine, presumably for him and Revie to share after the game.

He watches with Taylor as the Leeds team bus draws up and the players disembark and walk the 100 yards to the gates. Clough truly admires what Don Revie has achieved at Leeds, but his feelings are to change over the next few hours. Goals from Jack Charlton and Peter Lorimer see Leeds ease past Derby, but Clough is distracted. It's in his head that Revie is ignoring him. When the game ends, both benches exchanged the obligatory handshakes and commiserations, but Revie shakes the hand of Peter Taylor, totally snubbing Brian Clough. Clough is outraged.

My belief has always been that Clough's hatred towards Revie contained more than just a little jealousy. The seeds of anger were already germinating inside Clough. The following years saw a tense battle emerge between the two personalities. At every opportunity, Clough would accuse Revie's Leeds team of cheating, a taunt that Revie always refused to respond to. He criticised Leeds' disciplinary record, claiming that Don Revie should be fined and Leeds relegated to Division Two. He told the *Daily Express*:

> The men who run football have missed the most marvellous chance of cleaning up the game in one swoop. The trouble with football's disciplinary system is that those who sat in judgement, being officials of other clubs, might well have a vested interest.

Clough was undoubtedly a good manager, though, and his Derby side quickly rose to the First Division. But he remained obsessed with the idea of putting one over on Revie. It is legendary, too, how he openly criticised the Leeds players. Clough also had disagreements with the football authorities, including Alan Hardaker, as well as other managers, Sir Matt Busby and Sir Alf Ramsey among them. He fell out with his own directors at every club he went to. He had a particularly stormy relationship with Sam Longson, chairman of Derby County, not helped by the fact that in September 1973 Clough made a £400,000 bid to West Ham to take both Bobby Moore and Trevor Brooking to Derby without telling Longson. The offer was turned down, but Longson found out about it four months later while in conversation with West Ham's secretary Eddie Chapman about another matter.

But it was Don Revie who Clough hated. He constantly tried to undermine Revie's growing achievements with accusations of cheating and unfounded bribery allegations.

What is not often remembered, however, is that Clough's Derby County, in their first season back in Division One, were banned from Europe the following season and fined £10,000 due to financial irregularities.

While he was manager at Nottingham Forest in the early '90s,

Clough was implicated in one of the most famous 'bungs' scandals in English football. Tottenham Hotspur manager Terry Venables and his chairman Alan Sugar were involved in a deal that took Forest's Teddy Sheringham to Tottenham and which led to Clough being accused of having received illegal payments during transfer negotiations and of having made illegal payments to players.

Although Clough and Revie were alike in many ways, they were also completely opposite in many others. Clough was a very heavy drinker, while Revie hardly ever drank. Clough was very much involved in politics. He was a member of the Labour Party and a committed socialist. Revie, on the other hand, although clearly proud of his working-class roots, very rarely discussed politics. Clough was an extrovert, putting over his opinion to anyone who would listen at every opportunity. Revie remained a very private man, preferring to talk mostly with his own players.

When Don Revie left Leeds to become manager of England, amazingly, Brian Clough replaced him at Elland Road. Only a few years before Clough arrived at Leeds United, a Yorkshire Sports Personality of the Year awards dinner took place at the Queens Hotel in Leeds.

Brian Clough had openly criticised Leeds United and in particular Don Revie for more than seven years, so it was astonishing when Clough was brought in by the Leeds directors, led by Manny Cussins, to replace Don Revie. Rather than holding a players' meeting immediately after his arrival at Elland Road, Clough waited a few days. It took place in the players' lounge, and it was a stormy introduction to say the least.

'Right, you fucking lot,' said Clough, 'as far as I'm concerned, you can take all the medals you have won and throw them in that bin over there. As far as I'm concerned, you cheated for every one of them.'

He then pointed at Norman Hunter and told him he was a dirty bastard and told him that everyone hated him. 'I know everyone likes to be loved, and you'd like to be loved, wouldn't you?' Clough said to him.

'Actually, Brian,' said Hunter, 'I couldn't give a fuck.'

He then turned on Eddie Gray with those now legendary words, 'If you had been a racehorse, you'd have been put down years ago.'

Gray thought for a second and then pointed out to Clough that his own playing career had ended early due to a recurring knee injury. With that, Clough fell silent and the meeting was over, but not, by any stretch of the imagination, the ensuing drama.

It is a misconception that 'player power' forced Clough out of Elland Road and that Revie's players plotted to have Clough removed. In fact, it would have been quite understandable, but it wasn't the case. As Johnny Giles says in *A Football Man*:

> This is to misunderstand the huge level of self-interest in footballers, who may regard the arrival of a new manager as an odd appointment, even a completely mad appointment, but who ultimately want to keep winning things. If he fails, they are hardly going to succeed. Regardless of any ill-feeling that has occurred in the past, players know that a new manager is probably going to be there for a good while, which triggers that self-interest in them, to make the best of a situation.

Peter Lorimer says: 'In reality, despite what he [Clough] had said about us in the past, we as a team wanted to play well and add to our league title we had won only months before he arrived.'

Brian Clough could undoubtedly be a bully ('dominant' – as Giles puts it). He had forced his brash personality on his players at his previous clubs. Some players, on the other hand, found themselves snubbed completely. When Nottingham Forest signed John Sheridan in 1989, Clough completely ignored him. Sheridan recalled:

> I was signed by Forest whilst Clough was away on holiday and I got the distinct impression that Clough resented that and consequently me. He never once played me and totally ignored me in the dressing-room or whenever we passed each other at the ground.

Ironically, Sheridan's only appearance in a Forest shirt was on the back of a copy of *Shoot!*, a popular football magazine at the time.

Duncan McKenzie was another who felt the wrath, and the mischievousness, of Clough. He told me, 'I was in the team at Forest and had been playing well. Then, one day, as we waited to go out at Highbury, Clough called me over, with what I thought would be instructions for the game.' In a very passable Clough impersonation, McKenzie continued: 'He said, "Young man, I've heard that their number 10 is going to mark you tightly. Well, I've got news for him – and you . . . you're not fucking playing!"'

Clough was a law unto himself. When the 1991 FA Cup final between his Nottingham Forest side and Tottenham Hotspur ended all square, the players prepared for extra time. As the Spurs players received their pep talk and tactics from manager Terry Venables, the youngsters of Forest sat around on the Wembley turf chatting among themselves, while their manager totally ignored them and stood passing the time of day with an old match steward, giving not even a glance towards his inexperienced players. In extra time, Spurs beat Forest soundly, winning 2–0.

Don Revie often seemed uncomfortable when appearing on television, while Clough revelled in it. During the mid-'70s Revie appeared on Yorkshire Television in an interview with Richard Whiteley. Revie agreed to appear only on the condition that the discussion was to be about his football life and nothing else. But just a few minutes into the interview, Whiteley began probing Revie about his England career and payments from the Arab Emirates. Revie became annoyed and on more than one occasion began removing his microphone from his jacket lapel. Whiteley apologised and the conversation continued, but when once again Whiteley strayed onto the subject of the Middle East, Revie finally did remove his microphone and walked off the set.

In 1974, Revie and Clough came face to face in an ITV interview chaired by Austin Mitchell. Revie remained, as usual, pensive but open. Clough, although attempting to appear relaxed, was fidgety and strangely submissive.

During that TV debate with Revie, he looks sheepish, young and frankly inexperienced. Of course, underneath, Clough was none of these. The thing that always came to the surface and is not widely acknowledged is that in every confrontation between Clough and Revie, Clough was the aggressor – always the Revie-hater. And he never acknowledged Revie's phenomenal achievements at Leeds United. Revie, on the other hand, praised Brian Clough for his efforts at Derby. Clough built a very good Derby side in the late '60s and early '70s, and Don Revie refers to this in a Leeds United match-day programme from late September 1971. Leeds had drawn 0–0 in a League Cup game against Derby at the Baseball Ground and in the programme for the replay Revie wrote this about Clough's side:

> They are without doubt one of the most attractive sides in the First Division at the moment and if they keep this sort of form up over the whole of the season then they stand an excellent chance of winning something.

Indeed there were one or two impressive players around for Derby at that time, Colin Todd, Roy McFarland, Archie Gemill, Alan Durban, John O'Hare, Kevin Hector and Alan Hinton among them. In the replay that day, Peter Lorimer scored two goals to enable a 2–0 win to Leeds, and Brian Clough shunned the TV cameras, declining to give a post-match interview.

Personally, I only met Clough once. It was just before a friendly when Leeds played at Huddersfield in his first game as manager in 1974. I was only 18 years old and I vividly remember shaking his hand from my front-row seat as he walked towards the Leeds dugout. It was a very limp and somewhat insecure handshake. I realise that on the face of it that doesn't mean a great deal, but whenever I saw Clough on television after that, I saw, despite his bravado for the cameras, a very insecure man.

In another, much later television appearance, on *Sport in Question* hosted by Jimmy Greaves and Ian St John in the mid-'90s, Clough was very drunk. He touches on the subject of his alleged misdemeanours over illegal payments by slurring to the audience that Alan Sugar, 'a spiv from London', has made accusations against him and adding 'The second he's big enough, brave enough and gets a bloody shave and doesn't walk like a spiv ... I'll sue him if he repeats it!' He is then asked whether or not he thinks that, with him being the first manager to pay £1 million for a player (Trevor Francis), he feels responsible for the escalation in transfer fees. 'I felt responsible for Justin Fashanu,' he replies. 'It took me three months to twig him [referring to Fashanu being gay].' When asked how he would have handled Eric Cantona, he replies 'I'd have cut his balls off.'

Brian Clough's 44 days in charge at Elland Road was the subject of David Peace's 2006 novel *The Damned Utd*. It is a highly entertaining book, but its mixture of fact and fiction was controversial. Three years after its publication, it was adapted for the big screen by Peter Morgan. The film was directed by Tom Hooper.

The actors portraying the main characters were outstanding. Michael Sheen was absolutely perfect as Brian Clough. He said before the film's premiere in April 2009 that he immersed himself fully into Clough's intense character, so much so that at times 'it was frightening'.

Interviewed in advance of the film's release, he said:

> With all my characters [Tony Blair and David Frost among them] I always aim to play a rounded human being but with Clough there are so many contradictory things in his make-up. I hope in the film you recognise a real and complicated human being. That combination of confidence, the brashness and the 'old big head' that he gives on the surface while at the same time being able to inspire huge affection, admiration and respect from people. That's what made it interesting for me to play.

Sheen wasn't a Leeds fan, really:

> Leeds were the big team when I was growing up and that can inspire jealousy. I can't say my feelings about Leeds were based on their actual play, it was more to do with sideline issues – mainly Panini football stickers! If I was doing well with my Leeds United stickers, then I felt good about Leeds United. If I wasn't, I didn't.
>
> I supported Liverpool as a boy because I grew up there, but when we moved to Wales, my dad, who was a rugby man, never told me that you could still support a football team even if you didn't still live there.

The actor wasn't a bad footballer when he was young, even having a trial at Arsenal. This seemingly stood him in good stead for a particular scene in which Clough had to keep the ball up a few times and then volley it into the net, which Sheen did quite well, it has to be said. 'There was a lot of pressure that day,' said Sheen. 'The press decided to turn up that day and as well as doing interviews they witnessed my "football skills". But I think I came through OK.'

The supporting cast, including Timothy Spall as Clough's sidekick Peter Taylor, was flawless. The Derby County chairman at the time was Sam Longson, played brilliantly by Jim Broadbent. An unlikely candidate for the role of Don Revie was the Irish actor Colm Meaney, known from the film *The Commitments* and from countless *Star Trek* episodes as Chief O'Brien. Meaney's portrayal of Revie was pure genius. Although it did show Revie in a cold light and wasn't a balanced interpretation, it did display Meaney's undoubted talent as an actor.

However, the film, like the book, contained a large dollop of artistic licence and the fictional elements understandably annoyed the players who had been at Leeds during Clough's brief reign. One player who had more reason to be annoyed than most was Johnny Giles. Referred to only as 'The Irishman', he was portrayed as the man responsible for the plotting and scheming to remove Brian Clough from Elland Road. Giles took legal action against the author David Peace and his publishers Faber & Faber to have parts of the book that misrepresented him removed. Those parts were removed and he won all costs and damages.

Writing in his Irish *Evening Herald* column in March 2009, Giles commented:

> Peace set out to write about Clough's brief tenure at Elland Road from his own angle and with his own motivations ... Many of the things that Peace talks about in the book never happened and for that reason I felt it necessary to go to the courts to establish that this was fiction based on fact and nothing more.
>
> I won the case easily and one of the big by-products of that was that the Clough family, who had no voice at all on the subject, had their concerns aired. Nigel Clough has stated in public that he ... disagrees fundamentally with the depiction of his father. Just to give an example of that, it is obvious that Peace believes that alcohol was a huge problem throughout Clough's life. In his latter years it became the overriding aspect of his life but at the time when he signed up to manage Leeds, his drinking wasn't an issue.
>
> But Clough and his family are in no position to defend the man they knew as a husband and a father and that's why I was happy to contribute to a documentary for ITV which I believe

will show people a much more accurate version of reality ... Many people will be surprised to see that I am defending Clough's memory, even though it is well known that we didn't get on ... Because he came [to Elland Road] with the stated aim of changing everything that Revie had built, it was natural that he should put people's noses out of joint and that, in a nutshell, is what happened.

Essentially, what Peace did was to try to make fact out of fiction. The central plank of his yarn is that Clough came to Leeds United and in a fog of drink and eccentricity went head to head with the players that had worked for years under Don Revie and would now do it the Clough way. It is well known that Clough despised Revie and his methods and I think it is fair to say that he came to Leeds to prove a point.

The story of his time at Elland Road is undoubtedly a great subject for a book or a film but what we have in *The Damned United* is one man's interpretation of facts and not a true telling of events. I know this because I was there. According to Peace, I worked tooth and nail in the background to undermine Clough because I had wanted Revie's job in the first place. Peace wrote conversations between myself and Clough into his book that never took place but suited well enough the interpretation he wanted to portray.

... Clough was an arrogant man and I readily admit that I didn't like him or get on with him. But that doesn't mean I'm happy to see his memory battered this way, when he has no defence to offer. Read the book, go to see the movie but at all times remember that Peace and the filmmakers have created a production that may well be entertaining but is ultimately fictional.

I asked Allan Clarke what he thought of the film and he just laughed. 'Not a lot, really. Clough clearly had an agenda against Leeds United.

'But I remember one occasion when he had rung downstairs from his newly acquired office asking for two cups of coffee. Just by chance, Billy Bremner answered it. He took the order but ignored it. Fifteen minutes later, Clough rang again demanding to know where his coffee was.

"'Do you know who I am?" Clough bellowed down the line.

"'No," replied Billy. "Do you know who I am?"

"'No," said Clough.

"'Well, get your own fucking coffee then.'"

Paul Reaney has commented:

> There is one scene in the film taken on the training ground that used to stand to the rear of the West Stand in which Brian Clough takes part in a five-a-side game. Mark Cameron as Norman Hunter fouls Clough quite heavily and the new manager crumbles to the ground in agony and remains there motionless. This is totally inaccurate. In real life, Clough got up.

Of Brian Clough, Norman Hunter has told me:

> Although we were inaccurately portrayed as the culprits plotting against Clough, his appointment was never going to work. He had taunted and verbally abused Leeds United for years before coming to Elland Road, and he certainly set about the job totally wrong.

Of the film, he commented:

> Let's be honest, the actors who played us didn't look remotely like footballers, did they? It was a joke. The actor who played Billy Bremner looked like a dwarf with a ginger wig on.
>
> What isn't mentioned in the film but what really did happen is an incident when we travelled to a pre-season game at Aston Villa, just after the Huddersfield friendly [Clough's first game in charge]. Clough stopped the coach on a dual carriageway and ordered a team talk on the grassy bank. He then ordered us to sit down, which we did, but it was pouring with rain and we were in our suits so we started getting up. 'I'll tell you when you can stand up,' said Clough. Billy Bremner then said, 'If you think we're sitting out here in the rain, you've another thing coming.' I think he knew then that his bullying tactics weren't going to work with us.

Peter Lorimer remembers that incident on the wet grassy bank:

> This was his way of trying to belittle us. He would join in six-a-side games and we'd have to go on until his side won. I was consulted by the makers of *The Damned United* and I wanted the film to be made because I wanted everyone to see we didn't get Brian Clough the sack. Unfortunately, it didn't quite show that.

Gordon McQueen was a 22-year-old centre-half under Don Revie and played under Clough during those 44 days. He told Phil Hay of the *Yorkshire Evening Post*:

> Damned United? We were Doomed United under Brian Clough. If Clough had taken a different approach, things might have worked out for him. I think he tried to change too much too quickly.
>
> Everyone knows how meticulous Don Revie was about training and match preparation. He was the first at the training ground and was the last to leave. Every minute of our training was planned and before matches we'd be given dossiers detailing everything we needed to know about our opponents. Clough was quite the opposite. He would turn up halfway through training and it's fair to say that the senior players didn't take to his methods.
>
> The night before matches, Revie would have the team stay in a hotel – even if the game was at Elland Road. He didn't want players to lose sleep if they had young children at home.
>
> We'd heard stories about how Clough would get his players to go to the bar and have a few beers before a game. But that wasn't the Leeds way and he wasn't going to take away the professionalism of the team. One other thing that was unsettling was that, when Revie was boss, there were never any stories in the media about players coming in or going out. But when Clough arrived, there were loads of them.
>
> Clough's pre-match talks didn't go into anything like the detail of Revie's, but he would want us to go out and play football. Leeds had their worst start to a season for 15 years, winning just one and drawing two from the first six matches, and behind the scenes

there were rumblings. Chairman Manny Cussins was asking the senior players what they thought of the new manager and they said what they thought – that it was a mistake. But there was definitely no delegation from the players to the chairman or anything like that.

There were, of course, many harmless and quite funny inaccuracies throughout the film. The Leeds team bus is shown arriving at Derby County for the aforementioned FA Cup game – the players are made to walk the final 100 yards to the ground under Revie's instruction as part of his superstitious nature. Revie was, of course, deeply superstitious, but according to the team bus driver at the time, Jim Lister, this incident never occurred. Leeds midfielder Johnny Giles was around 5 ft 5 in. and the centre-half Jack Charlton was 6 ft 3 in., yet in the film, they are exactly the same height. Dave Mackay appears as a Derby player even though he had left the club three years previously. During one scene, Clough is shown in the tunnel remonstrating with the players; in the background is the East Stand, the largest cantilever-type stand in Europe. The fact that the film is set in 1974 and the East Stand wasn't built until 1993 seems to have escaped the film's makers.

All in all, the film is an entertaining account of Clough's turbulent stay at Elland Road, but it is important to keep it in its context. To my mind, a film should be all fiction or all non-fiction.

In August 2009, David Peace, a Huddersfield Town fan, wrote an article for *The Guardian*'s book club about how he came to write *The Damned Utd*:

> In the summer of 1974, my dad took me to see my first football match; Huddersfield Town v. Leeds United . . . I remember Brian Clough as I stood with my father in the Leeds Road car park and watched the Leeds players and staff get off their coach. Brian Clough looked different. Brian Clough looked friendly. He shook hands with people. He signed autograph books. He ruffled my hair. He winked at me.
>
> He said: 'You'll never forget this day.'
> Or at least I think he did.

Many years later, Peace had an idea for a book about Leeds United, 'a secret grimoire of the Dirty Whites, told through a chorus of voices':

> I began to read; the history of Leeds United and the life of Brian Clough, all the football books and all the local newspapers. And also all the novels that I wanted to pay homage to: *Room at the Top, Saturday Night and Sunday Morning, A Kind of Loving, This Sporting Life, Christie Malry's Own Double-Entry* and *Alma Cogan.*
>
> And then there came a point, when and where I stopped reading and I started writing; different lives, different voices ...
>
> But gradually, very gradually, day by 44-day, one voice, one life, triumphed over all the other voices, all the other lives; the voice and the life of Brian Howard Clough ...
>
> In the first person present; present in those 44 days in 1974. And in the second person present; present in the memories that brought him to those 44 days in 1974. Present and incorrect. A character in a novel; a novel about a man and a job and a place and a time; Brian Clough as the manager of Leeds United in 1974. And how he came to be there ...
>
> A novel about fact and about fiction, about dreams and about nightmares, about defeat and about revenge, about tragedy and about farce, about wings made of wax and rays made of sun.

Brian Clough had a liver transplant in 2003, but died of stomach cancer a year later, on Ward 30 in Derby City Hospital.

13. The Press Gang

The *Daily Mirror* and its sister newspaper the *Sunday People* had a clear vendetta against Leeds United Football Club and Don Revie; that in itself is indisputable. To this day, thousands of Leeds fans refuse to buy the *Daily Mirror* or the *Sunday People*, and many of the players of the '60s and '70s were so incensed by allegations of match-fixing that they will not read the newspapers ever again either.

Investigative journalist Richard Stott hated Leeds United with a passion. He was instrumental, along with the *Daily Mirror*, *Sunday People* and the *News of the World*, in hounding Leeds United at every opportunity. He claimed to have passed a dossier to the Football Association in 1977, once again alleging that Don Revie had attempted to fix games. Twenty years later, he was still at it. Only days after Billy Bremner's untimely death in December 1997, Stott reared his ugly head yet again. Despite all the bribery allegations from 1972 having been dismissed and £100,000 damages awarded to Bremner, Stott wrote an article in the *News of the World* once again claiming that Bremner and Revie had attempted to bribe other players. In the damning article, he called Bremner an 'unprincipled man' and branded Revie 'corrupt'. He also added in his column, which had the strapline, 'The columnist whose bite is as bad as his bark', 'Until the FA finds someone brave enough to root out the cancerous greed at the heart of the game, it will continue to stink of corruption and double dealing.' Incidentally, Bremner donated his damages to a Leeds hospice.

After that article was published, I contacted Stott and asked him why he had waited for Billy Bremner to die before raking up the past yet again. In his reply, dated 21 December 1997, Stott claimed: 'Newspapers exist to tell the truth, it is their duty not to shrink from it, even if Leeds United fans do.' I wrote again and asked him why he had not addressed my original question of why he had waited until immediately after Bremner's death to bring the story up again. I ended my letter by saying, 'As you seem so fond of unearthing corrupt dealings, may I suggest that you investigate the life bans and suspensions given to referees across Europe that robbed Leeds United of more than one major European trophy.' Perhaps not surprisingly, I never received a further reply.

I sent a copy of both my letter and Stott's reply to the then chairman of Leeds United, Peter Ridsdale. On 23 December I received this reply from Mr Ridsdale:

> Dear Gary,
>
> Many thanks for your letter regarding the recent article in the *News of the World*. Clearly, as Chairman of Leeds United and someone who knew Billy well, I like you am appalled by both the content of the article and the timing. As you correctly point out, it appears that any success by Leeds United is begrudged by some sections of the media. This is something that over the years has stopped surprising me but nevertheless continues to disappoint me. Thank you for writing to me personally and let's hope that we can give the best response possible to articles such as the one in question by going out and winning trophies again.
>
> Yours sincerely,
>
> Peter Ridsdale, Chairman

Unfortunately, since that letter was written neither Leeds United nor Peter Ridsdale has won any trophies. One day, maybe.

Towards the end of the 1963–64 season, Good Friday to be precise, Leeds beat Newcastle United 1–0 at St James's Park. Considering a number of Leeds players were out through injury, this was a vital win as Leeds closed in on the Second Division championship. In 1977, the *Daily Mirror* unearthed more 'evidence' of bribery and match-fixing, this time in relation to this game at Newcastle. The *Mirror* claimed that before the game Don Revie had telephoned a former teammate of his at Sunderland, Stan Anderson. Anderson was the captain of Newcastle at the time and it was alleged that Revie asked him to offer £10 to each Newcastle player to throw the match. An unnamed reporter, who just happened to be visiting Anderson at the time of the call, supposedly witnessed this telephone call.

The subsequent report by the *Daily Mirror* contained no hard facts and absolutely no confirmation from Anderson that the exchange had occurred. Anderson's reaction is recorded in *The Unforgiven* by Rob Bagchi and Paul Rogerson:

> The stories are a tissue of lies. The press were gunning for him [Revie]. I denied it from the start – it was all innuendo – and I deny it now. I went to see my solicitors about it and they said the story hadn't damaged me. The whole thing was based on a telephone call that never took place.

Authors Bagchi and Rogerson write of the Wolves bribery saga discussed earlier:

> It's a strange tale, full of claims and counter-claims. But given the court's verdict and the findings of the police and the FA, it's difficult to see how we're supposed to believe in Revie's guilt. It just doesn't add up.

Even to this day, the *Daily Mirror* continues with its attempts to besmirch the name of Leeds United Football Club. Right up until his death in 2004, Emlyn Hughes regularly received payment for providing two or three pages of highly amusing stories about how much he hated Leeds.

Former Leeds player Mike O'Grady says, 'I am amazed and bemused over the abuse that Emlyn Hughes gave Leeds United in the *Daily Mirror*. He would slag Leeds off on a regular basis and then have the hard-faced cheek to turn up at Leeds events.'

Hughes was known by Liverpool fans as 'Crazy Horse', but away from Merseyside opposing fans knew him as 'Tiny Tears' as a result of him always crying during TV interviews. Hughes' one-time teammate and captain at Liverpool, Tommy Smith, was famous for his clashes with Leeds' Allan Clarke, but I was at an after-dinner speech given by Billy Bremner where he told the audience that Smith had once told him that he and several of his teammates had hated Emlyn Hughes much more than they hated the Leeds players, or any other players for that matter. Smith readily admits he didn't like Hughes, and has written:

It was Emlyn Hughes who in 1993 wrote in the *Daily Mirror* that Brian Clough was a better manager than Bill Shankly and Bob Paisley. That pearl of wisdom left me speechless! . . . As for his illness, I see a reader in the *Football Echo* on Saturday had a go at me for not sending him my good wishes. Well, a few years ago, I was left on death's door after a car crash and I'm still waiting for the get-well card from him. Everyone knows we don't get on . . . there's one thing I am not – a hypocrite.

Hughes regularly filled the *Daily Mirror*'s sports pages with his hatred of Leeds United, and much of what he wrote was often repeated. It just appeared that the *Daily Mirror* was determined to get across its own message. Hughes' hatred wasn't confined to the Revie squad of players from the 1960s and 1970s, either; he continued to smear the club's name well after Don Revie had passed away in 1989. During the reign of Howard Wilkinson at Elland Road, Hughes wrote an article in the *Daily Mirror* previewing the following day's televised game at Hillsborough. 'If Howard Wilkinson sent out eleven vestal virgins and whistled up the Angel Gabriel to captain them,' he wrote, 'folk would still hate and loathe Leeds United. Me included. And, oh, how I hope they get torn apart tomorrow at Hillsborough.'

A Lee Chapman hat-trick helped Leeds to a 6–1 victory over Sheffield Wednesday, who at that time were fighting for a European place in the league. Leeds went on to win the league championship.

A journalist with *The Guardian*, Roy Greenslade, recently wrote, 'Revie angered the Football Association by selling news of his resignation to the *Daily Mail*, before the FA received his formal resignation letter.' To put this in context, it might be more accurate to say that it was other newspapers that Revie angered by selling the story, not just the FA. The full and correct details of Revie's resignation are covered later in this book, but could the *Mail* exclusive be the real underlying factor for the other newspapers' hatred of Revie – and in particular the *Daily Mirror*'s long, ever so long, vendetta against Leeds United and Don Revie?

Greenslade was writing in reaction to a piece in the *Sunday Telegraph* by fellow journalist Henry Winter, who had covered the 50th anniversary of Revie becoming Leeds United's manager with a glowing tribute:

They sang Don Revie's name at Elland Road on Saturday. They remembered the great times he brought to Leeds United and recalled how the rest of the country never appreciated him.

...The memory of that exceptional Revie team lingers on from Clarke's goal poaching to the thunderous shooting of Peter Lorimer, from the elegant wing-play of Eddie Gray to Billy Bremner's indefatigability and the utter indomitability of Johnny Giles, Norman Hunter and Jack Charlton. Among other iconic names.

Greenslade, who replaced Richard Stott as editor at the *Daily Mirror* in 1990, objected to what he considered glaring omissions from Winter's article with these comments in his *Guardian* blog:

It was remarkable for what it did not say, omitting from what Winter called Revie's controversial life story the most controversial episode of all. For those of you who don't know, Revie made an enormous success of managing Leeds from 1961 to 1974, winning league titles, several cups and European trophies. He then became the England manager, where his record was anything but spectacular, and in 1977 he suddenly resigned – the first man to do so from that post – to manage the United Arab Emirates team.

...The FA then suspended Revie from football for ten years on a charge of bringing the game into disrepute. All of this is recounted by Winter but – as with Revie's Wikipedia entry – the real reason for Revie's downfall is airbrushed from history.

For the true situation we have to turn to the *Daily Mirror* cuttings library and the memoirs of the late Richard Stott, a former editor who, in 1977, was one of the paper's senior reporters. With evidence from the former Leeds goalkeeper, Gary Sprake, he exposed Revie as a match-fixer. In fact, it was when Revie discovered that Sprake was about to spill the beans that he vanished to the UAE.

...Once Revie had taken up his job with UAE for £340,000 a year (a colossal sum in those days), other witnesses came forward. One of them, a respected player and manager, Bob Stokoe, told how Revie tried to bribe him to lose a game. By the time Stott had completed his investigation he was able to present the FA with a 315-page dossier cataloguing Revie's long period of corruption. Revie sued the *Mirror* for libel, but he did not pursue his legal action. The FA simply swept it all under the carpet, though it did issue the ban on Revie.

I just can't understand how, in a piece of more than 1,500 words, Winter managed to overlook this key incident, the real reason for Revie's downfall.

Once again, Stokoe's comments were unfounded and remain so today. As for the alleged reason for Revie's resignation, this will be addressed later in this book. Here, meanwhile, is just a selection of the hundreds of comments posted about Greenlade's article:

Talking of omission, why haven't you mentioned 1982 – when the *Sunday People*, the *Mirror*'s sister paper, repeated the allegations and was successfully sued by Billy Bremner for £100,000 . . . ?

If the *Mirror* scoop has been airbrushed from history it's because it didn't stand up. Bremner sued the *People* afterwards, and won, so the entire issue was put to bed – by most people.

Revie wasn't banned for disrepute. He was banned for refusing to face the charges of disrepute. If, in 1977, the FA knew he was guilty of match-fixing, why wasn't he sacked for it? Why was he banned only after he quit to take up a job with the UAE?

I'm a Lincoln City fan, but the 1970 FA Cup final was won by Chelsea kicking Leeds off the park. In the 1973 Cup-Winners' Cup final, they were again kicked off the park, then there was the 1975 European Cup final – the Clarke penalty, the disallowed Lorimer goal – bad, bad ref. Leeds United were sinned against a hell of a lot more than they sinned.

Shortly after Revie's death in 1989, conveniently, Malcolm Allison claimed that Revie 'used to leave £300 or £400 in an envelope in the referee's room and they could take it or leave it'. In *The Unforgiven*, Bagchi and Rogerson say of this:

Over the 13 years Revie was manager of Leeds and nearly 500 games in all competitions, wouldn't at least one referee, one might think, have corroborated Allison's claim? Yet the allegation is left unchallenged. Revie's death has meant his reputation is fair game for anyone.

It's true to say that Don Revie was deeply mistrustful of most, though not all, forms of media. During Leeds' rise to fame in the early 1960s, the southern-based press especially were extremely critical of Revie's side. This is one of the main catalysts behind the anti-Revie and Leeds feeling that clearly exists today, and where the 'Dirty Leeds' tag that is still attached to the team comes from.

It was claimed that Leeds had 'kicked their way out of the Second Division' in 1963–64, but what is never remembered is the fact that just about every team of that era could be extremely physical. Rough and tough encounters occurred against Preston North End, Sunderland and Bury – in fact, almost all the teams in the Second Division. Peter Lorimer has said: 'If a team wanted to mix it with us, we could mix it; if a team wanted to play football, we could play.'

On 31 August 1963, Leeds played host to Bury, who had Bob Stokoe playing at centre-half. It was a physical game, and one incident in the first half saw referee Maurice Fussey influenced by Stokoe. Johnny Giles had threaded a lovely ball through to Albert Johanneson just inside the penalty area; he rounded the Bury keeper, Chris Harker, and just as he was about to slot the ball home he was upended by the keeper. Fussey saw it and was about to give a penalty when Stokoe manoeuvred the official away from the incident and, with his arm around him, walked him away from the penalty area, while quietly talking to him. The *Green Post* wrote: 'The crowd claimed Johanneson had been pulled down by the keeper, and a towel thrown which came flying out of United's trainer's box showed that they were not the only ones who thought so.' Mr Fussey, however, had been persuaded otherwise, and Bury remained on level terms.

Another bloodbath occurred when Preston North End arrived at Elland Road on 16 November 1963. The *Daily Mail* reported:

So much violence erupted over the playing area at Elland Road on Saturday that a fight between grandstand patrons when

Preston conceded a penalty served almost as light relief. But it was not the tragic sight of two grown men who play football for a living trying to knock lumps out of each other that was disturbing. It was the apparent resignation, almost condonation, of officials that this had to be when two teams met while fighting for promotion.

When Leeds were defeated 2–0 at Sunderland just after Christmas 1963, Eric Stranger of the *Daily Express* wrote:

> Whatever is in store I hope there are no more games like that at Roker Park on Saturday. It was so full of spite and malice that it did no credit to the 22 players, the referee (Mr Cattlin, Rochdale) or the huge crowd of 55,046. Two Sunderland players threw punches and got off scot-free; so did a Leeds player who deliberately kicked out at an opponent. As for the crowd, it sickened me to hear them cheer when a stretcher was called for Jim Storrie, the Leeds inside-right, cheers which increased in volume as he was carried off 25 minutes from the end with damaged knee ligaments.

Another ill-tempered match took place that season when Leeds played First Division Everton in the fourth round of the FA Cup. United held Everton 1–1 at Elland Road in the first game, in which Bremner was booked for a foul on Alex Scott that lead to a penalty to Everton. Scott himself took the penalty, which Gary Sprake saved, but was judged to have moved by referee Tom Langdale of Darlington. Roy Vernon retook the spot-kick and this time Everton equalised.

Rumours circulated after the game that someone had tried to punch Langdale after the match and that he had locked himself in his dressing-room, which was then guarded by two policemen. But Langdale said later, 'I have no complaints about my treatment at Leeds. Nobody attacked me or said anything out of place.' Don Hardisty of the *Daily Express* then asked him why he had stayed in his dressing-room for an hour after the match. Langdale explained:

> That's simple. I certainly wasn't sheltering from anybody. I listened to the cup results and reports on the radio. I have no reason to

submit a special report to the FA. The only report I will be sending will be about my booking of three players.

On the evening of the replay, Billy Bremner, 21 at the time, was warned by the FA that he faced an automatic ban if he was booked again. He commented:

> I can't understand what all the fuss is about. I play hard. But I don't grumble when opponents play hard against me. The trouble is that when you're top of the table, like Leeds, players, crowds and, in some cases, referees sort you out for special treatment.
>
> You have to take it. Football is a man's game and is meant to be played hard. But I never set out with the deliberate intention of injuring an opponent. Any professional footballer who does that is crazy.

Leeds lost the replay, but in exactly the same round the following season they were once again drawn at home against Everton. It was another hot-tempered game and the score, once more, was 1–1, so Leeds had to travel to Goodison Park again for the replay. This time, however, goals by Jack Charlton and Don Weston saw Leeds go through 2–1. But it was a clash between the teams two months previously, in the league, that had grabbed sensational headlines. It was dubbed the 'Battle of Goodison'.

Despite overwhelming evidence that Leeds United were not the only physical side in the division, the vast majority of the press hated them. That was obvious. In simple terms, it seemed that Leeds were the 'new kids on the block' and the media didn't like it.

A clear campaign was mounted against this young Leeds United team, and in November 1964 figures revealed by the FA claimed that Leeds had more players sent off than any other team. What it didn't reveal was that these figures included all reserve games and even junior matches. In fact, Leeds United had not had one single first-team player sent off all season, while just about every team around them had had an average of five players sent off in that same season. 'Dirty Leeds' was a name that became indelible, and the press loved it.

The 'Battle of Goodison' had to be stopped by the referee as tempers and fists flew in all directions. Johnny Giles played that day, and, in his autobiography, *A Football Man*, he remembers:

> We had already gained a reputation as a tough squad, largely on the back of a report in the FA News . . . Everton were clearly waiting for us that day in November, to teach us a lesson . . . From the kick-off the crowd was hostile, as crowds were towards Leeds so many times . . . I was playing on the right wing, close to the Everton supporters . . . They called me names I had never been called before, well beyond the regular 'pig' or 'bastard', and always with the word 'Irish' attached . . . Then it boiled over just before half-time . . . It was the only time in my career I thought the supporters would invade the pitch. It was really scary. The referee obviously felt the fear too, and brought the teams off the field to allow the ugly mood of the crowd to subside.
>
> If the Leeds dog had a bad name before coming to Goodison, it was now more or less established in the public mind that we were bad to the core, even though Sandy Brown had punched me.

Despite unfair criticism levelled at Leeds by the press, some within the game admired what Leeds were trying to accomplish. Bert Head was manager of Swindon Town when Leeds drew there 2–2 on 18 January 1964. Speaking after the game, Head said, 'Leeds play the game as I like it to be played. They play hard and they never give up fighting.'

Reporting on that game was Ken Jones of the *Daily Mirror*. He wrote:

> I left this game satisfied that Leeds have faced and played in front of too many cowards this season. They are tough and sometimes awkward. But they always have one saving grace: they are honest. What they do, they do openly. And if they come off second best, there are no squeals. The knife-edge tackling of right-half Billy Bremner is undoubtedly the most controversial issue in any Leeds performance. But I like Bremner. He plays with a tremendous, natural talent that underlines his skill with great heart.

As Leeds steadily grew into one of the best teams in Britain during the 1960s, some newspapers began to take note. The *Daily Express* brought out a souvenir edition to commemorate United reaching the final of the Inter-Cities Fairs Cup in September 1967. James Lawton wrote:

> Leeds United have come up from the lower reaches of mediocrity to be a major force in England and across the face of European soccer.
>
> The Fairs Cup is a competition that has soared from a salesman's idea of an international trade boost to a tournament ranking second only to the European Cup. It is a trophy in fact that would find a fitting home at Elland Road. For though Leeds are not the foremost of pretty-pretty stylists, what stature, what power, and what a long way they have come in such a short time.
>
> They roared like a juggernaut to the Second Division Championship in 1963–64; surged to Wembley in 1965 and an extra-time defeat by a Liverpool moving towards their peak; lost the First Division title only on goal average the same season, and then finished second to Liverpool in the league the following season.
>
> Last season in the FA Cup semi-final against Chelsea, a referee's decision blocked them from Wembley at the last hurdle.
>
> A welter of fixtures drained their strength at a vital stage of the championship and United finished fourth. But they still reached the final of the Fairs Cup.
>
> This was a team growing up! Like every adolescent, delight has been studded with desolation. They have known failure when teams with only half their heart would have sailed to success.
>
> But Revie's pride, and belief, is that losses over these short years have, in fact, been gains and that the boys have taken them like men.
>
> It is a remarkable story.

But even today, there is very little love for Leeds United in the media. Martin Lipton from the *Daily Mail* was at Bolton on the day they won to relegate Leeds from the Premiership in 2004. Lipton was heard to say, 'Lovely day for it.'

'Lovely day for what?' someone asked.

'To see this lot get relegated,' was his response.

David Conn of *The Guardian* can't really be regarded as a Leeds United fan either. In 2007, as Leeds were in the midst of clawing back their 15-point deduction on the field, all he wrote about throughout was 'Who owns Leeds United?' It seemed to be a deliberate attempt to divert attention from Leeds' phenomenal ongoing achievements out on the pitch.

In May 2010, the *Daily Mail* even used the British Airways strike as an excuse for a sly dig at Leeds and their fans. Remarking on the BA industrial dispute and the attack on Acas offices by demonstrators, Richard Littlejohn said:

> In my day, though, [demonstrators] all wore Che Guevara T-shirts and little hammer-and-sickle lapel pins. One of the thick revolutionaries at Acas this weekend was wearing a replica Leeds United football shirt. Any excuse for a punch-up.

In 2009, Patrick Collins wrote an extremely damaging and scathing attack on Leeds United in the *Mail on Sunday*, totally and utterly without provocation. I got in touch with Collins to ask if he could explain his obvious hatred towards Leeds, pointing out that Leeds fans were without doubt amongst the most loyal and dedicated in the country. He replied by saying that he disagreed with everything I had said. When I was researching this book, I contacted Collins asking if he would elaborate on his dislike towards Leeds United. He replied: 'Given the tone and content of one or two of your previous messages to me, I am amazed that you feel able to ask for my help in this matter. Good luck with the book.'

Sadly, some television stations also neglect to mention the huge achievements made by Leeds United Football Club over the years. *Match of the Day* is, of course, a world-famous football show that has thrilled and excited fans since 1964. When *Match of the Day* celebrated its 40th anniversary with a special tribute programme to the past four decades of domestic football, I watched with great anticipation. Surely the programme would feature Leeds United? After all, during the existence of *Match of the Day*, the club had won the league title three times and broken three league records: twenty-nine unbeaten games; only two defeats in a season; and the record number of league points under the two-points-for-a-win system (sixty-seven). They won the League Cup in 1968, the FA Cup centenary final in 1972, the Fairs Cup twice, the last-ever league championship before the start of the Premier League. They were top of the league for the millennium. They won the *Match of the Day* Goal of the Season award for 1991–92 (Rod Wallace v. Tottenham Hotspur) and 1995–96 (Tony Yeboah v. Liverpool). Also, in 1972, Leeds thrilled the *Match of the Day* audience with an absolutely flawless and unforgettable display against Southampton at Elland Road. Leeds annihilated their visitors and ran out 7–0 winners. They even stepped off the gas near the end, thrilling the crowd with an exhibition of supreme football, stringing together 20-odd passes without a Saints player touching the ball. 'It's almost cruel,' exclaimed commentator Barry Davies. Almost 40 years on, people up and down the country still talk about that Saturday night. But it wasn't even mentioned on the *Match of the Day* anniversary special, and nor were any other of Leeds United's achievements. In the event, Leeds appeared only twice on the programme: it featured the FA Cup final defeats against Chelsea in 1970 and Sunderland in 1973.

I wrote to *Match of the Day* presenter Gary Lineker to ask why Leeds' phenomenal achievements had been completely overlooked. Lineker replied, claiming: 'I was absolutely shocked that you found our programme biased against Leeds United. We have many backroom staff here that are Leeds fans and they were amazed at your letter.' I was left wondering how much input those backroom Leeds fans had had in the programme.

14. Don Revie: Part 1

Revie the Footballer

Born in Middlesbrough in 1927, Don Revie was football daft from the age of four. He went to his first-ever football match (Middlesbrough) two years later, and three years on was picked for the school team. When Revie lost his mother in 1939, as a way of coping, he found solace in his football. He left school at 14, just as the Second World War began. Working as an apprentice bricklayer, he played for Newport Boys' Club before being transferred to Middlesbrough Swifts for two shillings – Revie's first transfer deal.

By the time he was 17, he was attracting a lot of attention from scouts for some of the top league clubs. Middlesbrough, naturally enough, were the first club to offer young Revie a trial, but Don was being watched from afar. Johnny Duncan was manager at Leicester City and had been monitoring this 'youngster with the lean build of a greyhound and almost the speed to match', as he described him. Duncan had also noticed that Revie was improving fast and decided now was the time to approach him, before it was too late. Revie thanked Middlesbrough for their interest but headed to the Midlands club. Even while he was at Middlesbrough Swifts, he had shown himself keen to learn everything there was to know about football, inside and out, and during his time at Leicester Revie picked up valuable advice and help from Johnny Duncan. It was here that Don met and eventually married Johnny's niece Elsie.

At 18, Revie received a bad injury while playing against Tottenham, breaking his ankle in three places. The injury was so serious that specialists were in no doubt that he would never play again. It was the support and help of Elsie, along with the expert influence of Johnny Duncan, and, of course, no small amount of determination from Revie

139

himself, that saw him back to fitness in less than five months.

A lot of the bad luck evident in his days as manager of Leeds United seems also to have plagued Revie in his younger days. Leicester reached the FA Cup final in 1948; meanwhile, Revie had sustained a nose injury in a match with West Ham on Easter Monday. Remembering it in his 1955 autobiography, *Soccer's Happy Wanderer*, Don wrote:

> My nose came into contact with the head of West Ham defender Walker. I spent the rest of the game with a sponge in my hand mopping up blood from my nose. Of course, I was eager to play in the cup final, so as a precaution Johnny Duncan rested me for our final league game at Plymouth Argyle. I still travelled with the team to Devon and after the game and a light meal, I retired to bed early. I used to room with Ken Chisholm and he arrived back at the room at around 10.30 p.m. He found me hunched over the wash bowl with blood streaming from my nose.

The club's trainer was called but by then Don's nose had been bleeding for ninety minutes and didn't stop for a further two hours.

The next morning, as soon as Revie got out of bed, the bleeding started again. He was rushed to hospital, where the nose was plugged, and once again the bleeding stopped. On the Monday, the Leicester team travelled to Skegness for a few days' light training prior to the final. Revie and Duncan remained in Plymouth. But the next morning, as Don climbed out of bed, the bleeding started again. By now, Revie was rightly concerned, and a specialist was called in.

The injury was diagnosed as a burst blood vessel at the back of the nose. It was recommended that he be admitted to hospital immediately, but Johnny Duncan insisted on taking him to see a specialist at Leicester Infirmary. Don was put in the back of a taxi with a load of packed ice and during the entire eight-hour journey his nose continued to bleed. On his arrival at the infirmary, Don said weakly, 'Can you stop the bleeding in time for me to play in the final?' He then passed out. After intense treatment, Don awoke the following day to be told that under no circumstances could he play in the final. Not only that, the doctor added that if he had been on the road for one more hour he might well have died, he had lost so much blood. Not only did this 'wretched' injury deprive Revie of an FA Cup final appearance, it also denied him a place on a European tour with England for which he had just been included.

After five years at Leicester, Revie moved to Hull City, but prior to that he turned down the chance to sign for Arsenal. Don arrived at Highbury amidst great secrecy but decided not to sign for the Gunners. When the Arsenal manager was told of his decision, he said something to Revie that he would never forget. He wrote:

> Tom Whittaker shook my hand and said, 'We would have liked you here at Arsenal, Don, and never forget if I can be of any help to you in the game or outside it, you only have to ring me. I'll be only too glad to give you any help or advice I can.' I returned to Leicester wondering whether I'd just made the biggest mistake of my life.

Hull's player-manager, the legendary Raich Carter, had been tracking Don for some time. Many believed this was because he wanted Don to succeed him as manager as he himself neared the end of his illustrious playing career. In *Soccer's Happy Wanderer*, Carter wrote:

> Don is what I call an old-fashioned footballer. He is not afraid of hard work, and his passing is a model for all young players. The remarkable thing is that Don Revie has taken so long to be recognised by the general public for the great footballer he is. Perhaps it is because he is a footballer's footballer: often unobtrusive but always in the right place at the right time.

Revie eventually moved on to Manchester City before he could fill the player-manager role that Carter had planned for him. After his departure from Humberside, Carter reiterated his belief in Don Revie: 'Whilst he was with me here at Hull, he never ceased asking questions. He was always wanting to learn something new.' Referring to Revie's key role in the Manchester City side, Carter wrote:

> The so-called Revie Plan has been a shot in the arm for our game of soccer. It has brought back the memories of how the great game used to be played in this country. I sincerely hope that more

British teams try to follow their example. It is a tribute to Don Revie that despite all his ups and downs in the game he has never stopped trying to play pure football all the way. The lesson Don Revie has taught the football world is this: it is not the man who does a brilliant body swerve in midfield who counts; it's how he parts with the ball to split the opposing defence that makes the master player.

Revie had been at Boothferry Park for only a couple of years when City offered a little over £20,000 for his services. It was in fact City's second attempt to secure the services of Revie, but with Arsenal about to pounce, they made another offer. Hull simply could not afford to turn it down and reluctantly agreed to the sale. Revie's value went up to almost £30,000, making him the second most expensive player of that era (Sheffield Wednesday's Jackie Sewell was worth £34,000). It was during his days at Maine Road that Revie finally realised his full playing potential.

One of Revie's teammates at Hull was a Dubliner, Paddy Fagan. When Revie was transferred to Manchester City in 1951, Fagan soon followed. Talking to Phil Hay of the *Yorkshire Evening Post*, he said:

> I never think of Revie as a manager, or not like other people do. To me he will always be Revie the player – a connoisseur of football and 30 years ahead of his time. Actually, in my opinion he was a better player than a manager, even though he was a lazy bugger! God knows, he was lazy! If you knocked the ball 20 yards in front of him, he wasn't going to chase it. It was passes to his feet or it was nothing. But that was the perfectionist in him – the hard task-master that I came to know over the many years I played with him.
>
> We both played under Raich Carter at Hull City and I played 165 appearances for Man City, Don made 162. When I say he was a connoisseur, I mean it. He had it in him to be very, very critical. He was without question the best passer of the ball I'd ever seen. He could put it on a sixpence without thinking – long or short passes from anywhere on the field. But it wasn't just skill with Don. He understood the game and he read it brilliantly. He

was a highly knowledgeable man and someone who saw things in the 1950s that other people began to spot and take notice of many years later. You hear talk now about players who can change a game. Well, Don was someone who could change a game in 20 seconds. Just like that.

In all at Maine Road, we had a great team. Bert Trautmann, Revie, Jimmy Meadows and more. But at the same time, there were players at City who Don didn't rate and didn't think were good enough to be there. He had no time for these lads.

I don't think I'm talking out of turn by saying that he felt they were earning their pay under false pretences; that the wages they were drawing weren't backed up by their ability. It wasn't a personal thing. He just took the attitude that you should only be in a team if you deserved to be playing. In his opinion, a few of the lads at City weren't up to it. That was his way and that's probably why his Leeds United team were such a great side. In the dressing-room, he never held back. He never swore and he never got personal but he'd get stuck in and pull people up, saying things like, 'What the hell are you playing at?' or, 'From now on, you do it like this.'

Don was hard in his attitude and he couldn't help but be critical. But as with all good motivators, he was also very fair. We became great pals and I spent a lot of time with him and his wife Elsie. They were so accommodating and could never do enough for me. It was also a bit like being part of their family. I think when Don took to you, he automatically took to you in a big way.

A lot of people didn't like him but I always take people as I find them. In my experience he was a terrific man and a masterful player. These days I don't know whether people appreciate that or not. He's generally, and wrongly, remembered for other things. For me, Revie's gift in management was merely an extension of his rare talent as a footballer. It's the only way I remember him. I read about what he achieved as a manager but I saw with my own eyes what he did as a player. He played the game as a professional, devoting himself to being the best and beating the best. Even then, he was like a student. Everything had to be just so. But beyond all the thinking, he had a marvellous touch and a range of passing like nothing else I've ever seen. I think he knew how good he was. I'm just not sure how many others do.

In four years at City, Revie became one of their most outstanding players, winning six England caps and being named Footballer of the Year.

The 'Revie Plan', in simple terms, was a tactic using a deep-lying centre-forward. The original idea came from the reserve centre-forward at City, Johnny Williamson. In one particular reserve game, Williamson was tiring of the usual centre-forward role and dropped back behind the rest of his attack. From here, he would begin pushing the ball forward for others to have a go. It caught on immediately. Every now and again, Williamson would vary the plan and chase through the middle and pick up the odd one-two himself.

Williamson was a good friend of Revie, and he told him about the idea. The reserve-team manager also liked it and subsequently it was decided that Revie would try it in the first team in the opening game of the season. In his autobiography, Revie remembered:

> Our manager at City, Les McDowall, called us together one day after a 1954–55 pre-season training session. 'We are going to play football this season,' he told us: 'By football I mean football. Keep the ball down; no big kicking; no wild clearances from the defence. We want to aim for a smooth link-up from defence to attack, letting the ball do the work, and not leaving chaps to chase a long ball when a short and more accurate pass would suit the situation better.'
>
> This sounded much like the Hungarian style of play, or the old Scottish style that Johnny Duncan used to instil into us at Leicester. Mr McDowall then took me to one side and asked, 'Ever play centre-forward, Don?' I told him that I had back in junior football, to which he said, 'I want you to play there this season. Only you won't be playing an orthodox centre-forward game. You're always saying that you prefer the short square pass with the ball pushed straight to your feet. We're going to give you that chance. I want you to play deep, and I want the other lads to play to you in the open spaces. It's all going to need a lot of stamina from you to chase all over the field, but the other lads

will have to do just as much running about too. I want a man as a midfield schemer who is prepared to wander about all over the field, and I think you are the man who can do it!' If the club wanted me to play that way, that's what I'd do.

The plan wasn't an instant success. In their first match playing in the new style, City were soundly beaten 5–0 at Preston North End, and *Daily Mirror* reporter Archie Ledbrooke suggested quite brutally afterwards, that the manager should 'kill this plan'. McDowall stuck with it, however, and the very next game saw a 5–2 victory over Sheffield United.

Even though it was based on a Hungarian idea, the plan was superbly executed by Revie, who added his own imitable style. Starting at the back with former German paratrooper Bert Trautmann in goal, the ball would be thrown short to Revie and moved about quickly on the floor, with short, accurate passes all involving Revie as he moved upfield. This particular part of the plan would occur just after Trautmann had made a save and Revie had dropped short; while the opposition struggled to get back from the attack, the plan would form a very effective counter-attack. Of course, there were various alterations to the scheme. Sometimes Revie would take the pass from his full-backs or half-backs. Revie was of course central to the plan, but it also relied heavily on other attackers moving into fresh positions and in doing so becoming the spare man.

Inevitably, some opposing teams would try to combat the Revie Plan by heavily marking the City man and attempting to take him out of the game. When this happened, Revie would go to the left wing, taking his marker with him. The left-winger would then go deep as the linkman instead of Revie. The right-back marking City's winger would be reluctant to follow his man that deep and would very soon be caught in no-man's-land, and then, with a few other players switching positions, City could very soon have even the best organised defence in the country all reshuffled whether they liked it or not.

About 15 years later, a similar style to the plan would become evident at Elland Road after Revie became manager at Leeds United. A short throw to full-back Paul Reaney on the right or Terry Cooper on the left from keeper Gary Sprake would be followed by short passes as the ball was moved upfield. One such move at Hillsborough saw midfielder Johnny Giles dropping back before, in just five passes through the team, Eddie Gray scored against Sheffield Wednesday.

A journalist at the time Revie was playing at City, Eric Thornton, became close friends with the player, and it was he who coined the phrase 'the Revie Plan'. The scheme soon developed into a fine combination, and at the end of the 1955 season Don Revie was awarded Footballer of the Year. The following year Revie was once again the star of the show as City lifted the 1956 FA Cup at Wembley.

In November of that year, he moved to Sunderland, and two years later he was on his way to Leeds.

15. Don Revie: Part 2

The Early Days at Leeds

Bill Lambton was the Leeds manager in 1958 and he made Don Revie the captain in place of Wilbur Cush. After a couple of pretty poor results, Revie, feeling he wasn't quite ready, relinquished the captaincy to Freddie Goodwin. Lambton then made way for Jack Taylor to become the next manager. As a player, Yorkshire-born Taylor had guested for his home-town team, Barnsley, and also for Watford during the Second World War, but it's fair to say that he struggled as manager of Leeds to get the right formula to take the club forward. Revie scored his first goal for the club in a 3–1 defeat at Preston in January 1959.

My uncle Frank remembers this period in Leeds United's history very well. 'It was very poor back then,' he told me. 'Towards the end of the '61 season, I remember, Jack Taylor resigned and Revie took over as player-manager, but things didn't improve; in fact, they got bloody worse!' He held up his thumb and index finger. There was a hair's breadth between them. 'We were that close to dropping into the Third Division.'

It is well documented how Don Revie was first appointed to the Leeds job. Bournemouth had shown an interest in him as player-manager, and Leeds chairman Harry Reynolds agreed to give them a written reference for him. While recording all Revie's attributes and talents, it occurred to Reynolds that the man he needed to replace Taylor could be right under his nose. He tore up the reference, summoned Revie to his office and offered him the manager's position. Another major factor in keeping Revie at Elland Road might just have been the £6,000 transfer fee that Reynolds had placed on Revie's head, forcing the south-coast club to look elsewhere.

The first thing Revie did was to surround himself with arguably the best backroom staff anywhere in Europe. Taylor had left him with three vital assets. The first was Les Cocker, a former professional with Stockport County and Accrington Stanley. Cocker's time as trainer at Leeds became legendary, and he went on to assist Alf Ramsey at England. Then there was coach Syd Owen. A former distinguished member of the RAF, Owen was a full England international, and his shrewd approach offered Revie yet another dimension. And finally, physiotherapist Bob English had been at Elland Road since 1957 and was widely recognised as one of the best in the business.

Syd Owen had been manager at Luton Town when Les Cocker applied for the trainer's job there. As mentioned earlier, Cocker was a very good player. Surprisingly, perhaps, given his relatively small stature, he was an efficient centre-forward. He had great belief in his ability as a trainer, too. When Owen read Cocker's letter applying for the job, he was immediately impressed. Although they had never met, Owen recognised a quality in Cocker. As well as the confident letter, it was the handwriting that appealed to Owen. 'That handwriting was like the man himself – unshakeable. It simply oozed character,' Owen wrote in 1969's *Leeds United Book of Football*. 'He explained in great detail how he would tackle the job at hand and I invited him for an interview.' Cocker, of course, got the job. However, it wasn't long before Owen was lured to the vacant coaching job at Leeds, and it wasn't long either until he recruited Cocker to follow him.

So when Revie arrived, the team behind him was almost complete. Maurice Lindley had briefly been a scout at Leeds but moved to Sheffield Wednesday before Revie took over as manager. When Revie became boss, he brought Lindley back as his assistant and chief scout. His job was to follow up information that could lead to the discovery of a promising young star. His journeys took him far and wide, across the country and into Europe. The trips to the Continent were usually to have a close look at United's next opponents in the Fairs Cup or European Cup. It was Lindley who inspired Revie's famous dossiers. During the early forays into Europe, Syd Owen usually accompanied Lindley. Between them, they would meticulously study the opposing team. Every player, every strength, every weakness, their favourite colour and even what they'd had to eat the night before.

By the time the players had read these dossiers, they knew more about the opposition than the opposition knew about themselves. Some criticism was levelled at Revie and his dossiers; there were those who claimed that Leeds should 'let their own players do the talking', and in many ways it was a valid point. In Revie's later days, as England manager, these dossiers had a mixed reception, but there was no doubting the detail that went into these reports.

On their assignments in Europe, Lindley and Owen came across many obstacles. On one occasion, Valencia were to be Leeds' next opponents and Lindley was sent to watch them in Las Palmas, in the Canary Islands. The club sent countless cables and letters stating that a Leeds representative would be there and needed a ticket. It was and still is customary to accommodate scouts, and Lindley was assured that he would be met at the airport and 'looked after'. Hours after he arrived, however, no one had met him, and with the kick-off looming, he had to buy a ticket for well over the asking price on the black market. He sat alone in some obscure stand, but still managed to deliver his report back to Elland Road.

Another time, Owen had difficulty whilst 'spying' on Valencia. He faced the same problem as Lindley had done previously, but he didn't even manage to get a stand ticket. He ended up paying to get into an open terrace behind the goal, where he was surrounded by screaming, frantic Spanish fans. He, too, duly delivered his report.

The final piece of the puzzle, Cyril Partridge, a former QPR player, was brought to Elland Road as youth-team coach, and, with the foundations in place, it was time for the next stage.

Revie created a youth policy that has been copied by almost every club in the world today. He brought in a 16-year-old Welsh keeper called Gary Sprake, who made possibly one of the most bizarre debuts of all time. On the morning of Saturday, 15 May 1963, Sprake was in bed ahead of a reserve game that afternoon at Elland Road when he was contacted by Leeds United and ordered to attend the first-team fixture Leeds were due to play . . . at Southampton. First-team keeper Tommy Younger had been taken ill shortly before kick-off and Sprake was whisked by car to the airport and flown to the south coast in a tiny two-seater aircraft.

He went on to make more than 500 appearances for Leeds and was a superb goalkeeper albeit prone to the odd mistake. As we have seen, Revie admitted many years later that he should have been quicker to replace Sprake with his loyal reserve goalkeeper David Harvey. Leeds-born Harvey made only a handful of first-team appearances in around seven years. He played only 11 games during the 1971–72 season, but Revie, who had finally lost patience with his Welsh keeper, put Harvey in goal for the FA Cup final against Arsenal, and he went on to record 447 appearances for Leeds.

One man who became famous for getting Gary Sprake out of quite a number of embarrassing scrapes was full-back Paul Reaney. The number of times that Reaney cleared the ball off the line behind Sprake has been lost in the mists of time, but it was considerable. Reaney was born in Fulham in 1944 but considers himself very much a Yorkshireman, and the fact that he was only two weeks old when he moved to Leeds makes that quite acceptable. Playing a pivotal role in the defence, Reaney racked up no fewer than 558 appearances for Leeds United, and it is nothing short of a scandalous that he received only 3 caps for England. Paul Reaney was probably the only defender in the league who consistently got the better of George Best, and in countless interviews Best always cited Reaney as the most difficult opponent he ever played against.

Just across to Reaney's left was another local lad. Terry Cooper occupied the left-back position under Don Revie after coming to the club as a left-winger. Revie converted Cooper into one of the best left-backs this country has ever seen. His winger's instinct was evident in his play, as he would regularly overlap down the wing, and it was his solitary goal that brought Leeds their first-ever major trophy with a 1–0 win over Arsenal in the 1968 League Cup final at Wembley. Famously, Cooper has told how he dreamed of scoring that winner for several nights leading up to the final.

Back in the late 1920s and early '30s, Leeds United had a formidable half-back line in Edwards-Hart-Copping. Willis Edwards played 444 times for Leeds and won 16 caps for England. Centre-half Ernie Hart appeared in the heart of the defence 472 times and received 8 caps for England. 'Iron Man' Wilf Copping completed the trio and he cut an awesome figure. Known for not shaving before a game, Copping was famous for his hard but always fair tackles. He played 183 times for Leeds and 20 times for England. Revie also knew the importance of a good half-back line. Jack Charlton had made his Leeds debut at centre-half in 1953 against Doncaster Rovers. In the early '60s, as the football world looked on, Revie's playing squad was coming together, and Charlton would become an integral part of it.

However, it wasn't all plain sailing with Big Jack. By his own admission, he was an 'awkward bastard'. He wouldn't conform and thought he was too good to be at Elland Road. In fact, his attitude was so rebellious that one Leeds fan actually telephoned Don Revie and told him that if he didn't drop Jackie Charlton, 'I'll shoot you'! Thankfully for everyone concerned, Jack knuckled under and became one of the world's greatest centre-halfs, winning Footballer of the Year in 1967.

Charlton was a one-club man. Towards the end of his playing career, he was approached by Hull City to become their manager. He declined, saying that it was a little early for him to move into managership. 'Besides,' he told them, 'Don Revie still believes I can play top-class football for some years, and he's the man whose judgement I accept in everything associated with football.'

Alongside Jack Charlton in defence was 'Iron Man' Norman Hunter. Many nicknames have been attached to Hunter down the years – 'Tarz' and 'Bites Yer Legs' spring to mind – but they don't portray the real Norman Hunter. Spotted by the ever reliable scouting staff of Leeds United when he was just 15 and playing for his school team, Hunter would go on to be a prize asset in Revie's up-and-coming team and to grace the best football grounds worldwide in the white shirts of Leeds United and England.

As a player with Leeds, Revie had played alongside a youngster called Billy Bremner. The Scot had signed for Leeds despite approaches from Chelsea and Arsenal, who were both in the First Division. Bremner would later say that it was the honesty and frankness of chairman Harry Reynolds that impressed him and, although Leeds United were unheard of by many in England, let alone Scotland, he made his debut for Leeds at Chelsea in 1960. Bremner, though, was homesick in a big way. Revie could see this and took Bremner under his wing. When Bremner did decide to go home to Scotland, it was Revie, as manager, who drove up to Billy's family home in Stirling and persuaded him to return to Elland Road.

Revie soon moved Bremner to right-half. He possessed a high degree of skill and tenacity alongside tremendous goal-scoring ability, netting the winning goal in three FA Cup semi-finals. Bremner, whom the *Sunday Times* once described as 'ten stone of barbed wire', was voted Footballer of the Year in 1970. He was capped 54 times for Scotland and on 9 December 2006 was voted Leeds United's greatest-ever player on what would have been his 64th birthday. Bremner forged a midfield link with Johnny Giles that is still talked about today and is classed as one of the most feared ever in football. It was almost telepathic.

Another Scot was brought in by Revie. Bobby Collins was supposedly nearing the end of his career at Everton when Revie offered the Merseyside club £25,000 for him. Collins was 31 and only 5 ft 4in. tall, but he made a big impact at Leeds. The move angered many Everton fans and at the time Revie described Collins as 'probably our best-ever buy'. Bobby Collins won Footballer of the Year in 1965.

In 1963, after a 1–0 win over Rotherham United, Ronald Crowther wrote in the *Daily Express*, 'Two pint-sized Scots, Bobby Collins and Billy Bremner, pointed the way to victory in this rousing derby match. Twenty-year-old Bremner starred in the Leeds problem spot of right-half, and looks set to stay there.'

Also in 1963, Revie noticed that a player called Johnny Giles was unhappy over at Old Trafford. The Leeds manager added Giles to his squad, and the headline in the following day's *Daily Express* proclaimed, 'Revie Gets His Man'. On the same page, a smaller article was headlined 'Bremner Still Wants a Move'. Thankfully for everyone connected with Leeds United, Revie managed to keep Bremner at the club. Revie paid only £33,000 for Giles (beating a bid from Blackburn Rovers), £20,000 less than the biggest fee Leeds had ever paid, when they brought John Charles back from Italy.

After signing Giles, who was 22, Revie said, 'We're aiming high and we want to build a good pool of top-class players, who can not only take us into the First Division, but win honours for us once we get there.' Leeds chairman Harry Reynolds added, 'I hope this supplies ample proof of our intentions. The board will back Revie all the way in his efforts to build a side that can take us to the top.' Giles himself commented, 'I have no regrets about leaving Old Trafford after seven years. I'm young enough to look forward to the future with Leeds. I'm not looking back at the past.'

Giles's skill was mesmerising, and he could literally land the ball on a sixpence from the opposite side of the field. Known as the midfield general or the schemer, he was also the team's penalty-taker. I remember vividly one occasion when I saw Giles demonstrate his amazing ball skills. It was a few years ago at a banquet at Elland Road in tribute to the FA Cup-winning team of 1972. During the event, a penalty competition was taking place. A small six-a-side goal had been placed onstage, and members of the audience were invited to go in goal and face the United players taking penalties at them. The ball was nothing more than a light, orange plastic thing, which had a mind of its own when kicked. Jack Charlton, dressed in a pink fairy's dress, had taken three penalties, all of which went off in all directions except into the goal. Then Johnny Giles stepped up to take his three. Dressed in full lounge suit and shiny shoes, he placed the plastic ball down in front of him and looked up at the bulk of the man who occupied the goal, leaving little more than a foot of space at either side of him. Then everyone in the room gasped in amazement as Giles dispatched his first penalty coolly into the bottom right-hand corner of the net, then put his second into the opposite corner before slotting home the third in the right-hand corner.

Revie had signed another youngster earlier that season. Leeds had been tracking a young lad from Dundee for some considerable time. Fifteen-year-old Peter Lorimer – 'Hotshot', as he became known – was playing for Stobswell School, for whom he scored 176 goals in a single season. He was wanted by almost every club in Britain. Revie was tipped off that Manchester United were all set to sign him, so he and Maurice Lindley travelled by car through the night up to Scotland. At 2 a.m., Revie knocked up the whole house and convinced Lorimer's parents and Peter himself that Leeds were going places and that they were the club for him. When representatives from Old Trafford turned up at the Lorimer household at 8 a.m., Revie had been gone three hours and, more importantly, Lorimer was a Leeds player.

Revie had to spend money on Leeds' development and in 1967 he paid Sheffield United £100,000 for their talented centre-forward Mick Jones – Leeds' record signing at the time. Jones was an incredibly brave and strong forward; indeed, he was widely recognised as the best centre-forward in the First Division. The following season, Revie broke the UK transfer-market record when he paid £165,000 to Leicester City for their young striker Allan Clarke. Another fearsome partnership was set up in the Leeds team, and Jones's unselfish, tireless work enabled his strike partner Clarke to net 151 goals in 361 appearances for Leeds.

Over on the left wing was another young Scot found on the radar of the Leeds United scouting system. Eddie Gray had been spotted by John Barr, who specialised in finding Scottish talent. He made his Leeds debut at the age of 17 against Sheffield Wednesday at Elland Road – and scored. Gray was an absolute wizard with the ball and possessed amazing skill. One of the most memorable goals ever scored by a Leeds player was the spectacular one by Eddie Gray against Burnley in 1970. Although Gray was dogged by serious injuries throughout his illustrious career, he was, in my opinion, a far more skilful player than the aforementioned George Best, and in later years he was a phenomenal football coach.

Revie had an extraordinary eye for detail. He watched his Leeds United juniors play against the Leeds City Boys Under-18s and noticed a youngster by the name of Paul Madeley, who played for local team Farsley Celtic. After the match, Revie was knocking on Madeley's door offering him a trial at Leeds United. Madeley famously went on to play in every position except goalkeeper in more than 700 games for Leeds. He even played in nine different positions in one season. Revie called him his 'Rolls-Royce' because of his effortless, flawless displays, week in, week out.

Like all Revie's youngsters, Madeley could have walked into any other side in Europe, if not the world. During the early '60s, Leeds players such as Mick Bates, Rod Belfitt, Terry Hibbitt, Rod Johnson, Nigel Davey and later Terry Yorath all attracted interest from other First Division clubs, but all chose to stay at Leeds, despite being only what could be termed 'squad players' there. Revie told *Goal* football magazine in 1970:

> One of my most difficult jobs is keeping these players at Leeds when they know they could get first-team football elsewhere. I make sure I give them a good basic wage and good bonuses, so that in earnings they aren't that far behind those actually in the first team. I also have to let them know how important they are to the side and that without them we wouldn't be winning anything.

It has to be added that, unquestionably, above all, Revie's players chose to remain at Leeds because of the family spirit created by the manager. As soon as a youngster was accepted into the 'family', there were certain rules. In *The Leeds United Book of Football*, Maurice Lindley wrote:

> It's a hard apprenticeship. The hours at the ground are long, and the jobs the lads have to do can be tedious. For while they're learning to play football, they're also cleaning the boots of the established players. There's no room for a lad to get big-headed, but all the time the accent is on building character.

These days, when a new player comes to a big club, he's pampered and put in a hotel until his eight-bedroom house with six bathrooms and worth about £170 million is built. In the '60s, youngsters at Leeds were provided with lodgings, usually in a large terraced house close to Elland Road, and always with a hand-picked landlady. Lindley continued:

> The Leeds 'landladies' are vetted closely, and United lay down keen terms under which the youngsters are to be brought up as part of the family ... It's not so much a case of going into digs, in fact, as going to a home from home. At 15, as an apprentice professional, a lad draws about £7 a week. Not a fortune. At 17, in the last year of his apprenticeship, his pay has risen to £9 in the close season, £10 in the playing season. Once he's turned full-time professional he can earn as much as his talent demands. Leeds always look at other aspects apart from the footballing side. Apprentice footballers are taught the value of money. Each professional has a bank book, but Leeds United keep it for him, and from his weekly pay they deduct a sum which they put into a bank account. If they need to draw out extra cash, they have to have a good reason. The apprentice professional eats well. His food is closely supervised to ensure that he gets a varied and balanced diet. There are regular medical checks by the club doctor, Ian Adams, to make sure each individual is making satisfactory progress physically.

It may seem to the outsider as though the young players were being groomed as some kind of foot soldiers, and this may be true to an extent. Don Revie would not allow any of his players to have shoulder-length hair or indeed a moustache. There was a lot of ribbing from opposing teams, especially Chelsea. The King's Road was at the height of fashion and most of the London team's players took to the field looking more like film stars than footballers, practically tripping over their flowing locks and large moustaches. By contrast, Revie once gave Terry Cooper a major dressing-down because he had grown sideburns. But the important thing to remember is that Don Revie cared about his players. He cared deeply. He gave every one of his players a massage every Thursday.

The young players even received a sex talk – not the 'birds and the bees', but to make them aware of the temptations surrounding the 'glamour footballer'. Les Cocker was the man responsible for keeping the lads on the straight and narrow. He made sure every lad knew the pitfalls that lay in wait for him as he embarked on a career as a professional footballer, with all that that entailed. From the very start, the youngsters were taught to beware the temptation of 'loose living' as the management called it. The club's padre, the Reverend John Jackson, travelled from York every week to Leeds to give the lads guidance. A former headmaster by the name of Jeffrey Sanders was always on hand to advise the youngsters about courses available to them, to ensure that they had something to fall back on once their playing days were over. A keen eye was kept on all the youngsters' leisure pursuits, to make sure they didn't go off the rails, and commerce and trade classes were made available to every one of them.

Basically, Leeds United did everything in their power to ensure that every boy who arrived at Elland Road was treated as one of the sons of a large family. Even when a youngster failed to make it as a senior professional, the club would often receive glowing praise from they boy's parents. Maurice Lindley wrote:

> It's always hard to tell a youngster that we don't think he's going
> to make the grade. But the blow is often softened for us by the
> letter from his parents. The parents express their thanks to the
> club for the way we have looked after the youngster during his
> apprenticeship at Leeds. This encourages us to go on looking

after the lads, being ever careful about their welfare for when they do depart. They make the name of Leeds United known around the country, as a club which really cares about everyone in the family.

The 'family' was destined to become one of the most famous in Europe over the next decade. As Revie meticulously built a side with the promising youngsters he had collected from all corners of Great Britain, a ten-match unbeaten run at the end of the 1963–64 season saw Leeds storm the Second Division championship and return to the First Division after an absence of four years.

The name of Leeds United had up until then been a joke. Throughout the country, they were ridiculed, and even in their home city people were turning from football to rugby league. When Revie arrived, gates had been dwindling and the club's overdraft was just growing bigger. Relegation from the Second Division had looked imminent at one stage and the future at Elland Road seemed very grave indeed. The players had lost motivation, and team spirit was so low that every player wanted to leave the club. Billy Bremner, in *The Leeds United Book of Football*, wrote:

> The situation was depressing. No one cared and the players couldn't be bothered to train any more. They were so sick of losing that I'm sure they would have left the club at the drop of a hat. The word 'win' was never mentioned, in fact the whole conversation in the dressing-room concerned how many goals we would be defeated by in our next game. All our confidence had gone ... the stuffing had been knocked out of us. I was so desperate for a move that I was fully prepared to pay my own fare back to Scotland. That was how low things had become.

This was the state of affairs when Revie was appointed player-manager in 1961. But Revie was always determined as a player and wasn't about to give up as a manager. Leeds were already in debt, but he insisted on the very best. He ordered new equipment, new playing gear, and demanded that everything about the club was first class – first-class travel to away games, first-class accommodation and food.

In 1970's *Leeds United Book of Football No.2,*Don Revie wrote:

The first thing I told our players was that our club strip would be changed to all white – like Real Madrid's. And I told them that if they looked like Real Madrid in dress, then they must play like them. I wasn't going to be satisfied until we had reached that target. Players who didn't like it were told that Leeds United had nothing to offer them. Either they thought and acted like me or they left.

It was my belief that Leeds could become great and I wanted to instil the right attitude into everyone connected with the club. A successful club must think big, act in a big way, and I hoped by adopting this kind of approach off the park that the players would respond to it during matches. When I look back, I must admit that I thought we had no chance whatsoever of making it. But how can you tell a side to reach for the sky and then admit to them afterwards that you didn't believe in your own words? I was determined we could try. We had to.

In 1963, I was in my second year at Kippax Infants' School. I can clearly recollect running down Well Lane from school and through the ginnel at the bottom to my house on The Drive clutching a brand-new scrapbook, which I had been showing my classmates. Every Saturday, I'd get the *Green Post*, the sister sports paper to the *Yorkshire Evening Post*, which printed the results of all the games from that afternoon less than an hour after the final whistle. I'd cut out the match report and glue it into my scrapbook. I didn't know it at the time, but I was recording a monumental season in the history of Leeds United Football Club.

16. Don Revie: Part 3

The Glory Years

When Leeds stormed out of the Second Division on 25 April 1964 after beating Charlton Athletic at The Valley 2–0, no one could have foreseen the impact that this 'new' club from West Yorkshire would have on English football.

In their very first season back in the top flight, 1964–65, Leeds United came agonisingly close to winning the league and cup double, losing out on the championship only on goal average and being beaten by Liverpool 2–1 in the FA Cup final at Wembley in extra time. Leeds United had made their mark and people began to take notice. In the next two seasons, the team once again came close to honours but finished second in the league in 1965–66 and fourth the following season. Then, in 1968, United finally hit the jackpot, winning their first-ever major trophy, with a second one thrown in for good measure.

On 2 March 1968, Leeds met Arsenal in the League Cup final at Wembley, and although it wasn't a spectacular game, Terry Cooper's 25-yard drive was enough to separate the teams and give Leeds United their first taste of silverware. They followed that up with the Inter-Cities Fairs Cup, achieving a 1–0 aggregate win over the crack Hungarian outfit Ferencváros to become the first British winners of the competition.

The very next season saw Don Revie realise his ambition when Leeds United were crowned league champions in 1969 with a record 67 points, having been defeated only twice all season. Four months later, they added the Charity Shield to their haul, with a 2–1 victory over Manchester City. Leeds were pitched against Arsenal at Wembley once again in 1972 for the prestigious FA Cup centenary final. In

1974, United added a second league championship to their already impressive tally. Don Revie had finally received the much deserved rewards for his determined effort in guiding Leeds United to the top.

Someone who got to know the Leeds manager as well as if not better than most during this period was the team bus driver. Jim Lister, now 74, has been a loyal fan of Leeds United since 1948. He describes his role as team bus driver as 'the best job in the world'. Jim was a coach driver for Wallace Arnold back in 1966, taking tourists to the seaside and on other excursions. His traffic manager at the time was a man called John Fisher, also a keen Leeds fan and season-ticket holder at Elland Road.

John had heard that Leeds United's team bus driver had got married and emigrated to South Africa. The club had tried a couple of replacement drivers but hadn't quite found the right man. John asked Jim if he would like to have a go at driving the Leeds team. It would involve staying with the team at the Craiglands Hotel, in Ilkley, the evening before every home game. 'Would I mind?' Jim said to me when we chatted about his time with Leeds. 'I was in heaven.' Jim was very nervous when he picked the team up at Elland Road for the first time on a Friday tea-time. 'As far as I can recall, the only thing Don Revie said to me was "hello".'

'When we arrived at Craiglands,' says Jim, 'Don met me at reception. He asked me to put my gear away and join him for dinner. When I got there, he asked me to sit with him and Les Cocker. We were at the top table and the players were seated on a long table in front. I can't remember what was said during dinner because I was on cloud nine! After dinner, we went to a private lounge especially for the use of the team. They played bingo and carpet bowls to help them relax. Don always played bingo. At half-past nine the team would go to their rooms to watch TV.

'After that weekend, I thought, although it had been a fabulous experience, it was just a one-off. To my disbelief, I was asked to drive to the away game the following week. The week after, it was back to Craiglands. During dinner that evening, as I was sitting between Don Revie and Les Cocker, Don turned to me and said, "Jim, I would like you to be our regular team driver." I almost collapsed; I couldn't believe this was happening! He also asked me to call him "Boss". He told me

I would be part of the family and was just as important as anyone else associated with the club. He also said that I was driving a "lot of money" around on a coach and that he really trusted me to get them safely from A to B. He made me feel so important that I must mention an incident that occurred a little later.

'We were playing Liverpool and, as always, stayed at the Adelphi. I put the coach away, put my luggage in the room and joined the team for dinner. I always sat, at the Boss's insistence, between him and Les Cocker. During the meal, the Boss asked me if I would be watching the golf later on TV. I asked him where I could watch it. He asked if I had a TV in my room and I replied that I hadn't. He got very annoyed and asked a waiter to bring the hotel manager over. The Boss said that when the hotel had been booked it had been stipulated that every room was to have a TV. The manager agreed, although he said he didn't think it applied to the coach driver. The Boss told him that I wasn't just a coach driver and was every bit as important as the rest of the team. He also said that if there wasn't a TV in my room by the end of dinner Leeds United would never book the Adelphi again. Sure enough, when I got back to my room, there was a TV!

'Another time, when Leeds were at Wolves, during the after-match reception at the hotel the great Wolves legend Billy Wright was present. He sat down at the table next to Don Revie. Don said, "Excuse me, Billy, that's Jim's seat."'

I asked Jim if he was the driver for the FA Cup semi-final against Chelsea at Villa Park in 1967. 'Yes, I drove the coach that day. I'll never forget the disallowed goal. Johnny Giles took a free kick quickly, passing it to Peter Lorimer, who scored a cracking goal. Unfortunately, the referee, Ken Burns, disallowed it because Johnny Giles had taken the free kick before he was ready. After the game, the team was heartbroken. After boarding the coach, they had a moan, played cards and had a drink on the way home. But, like the true professionals that they were, they put the game behind them and started planning the next one.

'On the evening before every match, home or away, the team always stayed in a hotel. I would collect the team from Elland Road and they were always on time. During the drive, the team was always upbeat and in good spirits. Some of them played cards, especially Big Jack and Billy. The coach was "luxury", complete with four tables in the middle and a tea and coffee machine at the rear – nothing like the coaches of today, but for back then it was excellent.

'On the day of the game, while travelling to the ground, the team was usually very quiet. Billy Bremner always seemed to be first on the coach. Before we left the hotel, the Boss would have a team talk, so the players could reflect on it while travelling.

'As I mentioned, a separate lounge was always provided in the hotel so they could relax. At bingo, Norman Hunter was always first caller, and I usually called the rest of the games. These normally lasted about an hour. The first game I ever called was at the Adelphi. The players used to make up the kitty for the prize money and everyone, including the Boss and Les, played.

'The other favourite game, of course, was carpet bowls. The best and keenest player was Johnny Giles, who was brilliant. I actually partnered him a couple of times. He taught me how to play. A few years ago, I was on holiday at Barmston Beach in Yorkshire with my family. I won a carpet bowls tournament and received a trophy. As I was being presented with it, I remember thinking, "Thank you, Johnny Giles." Dare I say that Big Jack wasn't much good at carpet bowls? Neither was Terry Hibbitt, bless him. But everyone enjoyed themselves and I can honestly say that during all my time with the team, I never saw any of them touch a drink on the evening before a match.'

During the writing of this book, I took Jim back to the Craiglands Hotel in Ilkley, about 15 miles out of Leeds, for a look around. Nestled high above the town, the Craiglands is surrounded by its own luxurious gardens. As we drove into the car park, the memories from more than 30 years ago came flooding back to Jim. We walked towards the towering frontage, decked in creeping ivy, and as we arrived at the dark-green canopy that stretched over the outside steps leading to the reception, Jim was quiet for a while before saying, 'That bit over there is new, but I remember this.' And we looked up for a few moments at this monumental part of Leeds United's history.

We walked into the reception, which was to our right as we entered the building. Jim pointed straight ahead. 'That's where the reception used to be,' he said. 'It hasn't half changed.' We walked around inside and found the room where the famous carpet bowls games were played. 'I would sit over there in that corner with Les Cocker,' said Jim. 'We would call the bingo from there.'

Later, as we sat downstairs, he reminisced about the many times he had brought United here. 'Don liked the players to be in bed fairly early,' he said. 'They would have room service and watch TV, and the next morning they wouldn't rise until around nine-thirty to ten. By then, I'd have been sat chatting with the Boss in the reception and then have ordered his coffee while he did his customary walk around the grounds alone. He would return and by the time he'd drunk his coffee, the players and us would go into the dining room for a light breakfast.'

As we left, walking under the green canopy, Jim stopped. I turned and looked at him but he said nothing for a few seconds. 'This is where Billy (Bremner) would stand for a while,' he said. 'He would be drip white the morning before a match. That's where his nickname, 'Chalky', came from. He would board the coach and be almost silent for the journey to Elland Road.'

Then Jim pointed back to the 'new bit' and revealed a secret he had always kept from the Boss. 'That building wasn't there then, that was where I used to park the coach,' he said. 'I would bring it around to the front from there and load all the kit on before the players came out. But when the coach was parked there the night before, Gary Sprake would come to me in the hotel and quietly slip me a fiver for the keys, and he would entertain his latest "lady guest" on the back seat. I was in a real dilemma. If the Boss had ever found out, I'm sure he would have sacked me. But Sprakey had a real smooth tongue, and the Boss himself had got Sprake out of a few scrapes, especially one particular incident where he "had a word" with the local police when Sprake's sports car was involved in a crash and a girl was seriously injured.'

Despite 'smoothing things over' with the police, the Boss wasn't prepared to let his goalkeeper off the hook altogether, says Jim. 'After the players had boarded the coach for the very next game, the Boss said to me, "Close the door, Jim." He then really laid into Sprake in front of all the other players, who, of course, remained silent throughout Sprake's dressing-down. It was a demonstration that he would always remain loyal to his players, but he would also demand the same back from them. I started the coach and drove off. The Sprake incident was never mentioned again.'

Later, I asked Jim for more of his memories about his trips with

163

United. 'On away games, our hotel was always asked to have food prepared for us to take on the coach for the return journey. This would be the same menu practically every time: lamb cutlets, cheese and biscuits, chicken sandwiches and bottles of beer and lager. There was always a lot of food left and, after dropping the team off at Elland Road, I would take the coach back to the depot on Gelderd Road, where the night staff would have a party.

'The joker on the coach was always Big Jack. He and Billy would enjoy a cigarette now and again. As I was driving, when Billy wanted a smoke, he would reach into my jacket pocket and take one cigarette from the packet. Jack would take the whole packet.

'After Leeds won the championship at Anfield in 1969, I was driving towards the motorway when a hand came in front of my eyes for a few seconds. It was Big Jack standing next to me with the biggest cigar in his mouth that I have ever seen. He was absolutely ecstatic.

'With Jack and Billy, you got what you saw. I would often meet them at the Woodman pub for a few pints and a game of dominoes with the locals.

'That game at Anfield was probably my best game with the team. Everything about that day was brilliant – excellent football and wonderful camaraderie. Before setting off on the Friday, the Boss had asked me to load crates of champagne into the boot of the coach. He said if we won or drew I was to take the champagne into the dressing-room for the end of the match. I left my seat five minutes before the end of the game with the score at 0–0. As I was in the dressing-room, I heard an almighty roar. I felt physically sick because I thought Liverpool had scored. As it turned out, it was the end of the game and the Liverpool supporters were applauding Leeds United. You can imagine the atmosphere in the dressing-room. It was one occasion when I wished I wasn't driving so I could have joined the team in a glass or two of champagne.

'Afterwards, Bill Shankly came into the Leeds dressing-room with more bottles of champagne and shook hands with every one of our players, calling them "true champions"!

'Whenever we played at Liverpool, Don liked to arrive early to have a chat with Shankly, and I would be with him. Every time, he would greet me with a handshake and say, "Hiya, Jim, cup of tea?" Don and Bill really were two of a kind.

'That evening, a banquet was being held in the team's honour at the Queens Hotel. As we were coming into Leeds, the Boss told me that a few of the lads wanted to visit a nightclub called Intime to celebrate before going to the banquet. I dropped them off and made my way to the Queens. As we made our way to City Square, there were thousands of fans lining the route. On the steps of the hotel stood Alderman Rafferty, the Lord Mayor and various other dignitaries. I don't know what they thought when the Boss, Les Cocker and me were the only people who got off the coach.

'The banquet started and the Boss asked me to go to the nightclub and collect the team. I parked opposite the club and I had to tell them that, although they were enjoying themselves, they had to go to the banquet. One or two of them took some persuading, but they all eventually piled out of the club. By the time I got outside, my coach was missing! After a few minutes, it came down the road being driven by Mick Jones, who had fancied going for a spin!

'When we got back to the Queens, the Boss asked me to get another driver to pick up the coach. He then booked me into a room with one of his best friends, Herbert Warner, and we had a good few drinks. Needless to say, we got up very late the following morning. What a night!

'For the 1970 FA Cup final against Chelsea, we booked into the Hendon Hall Hotel. This was a favourite spot for the England squad. The team trained at pitches just off the A1 and the Boss even asked me to referee some of the five-a-side games. On the day of the game at Wembley the BBC filmed the whole of the journey to the stadium from inside the coach. I'd love to see a video of that.

'The game itself was brilliant and in my opinion we played Chelsea off the park. Eddie Gray was the man of the match that day. Gary Sprake was to blame for their first equaliser, as he let a harmless-looking shot from Peter Houseman go under his body and into the net. In the dressing-room after the game, Gary sat staring into space. He was so despondent that the boss asked me to help get his shinpads and boots off and get him in the bath.

'After the match, we were booked into the Royal Lancaster Hotel. As we were making our way there, I overtook the Chelsea team coach. As we were passing, Big Jack and a few of the other lads stood up, pointing their fingers at the Chelsea team. They shouted, "We've even got a better driver than you!" That evening, there was a banquet at the Café Royal. It was a bit muted because of the score, a 2–2 draw, but it was enjoyable nonetheless.

'The replay at Old Trafford was bad. The Boss asked me to sit in the dugout. Eddie Gray got kicked off the park that night. The opposing players did their best to shackle him. After losing the game, we made our way back over the Pennines and the atmosphere was very tense. Everyone, including me, was gutted. To try and cheer the Boss up one or two of the lads started a sing-song. When we got back to Elland Road, a few of the lads asked me if I could get them in for a drink somewhere. I telephoned a friend of mine who was the landlord of the Bridgefield pub in the East End Park district of Leeds. He welcomed us with open arms, as he was a big Leeds fan, and there the players drowned their sorrows for a few hours.

'The Boss very seldom drank himself, apart from the odd bottle of Carlsberg accompanied by a Hamlet cigar. One of his many superstitions was to always send me for a packet of Hamlet cigars before every away game, even if he already had some in his pocket.

'As I say, we always stayed in hotels before every match. The Boss had a set routine. As with the Craiglands for home games, when we were away I had to be in reception at around ten. On one occasion when we were playing Manchester United in the second replay semi-final of the FA Cup at Bolton, the Boss said to me on the morning, "Jim, the last two games I had Paul Reaney on George Best, but tonight I'm going to let Paul play his natural game and let whichever player is nearest to Best pick him up." We won the game that night and got through to Wembley.

'The Boss and Les Cocker were absolute salt-of-the-earth men, in my eyes. Don was a very compassionate man and made everyone feel important. But, as I said, he was very superstitious. I'd like to think that a lot of his compassion rubbed off on me. Many years later, after I left Leeds United, I started community groups to help people who were less fortunate than myself.

'The Boss became good friends with the late singer Ronnie Hilton, who, of course, recorded many Leeds United songs, as well as often training with the team. The Boss liked easy-listening music. He was very keen on golf and his favourite food was definitely potted shrimps or ravioli for starters, followed by fillet steak. He would always insist on a four-minute boiled egg. He knew if it wasn't four minutes and he would send it back.

'We would regularly have the top 1970s act the Grumbleweeds, all Leeds fans, travelling with us on the coach, and the actor Colin Welland, also a big Leeds fan, would often come along. When I married Christine in 1976, Ronnie Hilton sang at our reception at the Parnaby Tavern in Hunslet, Leeds.'

Jim Lister is a fascinating man with some great memories of the 'best job in the world'. I asked him about something Dave Cocker had mentioned about Don's 'stormy' relationship with the former Leeds director Bob 'Pearhead' Roberts. 'It wasn't just Roberts that the Boss had problems with,' said Jim. 'There was also Percy Woodward. We were playing an evening game in Burnley and we had left Elland Road at lunchtime. The Boss had booked the team into a hotel for the afternoon. I was having a cup of tea around four o'clock when Percy came into reception. When he found out that the players had rooms just for the afternoon, he became very angry. He told me that although the club didn't mind spending some money, he'd "be buggered if we were going to be so extravagant". This was said in earshot of the Boss and others, and the Boss in turn became very angry, and he and Woodward had words. I have often wondered if this persuaded the Boss it was time to move on.

'I used to enjoy the times when the Boss would take the team away to Scarborough and we would stay at the Grand Hotel for a few days. There was only very light training done, usually on the beach, and then it would be off to the Ganton Golf Club.

'I never took the coach abroad, but I would travel with them. I always drove the coach to the airport and another driver would take the coach back. When the team were on the coach, the Boss would always insist on me driving.

'In 1971, we went to Juventus for the final of the Fairs Cup. We travelled on the Monday and the game was on the Wednesday evening. On this occasion, two hotels were booked, one in the country for the players and another for the wives, girlfriends and the press. Don did everything to look after the wives of the players – birthday cards, get-well cards and flowers would be sent by his secretary, Jean Reid – but he wouldn't let them near the players before a game. After a game, though, was fine and the social gatherings after games were great.

Normally, I would have stayed with the players at their hotel, but the Boss asked me to act as chaperone and stay with the ladies. The following day, the ladies had arranged to go shopping in Turin and I was asked to escort them. In 1971, the latest fashion was hotpants and some of the girls were wearing them, so you can imagine the wolf whistles from the Italian men. I couldn't get back to the hotel quick enough!

'Heavy rain followed, however, and the game on Wednesday night was abandoned due to a water-logged pitch with the score standing at 1–1. The game was rescheduled for the Friday, which caused another problem. The Boss had arranged for the girls to move into the players' hotel for the Wednesday night before all departing for England the following day. But because of the game being called off, the Boss now wanted the wives to go home to allow the team to concentrate on the rearranged final two nights later. The wives, understandably, wanted to stay, but the Boss hated distractions before a game, and games didn't come any bigger than this one.

'During the after-match banquet at the players' hotel on the Wednesday night, some of the players, no doubt urged on by some of the wives, tried to persuade the Boss to let the girls stay on. The Boss very rarely showed anger, but he was livid and stormed out of the banquet. What is not widely known is that the Boss actually resigned as Leeds manager that night. In the reception, I heard him say, "After all I've done for you!" He then left the hotel and booked himself into another one alone.

'The players were visibly stunned and Jack Charlton, Billy Bremner and Les Cocker spent two hours trying to locate the Boss's hotel. Once they did, thankfully, they managed to persuade him to return to the hotel. The wives returned home the following day.

'On the same day, the Boss arranged for me to have dinner with the press at their hotel, the same one where the wives had stayed. Well-known journalists such as Alan Thompson of the *Daily Express* were there, so too was Frank McGhee from the *Daily Mirror*. I took a look at the prices – God, it was expensive! The Boss had said I wouldn't have to pay, as it was on the press expenses, but after the meal and a couple of drinks, one of the press – I wasn't sure who he was – came round with a kitty, which I felt obliged to put into. When the Boss found out that I'd paid out of my own pocket, he went mad. He went to the hotel and gave certain members of the press a right earful. It turned out that none of them had paid out of their own pocket, and my money was refunded.

'I remember vividly the day that I found out that the Boss was leaving the club. He asked me to go and have a coffee with him at Sheila's Café opposite the ground. It was there that he told me he'd taken the England job and was taking Les Cocker with him. This was before he'd told the press. I felt very upset, because these were the two men in my life who I had the greatest admiration and respect for.'

Jim had clearly been saddened by Don's departure. I bit the bullet and asked him how he got on with Revie's replacement, the infamous Brian Clough. His reply was quite surprising. 'In my opinion, despite their obvious differences, they were also alike in many ways. They treated everyone equal, including me. Cloughie certainly befriended me in the short period of time he was at the club.

'John Redmond and Eric Carlile from the Leeds United Supporters Club called me one evening and asked me if I could get Brian Clough to visit the Supporters Club at one of their meetings. Apparently, they were having trouble getting hold of him. Brian said he would only go because I had asked him. In fact, his words to the supporters were, "I'm only here with you bloody lot because Jim asked me."'

Jim also revealed a side of Clough that isn't widely known. 'We were at a hotel in Stoke on the day of a match when two Leeds supporters walked into the hotel. They looked like a couple of drowned rats. They had hitch-hiked from Leeds and had spied the team bus and wanted some autographs. Brian was stood at the bar and bought both the fans a pint. He then told them to go into the dining room, where dinner was on him.'

I asked Jim if he had seen the film *The Damned United*. 'The film got it wrong on a number of occasions. Billy Bremner and Johnny Giles never sat at the front. They always sat at the tables and played cards. The Boss and Les Cocker would always sit behind me.

'When Albert Johanneson played for the club, he always sat opposite me with the curtain pulled around him because he was embarrassed by his colour. It didn't bother anyone else at the club, but he was very upset about it.'

I asked Jim if he could remember any incidents with away fans and the team bus. 'Lots of fans didn't like us,' said Jim. 'QPR springs to mind. And after our title win at Anfield in 1969 we were passing Goodison Park and the Everton supporters threw bricks at the coach. A small window was shattered and Paul Madeley ended up with a slight cut to the side of his neck. This was despite the team receiving that wonderful ovation from the Liverpool fans after the game less than an hour earlier.

'After that incident, at every away game the Boss arranged for a police escort from the ground to the motorway. It was an experience to go the wrong way down a dual carriageway or round a roundabout following a police motorcycle with flashing lights. I can still hear the players shouting, "Go on, Jim!" As we approached the sliproad to the motorway, the police would pull away. The Boss would ask me to stop and he would get off the coach and personally thank them, putting a small gratuity into their hands. This was the generous nature of the man.'

On one of Jim's last trips with the club he saw the ugly side of a few of our own supporters. 'It was the European Cup final in Paris,' Jim remembered. 'Wallace Arnold had been asked to provide 20 or 30 coaches for the game. I was asked to take the team coach with members of staff, spare drivers and mechanics on board. The team had travelled in advance. After that game, although United were on the wrong side of some awful refereeing, I was heartbroken by the loutish behaviour of some of our fans. In my opinion, Leeds United supporters are fantastic and simply the best, but on that occasion, 36 years ago, a minority behaved appallingly.'

Finally, he recalled, 'The last time I ever heard from the Boss was in a letter from Dubai in 1979. He had moved there after resigning from the England manager's job. Unbelievably, he had met someone over there who knew me; I had moved house and the Boss didn't have my new address so he had asked him for it. Consequently, I received a lovely letter from the Boss and Les Cocker (who had moved out there with Don), saying how much they loved it out there, with the sunshine, golf and their families. They were in paradise.'

17. Don Revie: Part 4

The Board Game

When Don Revie left Leeds United to take up the England manager's position, the Leeds board of directors took his car from him. This was an absolutely staggering way for the board to behave, considering the huge debt that the club owed Revie for his efforts in turning Leeds from a struggling, foot-of-the-Second-Division side to one of the most feared outfits in Europe. But, given this same board's treatment of Johnny Giles, it was hardly surprising. They famously messed Giles about over the vacant Leeds manager's job. Giles was in line for the post, but the directors, fearing the wrath of captain Billy Bremner, who was also interested in the job, went outside the club and appointed Brian Clough instead, a decision that chairman Manny Cussins later admitted had been 'a disastrous appointment'.

Dave Cocker insists that one of the directors, Bob Roberts, was the reason why Revie decided to leave the club for England. 'I'm convinced to this day that if Bob Roberts had not been at Elland Road at the time, Don Revie would have remained at Leeds for many more years,' says Cocker.

When a young Don Revie trotted out for his England debut in 1954, he could have had no idea that he would one day go on to manage his country, just as he would have no idea when he took charge of his first England game as manager, against Czechoslovakia in 1974, of the turmoil that lay ahead.

Revie, who had not had the best of relationships with the media during his Leeds United days, immediately got the press on his side by issuing his home telephone number to many football journalists. Drinks and sandwiches were laid on whenever there was a press call at England pre-match conferences.

The new manager immediately increased the England players' wages and also ventured into the first-ever sponsorship deal. Many of the England board of directors weren't happy about this new venture with Admiral, but Revie was clearly ahead of his time, both on and off the pitch, and now, of course, every team in the world has sponsorship deals.

Revie also crossed swords once again with Alan Hardaker, when he asked that all Saturday games prior to an international be postponed. It was two years before Revie got his way and the Football League finally agreed to move a Saturday game preceding an important England international forward to the previous midweek. This is now a policy demanded by FIFA.

For his debut as manager, Don Revie introduced a rendition of 'Land of Hope and Glory' to the pre-match build-up and issued the 84,000 expectant fans with song sheets. The patriotic euphoria certainly seemed to work, as England stormed to an impressive 3–0 victory over Czechoslovakia.

Secretly, though, Revie wasn't entirely happy with the players at his disposal, and things started to go downhill fairly rapidly. Revie had amassed a huge squad (81 men were invited to attend his first players' meeting), but there was a lack of natural ability, and some players, such as Emlyn Hughes, Malcolm Macdonald and Alan Hudson, clearly resented the new manager. There was huge pressure from the fans, and indeed from the FA directors.

Revie brought in the carpet bowls and bingo sessions that had been so popular with his Leeds team, but the majority of the players hated these games. He also introduced the famous dossiers, but the England players were found using them as scoresheets for their card games. The squad constantly flouted Revie's strict rules about not going out of the hotel or drinking after 10 p.m.

In Richard Sutcliffe's *Revie: Reverd and Reviled*, sports commentator John Helm says of Revie's reign as national manager:

> Don never had those individual relationships he had at Leeds. Being the England manager was a very different beast and he had to be a lot more political. He wanted to be with his players on the training pitch, but instead he had to attend committee meeting after committee meeting.

Meanwhile, the knives were being drawn in the boardroom, and although FA secretary Ted Croker, an unlikely ally to Revie initially, said afterwards, 'I always thought Don was the right man for the job, but things behind the scenes were becoming impossible for him.' Certain directors were definitely becoming impatient. Revie's biggest enemy within was the new FA chairman, Sir Harold Thompson.

A pompous and domineering man, Thompson made no secret of his dislike of Revie. At dinner one evening, Thompson, then vice chairman, said to his new manager, 'When I get to know you better, Revie, I shall call you Don,' to which Revie replied, 'Well, when I get to know you better, Thompson, I shall call you Sir Harold.' It's certainly true to say that Thompson upset many of the employees at the FA, and he famously used to annoy Sir Alf Ramsey in the same way, calling him by his surname only.

In *Revie: Revered and Reviled*, Lord Harewood, former FA president and president of Leeds United, says of Thompson that he was 'in the very worst sense, a dour man. He did not respect anyone but himself. He was wholly lacking as a chairman of the FA.' He remembered:

> I was in the royal retiring room for one evening game, waiting to go into the royal box, with Thompson and Lady Thompson, and I said to Lady Thompson, 'Let's hope we win,' to which she replied, 'Let's hope we lose so we can get rid of that man [Revie],' to which her husband nodded in agreement.

I asked Duncan Revie if his dad had ever commented on Thompson to him. 'My dad hated everything about Thompson. It appeared that no one in or out of the FA got on with him. He was a horrible man,' said Duncan.

As England's performances remained below par, more pressure was heaped on Revie. He knew that certain people at the FA were plotting to have him removed. Behind his back, the FA even approached another club about their manager replacing Revie. Lord Harewood has substantiated this claim, saying, 'I knew for a fact that they were already negotiating with Bobby Robson to replace Don because the Ipswich Town chairman had told me.'

Revie, however, was one step ahead of the FA, and had negotiated a deal to become manager of the United Arab Emirates national team in Dubai. He then, some say unwisely, gave the story exclusively to journalist Jeff Powell of the *Daily Mail*. The FA found out via a letter of resignation that Revie had posted at their headquarters, closed for the night, before his departure to Dubai and the breaking story on the front page of the *Mail* on 12 July 1977.

Previously, Revie had sought and received assurances from the chairman of the FA international committee, Dick Wragg, that there was no conspiracy to replace him as manager. Wragg had told Revie that there was absolutely no plot – but it is now known that this was not the case.

The FA were seething about Revie's departure and an emergency meeting, chaired by Harold Thompson on 28 July, charged him with bringing the game into disrepute. The case was to be heard on the last day of August and four charges were to be levelled at Revie:

- By breaching his contract, he had set a bad example to all.
- He had acted deceitfully by failing to tell the FA of his dealings in Dubai.
- By his alleged attempt to conceal his visit to Dubai, he had debased his official position in English football.
- By telling the *Daily Mail* before the FA, he had breached his contract.

Revie's solicitors claimed that it was their belief that the FA had no jurisdiction over him and that they would not be attending the hearing. A commission was arranged for 17 September, with Harold Thompson presiding. Thompson had insisted on this, despite protests from Ted Croker that Thompson, as chairman of the FA, would not be considered impartial. The result of the commission was that Revie was suspended from any involvement in English football until he appeared before them in person.

Finally, he agreed to attend on 18 December 1978, a year later, and to answer the charges, with Gilbert Gray QC acting on his behalf. He too criticised the involvement of Harold Thompson, claiming that he was unfit to sit in judgement as there was a real likelihood of his being biased. Gray produced newspaper cuttings that showed Thompson openly attacking Revie and told the hearing that if it had been a court of law, the judge would have been debarred from sitting. Gray also repeated what Revie's solicitors had said: that the FA had no jurisdiction over Revie. Both objections were overruled and the case went ahead, with Harold Thompson giving evidence and asking Revie questions. It was a ludicrous situation.

Throughout the trial, Gray produced evidence of an obstinate board of directors at the FA, showing that Revie had been expected to travel second class, although his contract had arranged for first-class travel. Gray also told of commercial deals being lost because of the board's hesitancy. A more worrying concern for Revie, Gray told the hearing, had been his family. He had taken the Arab Emirates fortune (he received a four-year contract for £340,000) to secure his family's future. None of this had any effect on Thompson, and Revie was banned from involvement in English football for ten years.

Revie's solicitors immediately appealed and the case went to the High Court almost 12 months later. In November 1979, the case resumed with Mr Justice Cantley presiding. Unfortunately for Revie, Cantley turned out to be not a great deal more in his favour than Thompson. He referred to Revie as 'greedy' throughout the whole case; so much for impartiality. The former England manager was grilled, cross-examined and stripped of his dignity for the whole of he 18-day hearing.

Revie was not without support, however; his trusted friend Lord Harewood gave evidence on his behalf, as did Johnny Giles, Jimmy Hill, David Coleman, Jock Stein and Lawrie McMenemy – none of which seemed to impress Justice Cantley.

Nonetheless, it was with cast-iron certainty that Cantley, however reluctantly, found in favour of Revie. He then launched into a venomous, two-hour-long personal attack on Revie, calling him 'lacking in candour, utterly selfish, brooding on imagined wrongs, notorious and prickly'. He said of Thompson that he was satisfied to acquit him of bad faith, and amazingly called him 'an honourable man, who deplores the coarse comments and selfish greed which obtrude in professional football'. They were absolutely unbelievable comments. Cantley then went on to deny Revie any damages and even ordered him to pay two-thirds of his own costs.

Lord Harewood was stunned after the hearing as he told Richard Suttcliffe in *Revie: Revered and Reviled*:

I think it was agony for Don and the elements of character assassination on the part of the defence counsel grilling him were very unattractive. The summing-up by the judge was one of the craziest things I have ever heard. I think the judge was extremely ill-versed in human behaviour . . . he was an ass. If he really thought that Sir Harold Thompson had behaved admirably and Don hadn't, then he is a very, very poor judge of character . . . and of evidence. He plainly disbelieved every word I said but I don't give a bugger what he thought.

Even Ted Croker said that he hadn't liked the way Cantley had handled it: 'I thought his summing-up was very wrong, his assessment of various characters was wrong. He praised Sir Harold Thompson to the hilt as being an honourable man.'

I am in no doubt whatsoever that those 18 days of the trial, and the scathing, totally unwarranted comments made by Justice Cantley, are the underlying factor that has led to the pure, misguided hatred that continues towards Don Revie to this very day in people who will simply not listen to the truth.

Don and his lovely wife, Elsie, enjoyed possibly the best years of their lives in the United Arab Emirates. They played golf together and son Duncan and daughter Kim tell of how happy and contented their parents were in those precious years.

In 1986, the couple moved to Elsie's old stomping ground in Kinross, Scotland. And it was whilst playing golf near there that Don discovered the early signs of what was to become a fatal disease. In 1987, his medical consultants told him that he had motor neuron disease (MND). Back then, it was a relatively unheard of illness; actor David Niven was the only high-profile case of someone who had died of MND, a muscle-wasting disease that so far has no cure.

Despite many trips to specialists in the US, Don's health deteriorated and on 26 May 1989, he passed away.

His funeral took place at Warriston Crematorium in Edinburgh. Many names from the world of football were in attendance, including Kevin Keegan and Lawrie McMenemy. There were no representatives from the FA.

Also paying his respects was the ITV football commentator Brian Moore. In his 1976 *Book of Football*, Moore wrote this glowing tribute to Don Revie as England manager:

> If Don Revie wasn't a very good manager – which he undoubtedly is – he would be one of the most sought after men in the field of public relations. His capacity for getting people on his side and making them feel important is without equal in football.
>
> That may not be saying a lot in a sport where too many clubs and officials still believe that a half-cup of tea and a bun of doubtful origin pass for hospitality.
>
> But Don Revie sets a standard for others to follow. An example of the Revie brand of public relations came a year or so ago when half a dozen press and television reporters went with him to Switzerland to watch a match against Portugal, soon to play England in the European championship.
>
> We stayed in Zurich, though the match was in Berne. Don organised our transport, accepted dinner from us after the game, and made sure that, on our return to Zurich at 2 a.m., the hotel would call each of us at 6.30 a.m. for our early return to London.
>
> For some, that might have been the end of it – but not Mr Revie!
>
> When I staggered down at 6.30 to pay my bill, Don was already there, he had personally called every member of the party and, not content with that, had taxis ticking over outside to take us to the airport.
>
> 'Nothing brilliant about that,' you may say. 'Unique amongst football managers,' I would answer. 'Only getting the media on his side in case there are rainy days ahead,' you may counter. 'Uncharitable as that may be, it shows a man with enormous regard for the smallest detail,' I would reply.
>
> Indeed Don's eye for detail is well known. The protection of his players is equally famous. And his regard for them is warm and generous. For example, he keeps a list of the birthdays of all the England players and takes the trouble to send them all a card. He believes, too, that nothing is too good for his players. That's why an England player has a chauffeur-driven car at his disposal – no matter how far – after a Wembley game.
>
> His passion outside football is golf. He plays to a handicap of

eight and is now quite a catch for the organisers of the big pro-am tournaments, with Jimmy Tarbuck and Bruce Forsyth.

Don is a devoted family man. His son Duncan has a law degree and now works in London, where his sister Kim, 16, is at school. Even so, Don's house in Leeds still has a real family atmosphere about it. His wife Elsie has her mother and two aunts staying there, as well as 88-year-old Uncle Willie!

It's typical of Don to encourage this sort of family togetherness. After all, he had the same sort of thing going on for him at Leeds United. And we all know what a warm and worthwhile relationship that was.

In spring 2010, sculptor Graham Ibbeson, from Barnsley, was approached by Paul Robinson of the *Yorkshire Evening Post* to see whether he would be interested in creating a statue of Don Revie. There is a groundswell of Leeds fans wanting a long-overdue tribute to this legendary manager. A cost of £90,000 was estimated to build a seven-foot bronze statue of Revie, but a lack of investment saw Graham contacting a man in Stourbridge, West Midlands. Jim Cadman has an expert knowledge of marketing and fund-raising and has worked previously with Graham. He came on board with an injection of financial expertise and enthusiasm.

Graham's works to date include statues of Les Dawson, Freddie Trueman, Eric Morecambe, Laurel and Hardy, 'Dickie' Bird, William Webb Ellis and Cary Grant. In 2000, he was also commissioned by Leeds Civic Trust to design and produce a sculpture of 'the person of the millennium', as voted by the people of Leeds, Arthur Lois Aaron VC. It stands in Eastgate in the city centre. A maquette (scale model) of the Revie statue has been produced, with Duncan and Kim giving their full approval of the likeness and the pose.

Jim Cadman, although a fanatical Birmingham City supporter, is a lifelong admirer of Don Revie and considers him the most influential English manager of all time. He says:

> This statue will be for the fans of Leeds United and will be paid for by the fans of Leeds United. We have produced a top-quality magazine to mark the occasion, and countless events to raise funds from Leeds supporters groups all over the country are

being held almost on a weekly basis, culminating in a grand Don Revie Tribute Dinner at Elland Road, when over 50 guest players from other clubs during the Revie Era will be present. Any surplus money received over the target of £90,000 will be donated to the fight against motor neuron disease, which so cruelly took Don from us in 1989.

The statue, which will be unveiled at Elland Road in May 2012 to celebrate the 40th anniversary of Leeds United's Centenary FA Cup win at Wembley, will take 12 months to create. Graham Ibbeson will be working with a team of craftsmen at his London bronze foundry from May 2011. A seven-foot clay model will be sculpted, using the maquette for reference. When it is complete, Graham will then seek approval from the family before going to the rubber moulding stage. A wax replica of Don's sculpture will be produced from the rubber mould; this will then be invested using the lost wax technique, before a bronze cast is produced.

Writing in anticipation of the statue's creation, Jeff Powell, the aforementioned chief sportswriter for the *Daily Mail*, paid this tribute to Revie:

> Leeds United, under Revie, played some of the most wondrous football ever seen anywhere. They also reinforced their flowing talents with the fiercely competitive challenges which were born of an iron will to win.
>
> Their critics, especially those who envied their success, protested against their aggressive commitment to victory. With hindsight, it can be seen that Revie was pioneering all over again. Just as the Revie Plan took the blinkers off English tactics, so he laid the foundations for the Premier League football we witness today, a furious game in which even the most refined skills can only prevail if they come driven by physical courage. He left a modernising legacy. The Don was a quarter of a century ahead of his time with his meticulous preparations for matches, especially the reports he compiled on opponents. It is inconceivable now that any leading club would go into a match without that detailed analysis and planning which made Leeds United great. That is the one reason why Revie is revered in the city of Leeds to this

day. The folk there, unlike those who misunderstood him, knew the man as well as the master tactician. They knew a kind, warm-hearted, generous human being who would give of his time to the tea ladies and laundry women at Elland Road as freely as to the stars of his team.

If Don took a liking to you, you were blessed with the most loyal friend a man could wish to have, as I will testify personally for the rest of my days. To be befriended by Revie was to be wrapped in the warm embrace of the most loving family imaginable.

Far from the calculating creature he was portrayed as at times by those who didn't know him, Don was a sentimental romantic with an abiding passion for football and people.

That kindly bear of a man is the Don Revie who remains in the hearts of folk in Leeds. That, as well as a genius of the game, is the Don Revie whose statue they will soon stand and admire as they reflect on the glory days.

18. Beaten Hands Down

It's understandable for every fan to feel that their team is victimised. But the facts and statistics prove overwhelmingly that Leeds United *are* victimised.

It is almost impossible to comprehend that as we entered the new millennium Leeds United sat, quite comfortably, at the top of the Premiership and were competing in the Champions League. But even that incredible European adventure wasn't entirely untarnished.

In their very first game in that Champions League, Leeds were on the end of some bizarre refereeing decisions in a qualifying game at Elland Road against Munich 1860. Late in the game, Leeds had a comfortable 2–0 lead and were counting down for a valuable cushion to take to Germany for the second leg. The referee, from Cyprus, Costas Kapitanis, robbed Leeds of two players with successive dismissals for Olivier Dacourt and Eirik Bakke. Hassler pulled one back for Munich fully seven minutes into injury time. Afterwards, Leeds manager David O'Leary said, 'That was by far the worst display of refereeing I have ever seen in my life, either as a player or a manager.' No action was taken by UEFA.

Thankfully, Leeds United grabbed a 1–0 victory in the return game to progress to the next round. They continued to make good progress despite continual comments such as 'Leeds are only there to make up the numbers' and 'They won't keep winning' from opposition managers.

It is common knowledge that politics plays a big part in the European game and this season was to be no exception. Before the Phase One group match with Barcelona at Elland Road, it had become increasingly obvious that Barcelona (as a major draw in the competition) were required in Phase Two. A Leeds win on that night would have eliminated Barcelona. This resulted in yet another controversy.

Leeds were 3–2 in front with only seconds remaining when the fourth official began to punch into his board how much stoppage time there would be. Two Barcelona defenders approached the official, but they were waved away by the linesman. There had been very few, if any, stoppages so the crowd went absolutely berserk when the board was held up in the air: '4 MINS'. How could that possibly be? And with Leeds fans still venting their anger, the Spaniards, of course, got their equaliser. The official UEFA recorded time of the goal was 94 minutes and 37 seconds. I would love to have been a fly on the wall at UEFA headquarters when, two weeks later, Leeds drew with AC Milan in the San Siro to put both Leeds and Milan through to the next phase, eliminating Barcelona.

In a Phase Two game with Lazio at Elland Road, Leeds were once again leading 3–2. In the final minute, Lazio's Pavel Nedved launched a horrendous two-footed lunge at Alan Maybury. It was undoubtedly a red-card offence, but Leeds fans were left staring in total disbelief as the referee awarded a free kick on the edge of the Leeds penalty area – to Lazio! As Maybury was stretchered off, Sinisa Mihajlovic made it 3–3.

In the following group game, United had to travel to the famous Bernabeéu Stadium and face the mighty Real Madrid. Undaunted, Leeds sent the several thousand travelling fans into a glorious rapture as they took a 1–0 lead. It was short-lived, however, as Raúl pulled one back. We were situated at the opposite end and all we could see clearly was the Leeds defenders angrily chasing after the referee. Raúl had dived at the near post and punched the ball past Nigel Martyn. The Polish referee, Ryszard Wojcik, was only yards from the incident and yet awarded the goal, even though television pictures proved beyond all doubt that Raúl had used his fist to score.

The Leeds players were still simmering in the dressing-room at half-time when in walked Wojcik and apologised for giving the goal. Unbelievably, Wojcik had seen the 'goal' on the TV in his dressing-room and had decided to say sorry to the Leeds players. But the goal would stand!

Madrid went on to win 3–2. Although they stressed that the result would stand, UEFA fined Raúl £8,000 and banned him for one game. But, two days later, a UEFA appeals committee reversed the decision on Raúl. Their reason for the decision was: 'We could only act if the referee had been unable to make it a factual decision.' In other words, because the referee had allowed the goal at the time, believing it to be legitimate, he had made a 'factual', although incorrect, decision, which apparently could not now be overruled. Including the 'handball', Raúl's goal tally in the Champions League was six. This put him in contention for the Golden Boot Award. However, there was another player on six goals: Leeds United's Lee Bowyer.

A little more than 24 hours before Leeds' second-leg game at Valencia in the semi-final, David O'Leary received a telephone call from a UEFA delegate. Apparently, after watching the first leg on television, UEFA's disciplinary committee had looked at an incident between Lee Bowyer and Valencia's Juan Sánchez, after which they deemed that Bowyer had stamped on Sánchez. He was charged with violent conduct and would receive a three-match ban with immediate effect, ruling Bowyer out of the second leg and potentially the final, too. O'Leary was stunned, as he remembered in *Leeds United on Trial*:

> We couldn't afford to lose Lee, and it was a terrible blow for him as well as for our chances. We studied the video. It was ludicrous to claim that Lee had stamped on his opponent: the Valencia player had fallen underneath him, and the only genuine contact was when Bowyer accidentally trod on the Spaniard because he couldn't avoid him.

The referee that evening was arguably the best in the world at that time, the Italian Pierluigi Collina. A couple of yards away from the incident, Collina adjudged it 'an accident' and let the matter pass without a caution or a free kick. But UEFA overruled a referee who was elected to FIFA's referees list in 1995. He was voted the IFFHS World's Best Referee of the Year in 1998, 1999, 2000, 2001, 2002 and 2003. He also took charge of the 2002 World Cup final, the 1999 European Champions League final and the UEFA Cup final in 2004.

Incidentally, two weeks before, in the other semi-final, between Real Madrid and Bayern Munich, the Bayern defender Mehmet Scholl smashed his elbow into the face of Madrid's Míchel Salgado as he waited for a throw-in to be taken. Bowyer's crime had been described by UEFA as violent conduct and millions had seen this incident in Madrid. Leeds fans waited with interest for the outcome. Surely Scholl would receive the mandatory three-match ban? After watching a video of the incident, UEFA stated that 'as Salgado was standing behind Scholl, it was impossible to prove that the German had acted with malice.

A quarter of an hour into the second leg between Valencia and Leeds, Sánchez scored for the home team. With his hand. Leeds were 1–0 down and millions around the world, once again, witnessed television pictures of a player scoring with his hand against Leeds United. It will have been around then that Leeds gave up the fight. Valencia ran out easy 3–0 winners.

For all you sceptics out there still thinking that this is all just a bunch of sour grapes, ask yourself this: when was the last time that an English, British or indeed any team has been beaten twice in the same European competition by two handball goals seen by millions live on TV?

In 1966, Don Revie's Leeds side came face to face with Valencia in the Inter-Cities Fairs Cup third round. At half-time, Valencia were a goal to the good. Lorimer brought Leeds back into the game early in the second half and shortly afterwards all hell broke loose. An incident occurred in the Valencia area and the next second, Jack Charlton was chasing Spanish defender Roberto Vidagany almost down the tunnel. Just about every single player then became involved in a massive brawl. The police entered the melee and eventually Charlton, Vidagany and a second Valencia player were sent off. Allegations arose that one of the defenders had bitten Charlton and that that was what had led to the altercation. Subsequently, the Football Association held an inquiry and fined Charlton £20. This was despite the referee that night, Leo Horn, offering his backing to Jack Charlton, claiming that he hadn't caused the incident. Interestingly, the Spanish FA took no action against either of the Valencia players.

In March 2000, the draw for the semi-final of the UEFA cup was made in Geneva. Fellow English side Arsenal were in the draw with Leeds United, along with Turkish side Galatasaray and French outfit RC Lens. 'Galatasaray will play Leeds United.' Everyone was well aware of the fearsome reputation of the volatile Galatasaray supporters and their apparent immunity from any reprimand by UEFA, despite numerous accounts of intimidation and attacks on both Turkish and foreign visiting players and fans alike. It certainly was not the draw favoured by Leeds.

'Welcome to Hell' is the slogan that is daubed on flags and banners at Istanbul airport to greet any visiting teams and fans unfortunate enough to have been forced to play there. Holding these banners are hundreds of locals filled with pure hatred. And the police and security can't or won't do anything to prevent this ugly, threatening demonstration of venom.

Late in the evening of 5 April, I witnessed this antagonism at first hand as I landed with a plane full of Leeds fans and passed through customs. News had begun filtering through to many of our mobile phones that there had already been 'major disturbances' in Istanbul. By the time we arrived at our hotel, we knew that there had been fatalities and that the dead were Leeds fans, but we had no idea of how many or who they were.

Leeds United chairman Peter Ridsdale was one of the first people to see the body of Christopher Loftus at the hospital. Another Leeds fan, Kevin Speight, died in the same hospital shortly afterwards. Both had been brutally murdered in an ambush by locals brandishing large knives in Taksim Square – a place known to be popular with tourists.

Leeds fans were all over the city and there were no further incidents, although, understandably, the atmosphere was very tense. The distinct impression others and I got was that the police seemed to apportion all of the blame to Leeds fans, which, of course, was clearly not fair. The following morning, all Leeds fans were put under hotel arrest. The whole situation was ludicrous. It was the day of the game itself and we learned that any Leeds fans who were due to travel out that morning had been prevented from doing so.

Leeds United, meanwhile, had voiced concern to UEFA about the game going ahead and asked, quite reasonably, because of the dreadful circumstances, to postpone the game. Galatasaray, for reasons only known to themselves, disagreed, and UEFA backed them. The delegate from UEFA then announced to Ridsdale that if Leeds didn't fulfil the fixture they would forfeit the semi-final. A hasty decision had to be made and Leeds reluctantly agreed to play. It was a decision that Ridsdale later admitted regretting.

Arriving at the ground was unbelievable, as all the coaches carrying

Leeds fans were attacked by the locals while the police stood idly by and watched. It was absolutely incredible. The supporters showed no remorse whatsoever for the tragic events of the night before.

A further snub to Leeds came when they asked UEFA for a minute's silence in the names of Christopher Loftus and Kevin Speight. UEFA refused because they said it would provoke the home fans.

Leeds players, wearing black armbands (the Galatasaray team refused to wear them), had to emerge from the tunnel under the protection of dozens of shields held aloft over their heads by riot police as a barrage of missiles was launched at them by a frenzied pack of animals wearing yellow and red scarves. The Leeds team made their way over to the end where their fans were congregated and a very moving tribute to Chris and Kevin took place amidst an atmosphere that had to be experienced to be believed – a cauldron of hate. As the kick-off took place, all the Leeds fans turned their backs on the pitch and raised their arms aloft in protest against Galatasaray and UEFA.

In 2010, to mark the tenth anniversary of the murders, the families of the victims, along with friends and supporters, held a sequence of events, including the famous Three Peaks Challenge, a 60-mile bike ride, and a Tough-Guy Challenge, as well as many others, and raised well over £100,000, which was donated to Candlelighters, a charity for children who have cancer.

The match itself was a non-event, with Leeds playing almost on autopilot and clearly not wanting to be there. Galatasaray won 2–0.

It has to be said that had this dreadful event occurred the other way around, and two Turks had been killed on the streets of Leeds, there is absolutely no doubt whatsoever that Leeds United would have been thrown out of the competition immediately by UEFA.

In *Leeds United on Trial*, David O'Leary wrote:

> Given my own experience down the years of football Turkish-style, I have always questioned how UEFA and FIFA can allow matches to be held there without demanding greater security around visiting fans, players and officials.
>
> It cannot be deemed acceptable to ask an opposing team to run onto the pitch under the cover of riot policemen's shields to protect them from the hail of missiles and bottles cascading down from the terraces. If that kind of behaviour was seen in England,

you can be assured the FA would close down the stadium. In England we would not allow thousands of supporters to effectively bring a major airport to a standstill so that a visiting football team could be bombarded with abuse by people waving banners reading 'Welcome to Hell' and drawing their fingers across their throats in a threatening manner.

Turkish fans were banned from travelling to Leeds for the second leg, which finished 2–2. Arsenal played Galatasaray for the title. Once again, there was intense fighting on the streets before and after the final in Copenhagen.

Unbelievably, only months after the tragic events in Istanbul, Leeds were forced to return there when UEFA paired them with another Turkish side, Besiktas, in the Champions League.

To be honest, it was a stark contrast to the last time we had flown into Istanbul. There were no 'Welcome to Hell' banners or other such hostilities. Only 138 Leeds fans were allowed to travel, and the only welcome we received was from Peter Ridsdale, who shook hands with each and every one of us as we filed past him and towards customs. Inside the ground, the Besiktas players handed out flowers to the Leeds fans in memory of the two supporters who had lost their lives last time we were in Turkey.

19. New Century, Same Old Story

There were, of course, a number of reasons for the decline of Leeds United in 2004, not least the attack on an Asian student in the early hours of Wednesday, 11 January 2000. On the preceding evening, Sarfraz Najeib went out in Leeds with his brother and three friends. What happened a few hours later has been well documented. An argument took place and a group of five white men attacked a group of five Asian men, resulting in a chase from outside Majestyk nightclub in Leeds across City Square and culminating in an attack in nearby Mill Hill that left Sarfraz Najeib seriously injured. He was attacked in a doorway and was left with his face fractured in six places and a broken leg; there were teeth marks and a shoe or boot print on his face. Three Leeds United players were involved: Jonathan Woodgate, Lee Bowyer and Tony Hackworth. The other two white men were Paul Clifford and Neale Caveney, both friends of Woodgate from back home in Middlesbrough. All were charged with causing grievous bodily harm with intent and affray.

A trial at Hull Crown Court lasting almost two years ended on 14 December 2001. The multimillion-pound trial had been halted in April 2001 because of an interview with the victim's father in the *Sunday Mirror* suggesting that the attack was racially motivated. The courts ruled that the article would cause 'a clear and substantial risk of prejudice' and the trial was postponed until October. The editor of the *Sunday Mirror* at the time, Colin Myler, felt obliged to resign as a consequence, prompting a staement from the managing director of the Mirror Group newspapers, Mark Haysom:

> This review has established that the well-defined procedures in operation in the company were followed and that legal opinion was sought prior to publication . . . Whether publication of this

article is subject to contempt proceedings is a matter for the attorney general.

In fact, the attorney general had been assured by the *Sunday Mirror* that the interview in question would not appear until after the trial.

The eventual verdict saw Paul Clifford sentenced to six years in jail. Lee Bowyer was cleared of all charges but was ordered to pay more than £1 million in costs because of the lies he had told the police in interviews, said Mr Justice Henriques.

Jonathan Woodgate was sentenced to 100 hours' community service and escaped a jail term because, the judge said, 'you have suffered agonies . . . that is etched on your face'. Neale Caveney also received 100 hours' community service, but there was insufficient evidence against Tony Hackworth.

And so, finally, a trial that had seen Woodgate reduced to a haggard figure – whereas in stark contrast Lee Bowyer continued to turn in dynamic performances for Leeds – was over. Woodgate hadn't played for Leeds United throughout the trial, but Bowyer, courtesy of a helicopter from Hull supplied by Leeds United, had been heavily involved, and had scored, in some of the most memorable European games that United have ever been involved in.

The trial saw Leeds United facing the usual barrage of abuse hurled at them by the media and opposing fans, but, true to form, the club's fans stuck together, developing a siege mentality.

Manager David O'Learywrote in *Leeds United on Trial*:

> My suspicions of a political agenda were intensified by the debate surrounding the date of the trial. In September 2000, after the players had been committed for trial, the Crown Prosecution Service said that their case would be ready for January 2001. Leeds Uniteds lawyers had pointed out that if the trial took place during the season, the club would be 'severely penalised in financial terms from the loss of a number of players as defendants in the case, and to a lesser extent as witnesses'. Mr Justice Henriques decided to delay the court appearance until June 2001, explaining that the club's representations were one of the factors he had taken into account in choosing to wait until the end of the football season.

But Lord Dholakia, a Liberal Democrat home affairs spokesman and advisor to the Judicial Studies Board, objected to the delay. He was supported by the Lord Chancellor, Lord Irvine, who claimed that a quick decision was required. Mr Justice Henriques responded by saying that such a representation by any company chairman would have to be considered by a judge in setting a trial date.

O'Leary commented:

> Nevertheless, the judge's decision was overturned and the date was set for 29 January 2001. I imagine that the defence legal teams must have realised from that moment that the politicians would continue to involve themselves in the business of the courts.

Peter Ridsdale was the club chairman at the time and gave this statement at a press conference after the case had concluded:

> You can't quantify the damage that this has caused. None of us had wanted to go through this and despite the fact that we as a club were not on trial, the mere fact that we are here today demonstrates that the two have been linked together and at the end of the day people have perceived Leeds United to be as responsible as anybody else.
>
> But Leeds United have not been on trial. I would like to add also that there is not a hint of racism at this club and I was very happy to hear the judge in the case say that there were no racial motives in the attack. Leeds United have been in a very difficult position, but we allowed both men to play because we believe that they were innocent until proven guilty.
>
> The trial is now out of the way and we want to get back to playing football and try to get back to some kind of normality. We recognise that our players are in the public spotlight. If they do anything deemed inappropriate, we know that they are made sure of the consequences of that. We will be taking internal disciplinary action against Jonathan. We consider very carefully what we do in certain circumstances and we do not take this lightly.

This court case and the worldwide coverage were to have far-reaching implications for Leeds United and this, unfortunately, was to be only the start of a very uncomfortable slide from grace – and Messrs Ridsdale and O'Leary would both become major players in that slide.

Despite O'Leary having inherited the best crop of youngsters in the country – Jonathan Woodgate, Lee Bowyer, Alan Smith, Harry Kewell, Stephen McPhail, Eirik Bakke, Ian Harte and Danny Mills – he couldn't win anything. To be brutally frank, I believe that with these young players at his disposal any other manager in the country would have won something – not least Martin O'Neill, who could have joined Leeds before O'Leary but for the inadequacies of the bungling board, including Peter Ridsdale. Maybe 'bungling' is unfair, but I distinctly remember at the time Ridsdale declaring publicly that the board at Leicester City had refused Leeds permission to speak with Martin O'Neill (though O'Neill had clearly expressed his desire to 'at least talk to Leeds United') and saying, 'We will now do the gentlemanly thing and back off.'

It is my firm belief that Leeds United should have persevered with their desire to bring O'Neill to Elland Road. (Especially with the money we supposedly had at our disposal. Although, of course, everyone later discovered that it wasn't in fact our money, but a huge loan that would prove impossible to repay.) O'Neill was undoubtedly the man to take the club into the European spot that became a bridge too far for the club under O'Leary. Sadly, not many months after this, a certain Premiership club did exactly what I would have advocated regarding O'Neill, when they poached our star defender. Although Rio Ferdinand was under contract, he was whisked away to Old Trafford, leaving a record transfer fee in the Leeds coffers. This money, along with millions more, consequently disappeared into a black hole of debt.

Not getting O'Neill when they could and should have is one of the most significant parts of Leeds' subsequent downfall. O'Leary had been given almost £100 million for new players and bought many whom the club clearly didn't need, as well as others such as Robbie Keane, for £11 million plus £1 million on loan, who was a terrific forward but was always left on the bench by O'Leary, who had been offered Keane two years previously for £6 million.

The biggest mistake, however, was when O'Leary brought in Brian Kidd as youth-team development manager and then promoted him to first-team coach over Eddie Gray, proving the truth of the age-old saying 'If it ain't broke, don't fix it'. This is where I feel O'Leary began to get above his station. He claimed he had brought Kidd in to allow himself a more 'hands-off' approach. But the vast majority of Leeds fans have always been at a loss as to why this role wasn't given to Eddie Gray. Peter Ridsdale has always maintained that Leeds fans never liked Brian Kidd because of his previous connections to Old Trafford. This may in part be true, but the fact is that Kidd was never successful as a coach at Leeds, leaving the club in 2003 just as United continued their slide to the lower depths of the Football League. Kidd's performance at Leeds didn't go unnoticed at Old Trafford, either, where a popular chant at the time was, 'Oh Brian Kidd, oh Brian Kidd is still a Manc, is still a Manc. Oh Brian Kidd is still a Manc, he's fucking up Leeds United, oh Brian Kidd is still a Manc!'

I always liken David O'Leary to a poor player of Monopoly who has by far the most money. He was sacked at the end of the 2001–02 season and replaced by Terry Venables.

Meantime, a catastrophic, some would say self-inflicted, financial meltdown was hurtling towards Leeds at such a speed that no one would be able to stop it. In a nutshell, it became known that Leeds United, and in particular Peter Ridsdale, had gambled heavily on competing and staying in the Champions League and it had backfired with disastrous results. It is still very painful for Leeds United fans to this day; suffice to say, Peter Ridsdale gambled and lost. Undeniably a Leeds fan, Ridsdale had been elected as chairman, replacing Bill Fotherby, while George Graham was the team's manager.

It has to be said, the situation arose partly because of that match mentioned elsewhere in this book where Wes Brown scored an own goal in a fixture against Leeds at Elland Road only to have it, incredibly, ruled out for offside. That match played a massive part in Leeds not qualifying for Europe. Also, in the same game, keeper Fabien Barthez stamped on Leeds' Ian Harte and remained on the pitch to save the ensuing penalty that could have won Leeds the game. That game was drawn and Leeds finished it with a solitary point. Furthermore, it can be argued that one solitary point would have been enough to see Leeds finish the season in a Champions League qualifying position.

Failure to qualify left Leeds in severe financial difficulty and, with many of the top players being bought via offshore loan deals, the team began a spectacular break-up. Peter Ridsdale always denied that record signing Rio Ferdinand was being sold to pay off debts and famously told reporters, 'Where do you think he is going? Into thin air? Rio is going nowhere.' But the following day, Ferdinand made the short trip across the M62 and signed for Manchester United.

Ridsdale arranged several meetings with the club's supporters in an attempt to convince them that things were OK and there was 'no need to panic'. He claimed that they had let Ferdinand go for financial gain and that he was no longer needed because of the recent great form of Jonathan Woodgate. I attended one of these meetings, where we were told by Ridsdale's media director, David Walker, a former sports journalist with the *Daily Mail*, to 'keep what is said in this room to ourselves'. We were told not to tell the mass gathering of the media outside, barred from entering the meeting, anything that had been said.

Rumours were now rife that Woodgate would also be leaving the club, going to Newcastle for £9 million because the club desperately needed funds to fend off the debts that had accumulated. I asked Ridsdale about this putting it to him that the club should find the £9 million from somewhere else and not sell any more players, as we would soon have none left and could quite easily end up being relegated. To this day, I can still see Ridsdale smile and say, 'Come on, now, that's not going to happen, is it?' I still have that response on tape.

At the time of his arrival, the club had assured Terry Venables that he would not be forced to sell any of its players. Yet within months, the club was selling players at an alarming rate, many, if not all, without Venables' consent. Venables had threatened to resign if Woodgate was sold. When he was transferred to Newcastle, however, the manager was persuaded to stay by Ridsdale. Venables was then sacked himself in March 2003.

Peter Reid was the next man into the Elland Road hot seat and he orchestrated some fine results, including a thumping 6–1 win at Charlton Athletic. Leeds travelled to Arsenal for the final away game needing a win to avoid relegation from the Premiership. Arsenal needed a victory to secure the title. Leeds won 3–2, but it would be only a stay of execution.

On 26 March 2003, Peter Ridsdale stepped down as chairman of Leeds United, or rather he was, as he put it, 'hounded to hand in my resignation'. He was then recruited by Barnsley FC to assist in steering them out of administration. He did that, and then he took up a three-day-a-week consultant's job at Cardiff City in order, as Cardiff owner Sam Hammam said, 'to get us out of the shit'. Ridsdale was later appointed as chairman. After two years, and seeing Cardiff back on an even keel, Ridsdale stepped down. He is currently the acting chairman at debt-ridden Plymouth Argyle.

On Thursday, 5 May 2011, Ridsdale appeared in court. Cardiff Council trading standards department brought the case over concerns about a 'Golden Ticket' scheme promoted by Cardiff City in 2009, during Ridsdale's tenure as chairman. The scheme allowed fans to buy their season tickets for the 2010–11 season early, promising that they would receive a full refund if the club was promoted to the Premier League, and that the proceeds would be spent on players in the January 2010 transfer window. But no players were bought in the transfer window and the club was in fact under a transfer embargo at the time. A statement by Cardiff City on 27 January 2010 read:

> It was anticipated that if we launched these tickets early and had received new investment pre-Christmas or in January, we would have been able to invest in new players in January. In the absence of the new investment this will not now be possible. We have to ensure that other overheads and financial issues are properly addressed. Whilst we apologise for this, we do not apologise for ensuring that the viability and financial health of the club is the ultimate priority.

Ridsdale appeared in court only to confirm his name and address, and the case was adjourned until 22 July 2011, with the council indicating that it wanted the case to be heard in a crown court, where the maximum punishment would be ten years' imprisonment, rather than a magistrates' court, where the sentence could be no more than twelve months in prison or a fine.

Leeds United had obviously been struggling financially, but had received no help whatsoever from the FA, or anyone else for that matter, unlike Portsmouth, who received all sorts of assistance as they struggled to survive in the Premiership. Unfortunately for Portsmouth, it was not enough and they were relegated in 2010, but they had certainly received some form of help from the FA. Leeds United, on the other hand, had the heavy boot of the Football Association/ Premier League placed firmly on their heads as they slowly sank underwater.

Leeds were still in a dangerously poor financial state and Reid saw his board forced to sell Harry Kewell at a scandalous knockdown price. To make matters even worse, the deal was done by an unlicensed agent, who later claimed it was his brother who had done it, but the FA refused to investigate. Cheaper overseas players were brought in, which was never going to work, and Reid was sacked in November 2003. Eddie Gray had to take over as caretaker manager, but the inevitable slide had begun, and Leeds were relegated to the Championship, causing massive celebrations right across the country.

The few remaining star players jumped ship immediately, including local hero Alan Smith, who, amidst all the rumours, insisted, 'I'm not leaving the club I supported as a boy.' But as our 'hero' saluted the massive turnout of fans at Elland Road (38,986) after the final game in the Premiership (a 3–3 draw with Charlton) and was chaired around the pitch by his adoring fans, he knew all the time that he would be moving to Old Trafford for £5 million in a matter of weeks. In hindsight, I suppose some of what he said, however, was true. He wouldn't be leaving the team he'd supported as a boy – he was a Liverpool fan as a kid.

Kevin Blackwell was brought in as the new manager, but he initially struggled to get enough players to begin the season. The scratch side, however, performed admirably, and after their first season in the Championship, there was a glimmer of hope the following season as Leeds reached the play-off final of 2005–06. Alas, the team underperformed against a very average Watford side and were beaten 3–0.

The following season, disaster struck the club yet again. Leeds were relegated to the third tier of English football for the first time in the club's history. And, once again, the whole world, it seemed, celebrated.

Although the football authorities weren't entirely to blame for

195

Leeds' plummet to the depths of the Football League, they were certainly responsible for ensuring that they stayed there. The Football League had recently implemented a points deduction penalty for any misdemeanours, including those related to financial matters. The rules were clear: a team going into administration would be docked points for that particular season only.

After failing to beat Ipswich Town at home on the penultimate Saturday, Leeds United travelled to Derby for the final game already relegated. Ken Bates had taken over the club in 2005 (bringing Dennis Wise in as manager in 2006) and had slowly dragged the club back to some sort of stability. Bates continued to battle against what he called 'a legacy left by others', but Leeds were still heavily in debt and had no choice but to go into administration.

Leeds United, quite understandably, went into administration shortly before the Derby game, knowing that the ten-point penalty would be irrelevant, as they were already relegated. Most importantly, they would start on an even keel as they prepared for their first-ever season in League One (the Third Division).

The administrators were KPMG from Leeds, and they had already agreed to sell the club to a newly formed company led by Bates. KPMG issued the following statement:

> Shortly after their appointment the administrators agreed to sell the business and its assets to a newly formed club. This company is called Leeds United Football Club Limited, the directors of which are Ken Bates, Shaun Harvey and Mark Taylor. The sale of the club is subject to approval by its creditors, via a Company Voluntary Arrangement (CVA). The creditors' meeting to consider the CVA will be held before the end of May. The Football League will also need to approve the sale.

Ken Bates hailed this as a new era for the club, but continued to criticise the previous regime for incurring huge debts. He said:

> This action brings to an end the financial legacy left by the others that we have spent millions of pounds trying to settle. But the most important thing now is not to view this as the end, but the beginning of a new era.

The financial burden of the past finally pushed the club into administration following the issuing of a winding-up petition by HM Revenue and Customs, who will be one of the company's major creditors. The other parties who will suffer the biggest financial loss are institutions from which the board arranged funding: Astor Investment Holdings, Krato Trust and Forward Sports, who collectively will lose in excess of £22 million.

The Football League confirmed Leeds' ten-point deduction. Head of communications John Nagle added:

> Following confirmation that Leeds United have obtained an administration order, the Football League can confirm that the club has been deducted ten points from its 2006–07 tally.
>
> Given the recent reduction in the number of clubs resorting to formal insolvency proceedings, it is disappointing that Leeds United have had to seek the protection of an administration order. Discussions have already begun aimed at establishing how Leeds United intend exiting administration.
>
> This will have to include complying with the League's insolvency policy under which all 'football debts' must be settled in full.

Covering the story on 4 May 2007, the BBC said, 'It was confirmed today that Leeds United would not lose any points for the start of their first season in League One when it begins in August.'

But the Football League, under chairman Lord Brian Stanley Mawhinney, were said to be 'not happy' that Leeds had escaped a points deduction for the following season. One League spokesman even suggested that Leeds had 'bent the rules' or 'used a loophole'. There was no question that Leeds had acted within the rules, but Lord Mawhinney was believed to have been incensed, and within hours of the season coming to an end, the rule was changed so that this particular 'rule-bending' could never happen again. But, unfortunately for Leeds United, they hadn't escaped Mawhinney's anger.

As stated, Leeds had gone into administration in May and had the agreement with KPMG. However, when Ken Bates attempted to pay off the creditors using the CVA, he was legally challenged by the Inland Revenue (HMRC), who were owed £7.7 million in unpaid taxes.

As the season approached, KPMG scrapped the CVA and put the club back on the market, prompting other parties to make fresh offers, but Bates resubmitted his original offer and emerged victorious. However, winning back the club under another name meant more complications for Bates and Leeds United. The Football League objected to the fact that Bates had regained control of the club for a third time without a CVA meeting. Only weeks before the start of the new season, a further 15 points were deducted from Leeds United, resulting in an unprecedented 25-point deduction in just a matter of weeks.

After much legal wrangling, the League issued the following statement:

> We have no choice but to grant Bates's new company, Leeds United 2007, the right to kick off the League One season under 'exceptional circumstances', but the League has determined that this transfer of membership should be subject to a 15-point deduction.

All I can add here is that they must have used an exceptional amount of midnight oil down at League headquarters coming up with that little beauty.

The League also withdrew Leeds from League membership and the future of the club hung precariously in the balance. This suspension from the League meant that Dennis Wise and his assistant, Gus Poyet, were unable to operate in the pre-season transfer market and could not prepare for the new season – assuming, of course, that they would be allowed to compete in it.

Ken Bates and Shaun Harvey asked the Football Association to intervene in events that the club thought were dangerously wrong, but there was no surprise when the FA refused to become involved, claiming that 'the Football League are just doing their job'.

Leeds United did, of course, appeal against the latest points deduction. Meanwhile, manager Dennis Wise said, 'It's just not funny at all. We'd like to know, deep down, the real reasons.'

Ken Bates laid the blame at the door of the Inland Revenue, saying:

Over the past two and a half years, Leeds have paid the Inland Revenue between £15 million and £20 million, but our cash flow dried up and we asked for more time to pay. The Revenue said 'no' and put forward a petition to wind the club up. I'm sorry that small creditors have lost money but that is totally down to the Revenue. We were happy to pay everybody over a period of time. The fault for Leeds' creditors not getting paid should be laid firmly at the door of the Inland Revenue.

Leeds' appeal against the 15-point deduction was, unsurprisingly, unsuccessful, due in no small part to the fact that Lord Mawhinney invited the clubs in all divisions of the Football League to vote on Leeds' fate. Put simply: all the League chairmen, including all the teams that Leeds would be competing against that season, had Leeds United's future in their hands. It was an absolutely ridiculous situation.

Just imagine for one moment: all the clubs in the Championship above Leeds would vote against the presence of a club that could be a threat to any one of them, as Leeds proved they were in season 2010–11 when they returned to the Championship with all guns blazing. All the clubs below Leeds United, in League Two, would obviously want a 'crowd puller' like Leeds in their division, and, for the same reason, League One clubs were going to vote to keep United in their division, with the added bonus, of course, of having a points advantage over United from the start. Leeds United had sold out their entire away ticket allocation for the past four or five years at least. It was what could be called a 'no-brainer'.

On 8 August 2007, Ken Bates wrote to all the Football League chairmen before the vote, to give the reasons why he and Leeds thought that they should vote in the club's favour:

Dear Chairman,
Re: Leeds United
Lord Mawhinney was kind enough to send me a copy of his letter to you dated 3 August.

As you know our appeal against the deduction of 15 points will be heard on Thursday and I felt compelled to write to all the Chairmen of the Football League Clubs to set out the true facts relating to the administration of Leeds United Association Football Club Limited and the subsequent purchase of its assets. I am disappointed but not surprised to have to say that the standard of reporting of the process has been appalling and in the main has been based on guesswork.

First of all let me confirm that the administration of the club was not pre-planned. My staff at Leeds fought tooth and nail to get Leeds United through to the start of the coming season when the last of the contracts that remained from the days of 'Living the Dream' would have at last expired. We had procured external funding of approaching £25 million in our attempts to keep the club alive. We spent nine months looking for external partners but as our playing fortunes declined during last season investors waited to see what would happen but by the end of the season funding had run out. We paid the Inland Revenue some £25 million during the period from January 2005 to April 2007 but the Revenue would not allow us more time to pay the outstanding arrears and whilst acknowledging our efforts issued a winding-up petition due to be heard on 1 June 2007. Following the issue of the petition administration or liquidation was really the only option.

We approached one of the leading insolvency practices in the world, KMPG, to advise. They were concerned that with the close season upon us there would be no income to run the club and advised that administration followed by a sale to a party willing to fund the Club during the Administration process was the best approach to adopt.

We have attracted some criticism for going into administration before the end of the 2006–07 season, and thus triggering the ten-point deduction during that season when we were almost certain of relegation. I think this criticism is unfair. Lord Mawhinney has stated publicly that the approach we took was completely within the rules. As directors of the Club we had a duty to act in the best interests of the Club and we believe that in taking the actions we did we discharged our obligation properly. The supporters of Leeds United would have rightly been appalled if we had been relegated and then have taken the ten-point deduction that could have been taken during the 2006–07 season.

Lord Mawhinney's letter to you highlights the fact that the Football League have imposed 'a 15-point sanction'. 'Sanction' is defined in the Oxford English Dictionary as meaning 'a penalty for breaking rules'. We believe that Leeds United have broken no rules and have complied with the regulations of the Football League to the absolute extent it was in their power and control to do so. We have no reason to think that KPMG have acted other than in accordance with the law of the land in conducting the administration. In these circumstances we believe that no 'sanction' is appropriate.

KPMG put a Company Voluntary Arrangement (CVA) to creditors of the company on 14 May and this was approved by more than 75 per cent of the creditors of the Company as required by the Insolvency Act 1986, only just, but a win is a win.

Following approval there is a 28-day period during which creditors can appeal against the conduct of the CVA. During this period various parties made threatening noises but did not appeal. I think the reason for this was that KPMG had sought the advice of two independent counsels before admitting any claim to vote in the CVA. It is difficult in such circumstances to see how the Administrators could be said to have acted unreasonably.

The Revenue, however, were still making demands and in an attempt to placate them we increased the sum payable under the CVA. Creditors were now offered circa 8.5 pence up front with a further 30 pence if the Club attained Premier League status within the next 10 years.

Despite the improved offer the Revenue appealed at approximately 15.00 p.m. on the last day for appeals. Their appeal was based on the acceptance by the Administrator of three debts upon which the Administrator had taken independent advice.

In our view the appeal was a sham. The Revenue could have appealed against the admission of debts on day one but it chose to wait until the 28th day to do so. It is our view that the decision of the Revenue was vexatious, and I think that this is confirmed by what happened next.

At a directions hearing for their appeal on 6 July a representative of the Revenue told the Administrator's lawyer that they would withdraw what they described as a protective appeal provided

Leeds put all sums into the CVA immediately and instead of paying 'Football Creditors' paid the sum set aside for 'Football Creditors' into the CVA for the benefit of the unsecured creditors generally. At last the true motive of the Revenue had been revealed. Their appeal was yet another attack on the 'Football Creditors Rules', something the Revenue had sought to attack since their preferred status had been withdrawn in September 2003.

The Revenue knew we could not and indeed would not want to break the Football Creditors Rules, but I think that they were surprised when we agreed to do the next best thing. We met their demands by increasing our payment into the CVA by an additional sum equal to the sum being set aside for Football Creditors. We put the unsecured creditors of the Company in the position that the Revenue had required, but we were still paying the Football Creditors, which was unacceptable to the Revenue.

The question of the Football Creditors Rules has been litigated to the Court of Appeal in the Wimbledon case. For the Revenue to overturn that position the case would have to go to the House of Lords and whilst the Revenue have our taxes to pay for that litigation, the Club could simply not afford it.

In these circumstances we approached the Administrator and offered to purchase the Club unconditionally and take our chances with the Football League. We felt that the Revenue's position represented an attack on football generally and on Leeds United in particular. The circumstances seemed to us to be the 'exceptional circumstances' referred to in the Football League Insolvency Rules.

On Tuesday last week Leeds met with the Administrators and the League. Initially the League expressed the view that 'exceptional circumstances' did not exist, a position that frankly we found unbelievable.

The League did not dispute that the offer we had made was the best offer on the table but wanted it to be put to the new creditors' meeting. Because we had paid the players' wages and some players had moved on during the close season the 'football debts' had reduced, meaning the Revenue's votes as a proportion of the whole had increased. The Administrators were of the view that the Revenue now represented 24.4 per cent of the debt and this would enable them to block any CVA.

It was agreed to approach the Revenue to seek to persuade them to withdraw their objection. Their response was categoric. They stated on record that if a revised CVA was presented 'as a matter of policy, HMRC would vote against any CVA that resulted in Football Creditors being paid in full'. If the CVA was passed they would appeal again and would litigate all the way. Their position means that unsecured creditors generally including themselves will get a lower payment than they would have done under the CVA.

In the face of this intransigence by the Revenue the Administrators said a further meeting was futile and the League eventually agreed that 'exceptional circumstances' existed and agreed to transfer the League share subject to the sanction now under appeal.

So exactly what rules have been broken?

1. Lord Mawhinney has acknowledged that going into administration as and when we did broke no rules.
2. The League press release states: 'Notwithstanding the manner in which this administration has been conducted, the Club should be permitted to continue in the Football League.'

If that is a criticism of Leeds then it is misplaced. The Administration has been carried out by KPMG. If the League have complaints about the process they should be addressing them to the Administrators not the Club. The Club could have had no influence over the Administrator, who was independent.

3. Finally, the CVA was approved by the requisite number of creditors but completion of it has been blocked by the Revenue for what can only be described as political reasons. Leeds should not be punished because the Revenue are intransigent.

We have broken no rules. The 'exceptional circumstances' rules were introduced to cover exactly the situation that exists today. We can only speculate as to the reasoning behind the imposition of a sanction when no rules have been broken. We believe such a sanction is wholly unfair and a breach of natural justice. On Thursday we will be asking you to overturn its imposition.

With kind regards,

Yours sincerely

K.W. BATES

Here, then, was a cast-iron, compelling case in favour of Leeds United, yet it came as no surprise to anyone that only 5 clubs out of 72, including Leeds, voted in favour of United's deduction of 15 points being overturned.

A final appeal by Leeds United was rejected by a three-man arbitration panel appointed by the Football Association. The appeal had been delayed by the Football League, so much so that it fell into the latter part of the season and Leeds United, having started from minus 15 points, were now sitting firmly in the play-off position, with a very good chance of automatic promotion. However, clubs around Leeds in the table also competing for promotion, such as Doncaster Rovers and Nottingham Forest, threatened to sue if the appeal was upheld and Leeds were given their 15 points back.

Amazingly, the arbitration report revealed that if United had accepted relegation to League Two for the start of the 2007–08 season, the club could have avoided the 15-point penalty. Quite understandably, United had refused that option. The club stated:

> The decision to remain in League One was always correct from the club's perspective.
>
> The matter is now closed. However it was galling to have been criticised for the delay in bringing the appeal when it was the Football League that effectively backed us into this corner in the first place.

The Football League had done Leeds again, of that there was no doubt, but United had no further right of appeal. The club added:

> This is a perverse outcome, it defies all logic, and we believe it has arisen as a result of a serious misrepresentation of fact by the board of the Football League in their presentation. The only

NEW CENTURY, SAME OLD STORY

winner is the Inland Revenue and we believe the full ramifications of Thursday's decision will adversely affect football going forward for many years. The club is considering its options, but in the meantime we will be concentrating on starting its promotion campaign at Tranmere on Saturday.

Lord Mawhinney responded by saying, 'Leeds are starting the new season in League One as a valued member of the League's football family – but with a penalty of a 15 points' deduction.'

One post on a fans' forum by 'Jon P', summed the whole saga up perfectly:

> It was unfair. We didn't break any rules last season by taking the points deduction. It's nothing to do with the FA, it's down to the Football League. We couldn't complete the sale of the club in time because there was a 28-day appeal window on the original deal. The Inland Revenue appealed on day 28, meaning it would have been impossible for Ken Bates or any new owner to be ready for the start of the season.
>
> Letting the other 71 League clubs vote on our fate is not part of League rules and why should you let 71 chairmen who have a vested interest in having Leeds take a deduction vote on their fate? Every club in our division would have been crazy to give us any help, it would keep us out of the promotion places or keep us in the division for another season. It means big paydays all round when we turn up to their little grounds . . .
>
> One positive outcome of it all is that it's pulled the club's players and the supporters together. We have a cause and there is a passion about the club. It could be the best thing that could have happened to us. I can't wait till we start climbing the league and start passing all the rubbish who can't make the most out of a 15-point start. Hopefully starting this weekend.
>
> Oh yeah, and two fingers to the Football League.

Leeds United began that season in fine style. The pre-match huddle you see these days from players on the pitch began with United's visit to Tranmere Rovers for the opening. At a sun-drenched Prenton Park, Leeds United showed such solidarity that it had to be seen to be believed. A large banner that simply said 'FO to the FL' hung defiantly behind the goal, where thousands of Leeds fans were amassed. Leeds won the game with a late winner from Trésor Kandol, who treated ecstatic Leeds fans to his trademark overhead backflip. There then followed another huddle as the supporters celebrated. Leeds fans had found themselves in a truly bizarre situation: celebrating with Dennis Wise on the same side.

Leeds went on to win their first five games. After Tranmere, they beat Southend United, Nottingham Forest, Luton Town and Hartlepool United, all teams who would have voted for the 15-point deduction. The 2–0 win over Hartlepool sent Leeds 'up' to zero points. At last they had got their 15 points back, but no thanks to the Football League. The side went on to win their first seven games of the season, equalling a club record set by Don Revie's team back in the 1970s.

On Saturday, 29 September 2007, Leeds travelled down to Gillingham, who were struggling to find any kind of decent form. Sebastian Carole put Leeds in front after half an hour and United looked set to get a hatful. Andy Hughes was booked after six minutes, Trésor Kandol after about twenty-five. Then Kandol was fouled heavily by Steve Lomas. When Kandol received the free kick, he jokingly applauded the referee, Danny McDermid, and was sent off. Then Jermaine Beckford was booked for dissent early in the second half, and four minutes later he was booked again for a foul on Sean Clohessy and McDermid immediately sent him off. It was incredible. Within fifteen minutes' play Danny McDermid had sent off the division's two leading goal-scorers. Kandol spent the rest of the game stood behind the goal with the Leeds fans. Six and a half minutes into injury time, Gillingham equalised and McDermid blew for full-time immediately. The referee had to leave the field under a heavy escort, and Dennis Wise was incensed, as was everyone involved with Leeds.

It transpired later that Dennis Wise was to be charged by the Football Association with using foul and abusive language towards Danny McDermid. But Wise had already lodged a complaint claiming that McDermid had sworn at him first. Which way would the FA go, do you think?

Wise said, 'The big issue here is that, at the end of the game, the referee has told me to "fuck off"! I think it is totally and utterly unacceptable and we as a club will be making a formal complaint.' Wise called five witnesses.

The FA's response was:

> The charge relates to Wise's conduct towards referee Danny McDermid at half-time during the game at Gillingham on Saturday.
>
> The FA can confirm that it has received a complaint from Leeds United regarding the conduct of the referee towards Wise at the conclusion of the game. This is now under consideration.

Two weeks later, the FA announced:

> At a Regulatory Commission hearing last week, Leeds United manager Dennis Wise was fined £5,000 and given a three-match touchline ban. Wise was charged with using abusive and/or insulting words to referee Danny McDermid at half-time of Leeds' match at Gillingham on 29 September.
>
> The Commission invoked a previous suspended one-match touchline ban and issued a further two-match ban. In reaching its decision, the Commission took into account Wise's poor disciplinary record.
>
> Meanwhile the FA has today charged referee Danny McDermid with using abusive and/or insulting words towards Wise.
>
> The incident is alleged to have occurred following the match against Gillingham. McDermid has until 13 November to respond to the charge.

As you would expect, referees stick together and Graham Poll said this of the incident:

> No matter how badly Wise felt that McDermid had performed in Leeds' draw with Gillingham last Saturday, he should have kept his comments to himself. Now each has reported the other for swearing, which sounds to me like a playground tit-for-tat spat. Foul language is no longer an offence unless it is offensive, insulting or obscene. I don't want to belittle this but I never saw Wise as a shrinking violet likely to be offended so easily.

Danny McDermid was cleared of all charges.

Leeds continued to fly in the face of the Football League and remained unbeaten through the following month. United continued to climb the table and the division's top teams were extremely worried when the club launched another appeal.

If anyone is left in any doubt about the severity of the systematic abuse that Leeds United have been subjected to since 1919, here are just some of the incidents that occurred only last season, 2010–11.

There are far too many to mention here involving that team from Old Trafford with diplomatic immunity, but here's one. During a game against Wigan, Wayne Rooney elbowed James McCarthy. Plain and simple, you would have thought. But, no, referee Mark Clattenburg saw the incident 'clearly' and decided no action should be taken. The fact that the laws stipulate that you cannot raise your arm/hand towards an opponent under any circumstances seems to have been lost on Clattenburg. Rooney's manager, Alex Ferguson, claims that his team are constantly victimised, and yet when United were playing Tottenham a couple of seasons previously, Clattenburg disallowed a goal by Spurs that was shown by TV footage to be at least a foot over the line.

Of course, it's all kidology with Ferguson, very clever kidology. Ferguson refuses to speak to the BBC at any time, because they had the audacity to question decisions given in favour of his team. But recently he hasn't stopped there. After a defeat at Anfield against Liverpool last season, he refused to speak to Sky TV, and he has even shunned his own club's TV station, because he blamed them for the FA taking legal action in response to one of his many outbursts, this time at Stamford Bridge.

The reason that Rooney wasn't given an FA suspension and no kind of disciplinary action was taken against him was because the official saw the incident and thought that no punishment was necessary, other than giving a free kick to Wigan and giving Rooney a 'friendly ticking-off'. FA law deems that no action can be taken afterwards if the referee has seen and noted the incident, even if the referee's actions are wrong in the eyes of the laws

FA general secretary Alex Horne said:

FIFA regulations state that if the incident has been seen by the referee, then we can't review it. If you review everything, then you begin to undermine the referee. I check this regulation with the FIFA executive and with other national associations regularly.

Despite FIFA chief Sepp Blatter saying any decision made should be at the FA's discretion, FA chairman David Bernstein insisted that his organisation followed FIFA's rules. He said:

In the Wayne Rooney situation, under FIFA's regulations if the referee sees the incident – which in this case he did do – the FA has no authority except in what is called exceptional circumstances, really exceptional. If you open the door to 'halfway exceptional' the floodgates will open.

On the night of Monday, 9 February 2009, those 'exceptional circumstances' were enforced, and you don't need me to tell you that it was at Elland Road, and also not in Leeds' favour.

Leeds were playing Millwall in a crucial, televised League One game when in the 65th minute there was an incident in the Millwall goalmouth. Much pushing and shoving ensued as Millwall keeper David Forde clearly elbowed Leeds striker Jermaine Beckford from behind as they fought for a high ball. Undeniably, Beckford retaliated with an elbow, and they both fell to the ground. Referee Alan Wiley immediately booked Beckford. But there was no punishment for Forde. I remember thinking that both players could and probably should have been sent off. Simon Grayson, the Leeds manager, was apparently in agreement: 'I've not seen it, but there was a melee in there. People say that Jermaine elbowed him. The referee has seen it and booked him. Whether that can change or not I'm not sure.'

Two days later those 'exceptional circumstances' appeared, under the guise of Rule E3. An FA statement declared:

The FA have confirmed that Jermaine Beckford has been charged under FA Rule E3 (violent conduct) for an incident on the field of play which falls within Law 12 – not seen by the match officials but caught on video.

Despite the official Alan Wiley not seeing the initial elbow by keeper

David Forde, it was seen on video, yet he went unpunished. Beckford was given a three-match suspension.

On Monday, 25 October 2010, Leeds United entertained Cardiff City. During a crucial period in the first half, Cardiff's Jay Bothroyd launched a horrific tackle on Leeds' Luciano Becchio, which went unpunished by referee Michael Oliver. Certain decisions can change a game, and that particular Becchio incident, along with a seemingly perfectly good goal ruled out, could have changed things on the night. That said, Cardiff did eventually run out deserved winners, but crucial decisions can matter.

After the game, Leeds United launched an official complaint about the referee. On this occasion, the FA refused to get involved and handed the responsibility over to the Football Association of Wales (FAW). Within hours, FAW issued the following, quite predictable statement:

> The Football Association of Wales has reviewed footage of the Jay Bothroyd tackle on Luciano Becchio during the Npower Football League Championship game, Leeds United v. Cardiff City, played on 25 October 2010. Retrospective action can only be taken where an incident has not been seen by the match officials. If the match officials have seen an incident such as the coming together of two players in a challenge, then it is not possible to intervene retrospectively.
>
> FIFA's clear stance is that incidents seen at the time should not be 're-refereed' even where it is perceived by others that match officials have made an incorrect judgement of an incident.
>
> As a result of relevant consultations, the Football Association of Wales has decided not to take any further action against Jay Bothroyd.

Not a surprising outcome, one has to say, but is it right that the Football Association can completely ignore a complaint by an English club against a Welsh club and delegate it to the Football Association of Wales?

Leeds manager Simon Grayson said:

You could go into the depths of controversial comments, but as a manager you have to be careful what you say.

The Welsh FA have decided for whatever reason that no punishment is needed. They have said that the referee saw it and saw nothing wrong. But his positioning would tell me he hasn't seen it. If he has seen it, then he isn't doing his job properly. Luciano did him a favour by not rolling about on the floor. I still don't think the referee saw it because if he had it would have been a sending-off offence.

This isn't sour grapes because a suspension for Bothroyd wouldn't affect us in any way, but I have seen plenty of other players 'done' in this way and all I'm asking for is some consistency from the panels that make these decisions.

Three weeks after the Cardiff game, Leeds played Hull City at Elland Road, and yet another controversial incident dominated the game. Midway through the second half, with Leeds looking the more dominant side and the score at 1–1, Luciano Becchio turned with the ball and lost his marker, Hull captain Ian Ashbee. But instantly, Ashbee flattened Becchio with his elbow. Referee Kevin Friend claimed afterwards that he saw the incident but decided to take no action – this despite him having to call on the medics to tend to Becchio and the Argentinian having to leave the field with a swollen jaw, a black eye and a bandage to the head.

A Leeds statement was issued the following day:

The club confirms it is disappointed that no action has been taken following an elbowing incident involving Hull City's Ian Ashbee during Tuesday's game at Elland Road.

Like all clubs, what we seek and should demand from the Football Association is consistency. Trial by television is either the way forward or it is not. It cannot be used on an ad hoc basis.

We had very similar circumstances two seasons ago when Jermaine Beckford was suspended for an elbow which hadn't been seen by the referee.

As footage shows, even though the referee claims he saw the incident on Tuesday, he plainly cannot have had the view that we had and is shown on TV images, otherwise you would have expected him to take action.

If he didn't see it clearly, then in those circumstances trial by television should be used. Referees are human and we understand that they are as liable to make a mistake as a player is.

Any mistakes can be rectified by the FA without apportioning any criticism to the referee, but this needs to be done consistently.

The Football Association refused to comment.

Leeds United failed in their attempt to gain back-to-back promotions in the 2010–11 season. In not having achieved that, they can justifiably feel a little aggrieved about many refereeing decisions, but it must also be recorded that the players fell short of fans' expectations of their abilities and that a large proportion of the blame, for want of a better word, for not getting promoted lies within the confines of the club itself.

20. Marching on Together

Upon arrival at Elland Road, row upon row of coaches can be seen, having come from Plymouth and Darlington, from Maryport and Devon. But these aren't away fans; these are Leeds United fans. Isle of Wight, Isle of Man, Shropshire, Norwich, East Anglia, South Wales, Wrexham, Aberystwyth, Blackpool, Cheshire, Scotland, Nottingham, Northampton, Bristol and all over the south-west, Cleethorpes, Scunthorpe, Grimsby, Scarborough, York, Whitby, Darlington, Sunderland, Durham, Kent, Surrey, Sussex, Chiltern, Cambridgeshire, Barnsley, Coventry, Warwickshire, Hampshire, Hereford, Leicester, Essex, are Thames Valley, Stoke, Stockport, Preston, Rochdale, Lincolnshire, as well as several parts of London – these are just some of the places represented each week by fans who converge on Leeds together with hundreds of supporters from Ireland, north and south, from all across Scandinavia, throughout Europe, Australia, Brazil, the USA, Malta, Cyprus, Dubai, Taiwan and many, many other countries all over the world, week in and week out. And then it goes without saying that there are dozens upon dozens of supporters club branches in Leeds and throughout the rest of Yorkshire.

Leeds United Football Club has long been tarnished with a reputation for having unruly supporters. It's certainly true to say that during the 1970s and 1980s there was an element of hooliganism attached to the club. But, as with the besmirched name of Leeds United FC, the Leeds fans too are criticised by many to this day. It wasn't just Leeds United to which hooligans have been drawn. Without exception, every club in Britain, possibly the world, has a section of undesirables attached to them.

It is almost impossible to find a more loyal fan than a Leeds United fan, of that there is no doubt. Most of the Leeds fans today haven't seen United win anything, and few witnessed the glorious Don Revie days. Yet throughout the recent decline of the club, the fans have remained loyal – and with little, if any, recognition from the media. In League One, from 2007 to 2009, every single Leeds away ticket was snapped up. This trend continued as Leeds began their climb back up to the top of the football ladder, just missing out on the play-offs for promotion back to the Premiership at the end of the 2010–11 season.

Leeds United regularly receive letters from pub landlords and other football clubs praising the behaviour of the United fans who have visited their towns and grounds. In 1986, Alan Roberts, who was the general manager of Leeds United, forwarded me a letter from Mrs Doris Tilly, who was landlady at the Heart in Hand pub in Winchester. It was full of praise for the many Leeds fans who had visited en route to a game at Southampton. 'I have never come across a more polite bunch of people in all my 40 years as a landlady, even though they were a tad noisy,' wrote Mrs Tilly.

Once, when we were travelling to Newcastle, we heard that heavy snow had prevented the fixture going ahead, but we carried on north and stopped off at a pub we had visited on many previous occasions. The landlord at the Kicking Cuddy in Coxhoe welcomed us with open arms, but at three o'clock he informed us that he usually closed at this time. However, he said he would stay open if we ran the bar ourselves. Imagine that – 50 travelling supporters whom he was prepared to trust with his livelihood. Needless to say, we put two of our lads behind the bar and ran the pub until the landlord returned two hours later. Not only was the till in order, there was a small bonus, in the way of a generous collection for the landlord.

Of course, the vast majority of football fans are good people, and other fans will have similar stories to these two examples. But when was the last time Leeds fans ever received praise or recognition from anyone? It's quite the opposite, in fact. Leeds fans are persecuted almost everywhere they go. It is generally accepted that a football fan has almost no human rights – well, a Leeds fan has even fewer.

Leeds United were the first and only club to impose restrictions on their own fans. In 1985, they introduced an Away Card Scheme under which no Leeds fan could gain entry to an away ground unless they had their 'away card' along with their match ticket. Any trouble from a fan would result in the card being revoked and that fan would not be allowed to continue watching Leeds United. That rule is still in force today.

I firmly believe that Leeds United fans are second to none. The vast majority who attend these days have rarely, as I've mentioned, if ever, seen United lift a trophy. This, for me, makes them even more special. (Fourteen-year-old Danny Dovey, with his dad, Mark, is one of those special fans, as are eleven-year-old Matt Handley and his dad, Alex, and Richard Seymour and his son Tom.) I've seen Leeds win many trophies over the years and for this I owe United a huge debt. They gave me the best memories of my life and for that reason alone I will continue following the Whites for as long as I live.

Unfortunately, however, Leeds fans, unlike other supporters, are condemned wherever they go. In 1971, in the wake of the so-called pitch invasion after Ray Tinkler allowed that infamous offside goal to West Brom, Elland Road was shut down and Leeds United had to play the first four home games of the following season away. Never before or since has such a punishment been handed out. The 'invasion' had consisted of no more than half a dozen irate spectators, most of whom were clearly drawing their pensions. There is a much-publicised image of a Leeds fan, easily in his mid-to-late 60s, that is shown on TV whenever this incident is mentioned; he was about 5 ft 6 in. and wearing a suit and tie while being escorted from the pitch by two burly police officers.

Yet when Leeds played at Carlisle United in the Johnstone Paint Trophy semi-final in 2009, the home fans were absolutely unbelievable. The match went to a penalty shootout and throughout this lasers were shone in the eyes of the Leeds players taking their penalties by the fans behind the goal, while Leeds keeper Casper Ankergren was pelted with missiles. Unsurprisingly, Leeds lost the shootout. Then, as the players left the field, Carlisle fans invaded the pitch and three Leeds players were attacked.

There was an FA inquiry but no further action was taken, despite overwhelming TV evidence in Leeds' favour. Carlisle Football Club played down and almost dismissed the incident, with managing director John Nixon even praising the police, claiming, 'Things were handled in textbook fashion.' TV footage shows otherwise. The Cumbria police were more concerned with containing the Leeds fans (who were housed high up in a corner stand and nowhere near the front) than with preventing the Leeds players being attacked.

Mark Pannone, Chief of Cumbria Police, said, 'The policing and stewarding were conducted in a restrained and professional matter.' Unbelievably, the only people arrested on the night were a handful of Leeds fans who remonstrated with police outside the ground over the lack of protection to their players.

The fans of Millwall Football Club have a famous motto: 'No one likes us, we don't care.' Unfortunately, when it comes to hatred, vindictiveness, resentment and victimisation aimed at a club and its fans, nothing on this earth comes close to what is directed at Leeds United Football Club and its supporters. And just as the Carlisle club defended their hooligans, Millwall do exactly the same. In 1993, Millwall played their last ever game at the Den. After the game, fans ripped out the seats and hurled them at the directors' box, carved up the pitch and trashed the goalposts. Apparently, they were protesting at the closure of the 83-year-old ground. Yet Millwall Football Club saw this as normal. Chief executive Graham Hortop said, 'What we saw was supporters looking for souvenirs, and not a riot. Whole generations have watched the club at that stadium and wanted a souvenir. It was their way of delivering the last rites on the ground.'

When Leeds were defeated in the play-offs at the new Den in 2009, 200 Millwall fans invaded the pitch, accosting the Leeds keeper and pelting him with missiles. Despite these same fans rioting at Hull City two months before, the FA took no action. And once again, Millwall turned a blind eye, manager Kenny Hackett playing down the pitch invasion against Leeds, saying, 'There were one or two on. It was a couple of kids and very minimal.'

The FA took no action against Millwall when their fans waved hundreds of Turkish flags at Leeds fans in 2011 in reference to the murders of two Leeds fans in Istanbul in 2000.

Leeds supporters had to endure constant abuse at Cardiff City in 2002. United were there to contest the third round of the FA Cup. On paper, it was a tricky tie, but one that the Yorkshire side should have negotiated to their advantage. Leeds, of course, were in the Premiership then; Cardiff were in League One.

Tensions were high between the rival fans before and during the game, but they rose to fever pitch when the Cardiff chairman, Lebanese businessman Sam Hammam, began walking around the pitch doing his famous 'Ayatollah' head-patting and taunting the Leeds fans. Sensing the anger from the Leeds fans, the police and stewards advised Hammam to refrain from such antics and remove himself from the scene. But as he headed towards the tunnel, he kept returning to the pitch side and repeating his head-patting while looking over at the Leeds fans.

The blue touchpaper had been lit, but it erupted when Cardiff scored what proved to be the winner in the 86th minute. Then, when the final whistle blew, hundreds of Cardiff fans invaded the pitch and headed straight across to the Leeds end. The police and stewards were powerless to do anything about it and an uneasy stand-off between the rival fans lasted for around 15 to 20 minutes. When the Leeds fans were finally escorted from the ground, the police turned on them. I have witnessed police brutality at football matches all over Europe and the world, but this was the first time I had seen scenes like this, especially on this scale, in Britain.

I saw one officer assault a Leeds fan whose son was crying and screaming at the officer. I complained to the officer in question, who snapped at me, 'Fuck off! You English shouldn't be here in the first place!' Then I, along with several others, witnessed police officers covering the numbers on the shoulders of their uniforms before launching an attack on helpless Leeds fans. One fan was mauled by two police dogs as he stood near his coach and was so badly injured that he later received substantial damages.

I felt compelled to report this to the authorities, and I received this reply from South Wales Police:

> Further to our telephone conversation on Wednesday, 13 February 2002, may I apologise on behalf of the South Wales Police following your visit to Cardiff on 6 January 2002. Behaviour of the kind you have outlined in your letter is totally unacceptable, even more so when coming from a police officer. Whilst I am sure that you will appreciate that officers are under considerable stress it is no excuse for the type of behaviour you experienced. In order that there is no reoccurrence of such behaviour I will personally speak with the Inspectors in charge of the officers deployed in the areas that you have mentioned. This will be reinforced during the training of officers for duty of this nature.

Thank you for bringing the matter to the attention of South Wales Police and once again my apologies for the occurrence.

Yours sincerely,

Stuart J. Twigg

Detective Chief Inspector

Specialist Operations Task Force

One afternoon in April 2011, Glynn Snodin, Leeds' assistant manager, told me that every player who comes to United, even those on loan, is completely bowled over by the massive support. 'They've all heard about it from other players, but when they arrive and witness it for themselves, they can't believe it!' he said.

One of those players was Andy Hughes, a Mancunian. When he left Leeds to join Scunthorpe United in January 2011, he told the *Yorkshire Evening Post*:

> Playing in front of the Leeds fans – home and away – made me feel so lucky and honoured . . . in the good times – and the bad times. They are honest fans and if you give 100 per cent they are happy with that. The day we got promoted to the Championship in 2010 we initially went down to 10 men and suddenly 38,000 Leeds fans became our 11th man and helped us through the game – there's no doubt about that whatsoever. They are immense.

As mentioned, Leeds fans come from far and wide. Andy Starmore from Bournemouth works for the *Dorset Echo* newspaper and is a massive Leeds United supporter and author of a recent book called *We Are Leeds*, which looks at Leeds fans from all over the world:

> I've been a Leeds supporter all my life and I'm incredibly proud of that. I'm proud of the club, its history, the people of the city of Leeds and most importantly the supporters across the world who follow the club like no other. They really are a special breed. We really are a special breed. It doesn't matter where you go, you'll always see the famous white shirt walking down the high street somewhere. Leeds fans are everywhere – Singapore, Sydney, New York, Tokyo, Azerbaijan, Oslo (all of Scandinavia), Malta,

Holland, practically anywhere else in Europe, Zimbabwe, Brazil, Argentina and countless other nations around the globe.

Every Leeds away ticket allocation is sold out within hours. Some clubs change their kick-off times or even switch their home fixture against us to a midweek night in an attempt to reduce the number of travelling fans to their neck of the woods. It never works. I was at Plymouth in 2006 when Argyle had decided to switch their game against us to a Tuesday night. However, 3,500 vociferous white shirts descended on Home Park for a vocal night to remember. It was the same at Bournemouth, Bristol, Yeovil and many others.

Even when England had been playing at the same time as Leeds during the League One days, the Leeds attendance wasn't affected one jot. Some Leeds fans travel hundreds and sometimes thousands of miles to a Leeds 'home' game, like, to name but a few, Satoshi Tamura from Japan, John Mallinson from New Zealand, John Thompson-Mills from Australia, Andy Burniston from Azerbaijan, Hilary Attard from Malta, and Sven Anders Karson Moum from Norway.

Why do Leeds have such a fantastic fan base? I have two theories. First, we all owe a colossal debt of gratitude to the late, great Don Revie who transformed the city of Leeds from a traditional rugby city to a city where football was put firmly on the world map. Secondly, the people of Leeds have a unique passion running through their veins. Once you've tasted it, it will stay with you forever. Once you're a Leeds fan, as so many supporters have told me, you're hooked. On 16 April 2011, I introduced my two little boys, Russell (9) and Harry (7), to the cauldron that is Elland Road for the 2–2 draw with Watford. They were gobsmacked by the whole occasion and I can confirm that they are both now well and truly hooked.

At their first game, my two sons were introduced to something else – dodgy refereeing! Heading towards the final whistle in that Watford game, Snodgrass crossed the ball only for it be charged down by a blatant handball, right in front of the Kop and, more importantly, the referee and linesman. The Kop immediately broke into, 'Shit refs, we only get shit refs!' Injusticeto s aplenty – welcome to the world of Leeds United, boys!

219

Even some Leeds-based United fans never cease to be amazed by the vast following that the club enjoys, week in, week out. One fan spoke to me after that Watford match and said how he admired us because we'd driven up from Bournemouth for an hour and half of football. His journey to the ground is a five-minute walk. I think I can speak for any fan that doesn't live in Leeds when I say that as soon as you see the first sign on the motorway for Leeds, there is a buzz that suddenly encapsulates your whole body. It's time to switch the car radio off and replace it with 'Marching on Together'. It's the mixing with other Leeds fans before and after the game, the whole Elland Road experience and the adrenalin rush that invariably kicks in at 3 p.m. on a Saturday afternoon that make it so special.

Not all players will have that same feeling of passion for their club. For the majority of players, it's a job and that's it, but, as far as Leeds players are concerned, they never fail to acknowledge the incredible support that greets them from the terraces. It's always the first thing a player mentions when he puts pen to paper to join the Elland Road party. 'It's a massive club with a massive fan base' is the usual response to the question, 'Why did you decide to come to Leeds?'

The Premier League has clearly missed Leeds. It was a devastating experience when we all watched in horror as Bolton Wanderers hammered the final nail into our Premier League coffin in 2004. But travelling to new grounds, the Leeds fans never wavered for a second. Despite our ironic chant of 'We're not famous any more', Leeds is the very first fixture opposing fans look for, with sell-out crowds everywhere.

And the typical Yorkshire wit is never far away, like the time when the floodlights failed at Portsmouth in January 2011. During the ensuing blackout and in reference to Portsmouth's crippling debts (which Leeds fans know about only too well), the Leeds supporters responded with a spontaneous chant of 'Pay up, Pompey, Pompey, pay up!'

We as Leeds fans truly have, as our anthem says, 'had our ups and downs'. But whether Leeds have been playing AC Milan in the Champions League at the San Siro or being bundled out of the FA Cup by non-league Histon on a miserable cold and wet

Sunday afternoon, Leeds fans will always will be there.

Wives, girlfriends and partners cannot give you a lifetime guarantee that they will still mean as much to you if you live to be in your 80s and 90s as they did when you first met. Leeds United can. Once the hook has grabbed you, there's no getting off it. That hook may have given you and me many heartaches over the years, frustrations beyond belief and feelings of 'Why on earth do I bother with that shower?' Those moments are all part and parcel of being a Leeds United supporter and are well worth putting up with when we all finally do get some reward for being so loyal – a bit of success. The downs are usually spectacularly disastrous, making the ups euphoric memories to cherish forever. I like that hook. It's a terrific hook!

Eric Carlile, the former secretary of the Leeds United Supporters Club, still talks as passionately about the team now as he did when he went to his first Leeds match in 1943 – a friendly against York City during the Second World War. He became secretary in 1948 and only retired when he had held that post for 50 years. Eric is now 82 – rock-solid proof that Leeds United Football Club never leaves you.

Trevor Cusack from Waterford is just one of the many thousands of Leeds fans who regularly cross the Irish Sea to watch their heroes:

If following Leeds United is a drug, then I'm happily an addict. My love for Leeds United for the past 39 years has steadily grown, and it won't cease.

I have made regular visits to my beloved Elland Road since I was 15 years old, and those early trips hold my fondest memories. Pre-mobile phones, pre-email, etc., you had to take your chances when you set off that you would meet someone at the station who would be going across to Leeds too. As I said, I was only a teenager and when I think now what I put my parents through, I shudder. However, I did bring my dad over to Leeds a couple of years ago for a couple of games and he then understood perfectly what I was doing.

Times have changed over the years, but one thing remains – Leeds United. It's a way of life, nothing more, nothing less. I'm often asked by people back home when I'm about to make my next trip, 'Is it worth it?' The answer is, and always will be, the same – 'Damn right it is! M.O.T.'

Let's now hear from a local Leeds fan about his deep-rooted love of a great club and a great football manager. Mick Hewitt is the secretary of the South Kirkby branch of the Leeds United Supporters Club:

As a young man, the first Don Revie influence I had was the superstitions. In 1969, walking down to the pick-up point for our home coach departure for the game against Liverpool, I started to cross the road when a bread delivery van came from nowhere and I just made it to the other side. Leeds had won all the previous six home league games but only managed a 1–1 draw that day. I put one and one together and realised that if I ever crossed in the same place again and saw a bread van Leeds wouldn't win. I never crossed that road again.

When queuing overnight for a 1970 FA Cup final replay ticket at Elland Road, a group of us climbed the fence and had a football game on the pitch. One floodlight was on, I suppose for the people outside in the queue. I scored a penalty that night with a busted ball. That would have been the highlight of my evening, but I found one of Don Revie's discarded cigar butts in the home dugout from the Manchester City game that same afternoon. It remains in my collection to this day, along with a Gary Sprake chewing gum wrapper and a dossier on Stoke City done for Don by Syd Owen before a match in 1970–71.

I had the privilege of meeting Don and Elsie on a few occasions, but the first time was by chance. I had gone to a pre-season friendly against Bradford City at the start of the 1973–74 season and I was loitering by the players' entrance very early doors waiting for the match programmes to be brought out. As they arrived and I made my purchase, Don came out and started talking to me and a few others. After signing the programme, Don said, 'We will go one better this season and win the league.' A man true to his word. God bless Don Revie.

Revielogue

'The apprentices are now the masters' declared the *Daily Mirror* on the morning of Tuesday, 29 April 1969. The night before, Leeds United had claimed their first-ever league championship title with a 0–0 draw at Anfield. Two days later, they beat Nottingham Forest at Elland Road to be crowned champions with a record 67 points. They had been beaten only twice all season. In the *Mirror*, Derek Wallis wrote:

> The long, arduous and sometimes frustrating years of apprenticeship are over . . . Leeds United are masters, the new Kings of English football . . . at last. Like true champions, they finally won the title that has escaped them for four years on the ground of their nearest challengers.
>
> Don Revie, the master tactician who last night achieved his greatest ambition, is so superstitious that the only forecast anyone is likely to extract from him is that Tuesday will always follow Monday. Yet nine months ago, before a ball had been kicked this season, the Leeds United manager made a statement so prophetic that he should now be qualified as a contributor to Old Moore's Almanack. He revealed that he intended his team to be more adventurous away from Elland Road, that an injection of boldness might be the secret of success.
>
> Revie said, 'I intend to let the players off the leash and let them go.' And then the prophecy. 'We feel this could give us the edge we need to lift the major trophies.'
>
> This season has proved beyond doubt that Leeds, a young, inexperienced team when Revie took over, have now flowered into the greatest team in England. Leeds took football by storm in their first season back in the First Division (1964–65), finishing

runners-up in both the League and the FA Cup.

Since then no team has been able to compare with them for consistency. Rigid discipline and tactical awareness are still very much part of the approach but now Leeds are more flamboyant, more gifted in the field of entertainment.

They are still not fully appreciated because the dour defence of the early years in the First Division left a mark that even this season's change of tactics has failed to erase.

There has been no doubt in my mind for two seasons though that Leeds United are the best equipped of all English teams for the traps, tensions and special demands of the competition they will now enter, the European Cup.

They might still lack another scoring forward to support Mick Jones. All other compartments of the team contain if not complete players, men who are so well versed in tactics and discipline that better players would not necessarily bring any improvement.

I believe that Don Revie will try to buy a new forward for next season with the European Cup and the defence of the league title in mind. Some might think it a little early to be talking in terms of next season within hours of the club's peak achievement. But the Leeds motto might well be it is never too early to think ahead.

Such thinking is one reason why Leeds United are so successful.

The following season, Don Revie paid Leicester City a then record transfer fee of £165,000 for their talented young striker Allan Clarke. Clarke told me:

There is no doubt that the Gaffer was the best manager I ever played for, and I've had some pretty good ones along the way, like Sir Alf Ramsey, for example. When I first arrived at Leeds I was the 'new kid on the block' and the 'most expensive player in Britain' and it took me a while to be accepted into the ranks, but once I was, I was one of them. I used to room with Billy Bremner. What a player and what a man. When Billy died in 1997, I was absolutely devastated and there is not a day goes by even now that I don't think about him.

In 1970, Bremner, the inspirational captain, told the *Yorkshire Evening Post*:

> I owe everything to the Gaffer, everything. I ran back home to
> Stirling on numerous occasions, I just wasn't happy or settling in
> Leeds. But the Gaffer wouldn't give up on me; he called at our
> family home many times, often in the dead of night, which wasn't
> a very clever thing to do, especially in the Raploch area where I
> grew up. But he persisted and eventually persuaded my girlfriend
> Vicky to move to Leeds, where we later married, and the rest, as
> they say, is history.

After one of the most successful careers in football ever, Bremner
went into management. 'Once I had played all those years for Leeds
United, my next ambition was to manage them. Thankfully, I managed
that,' said Bremner in 1989.

But first he cut his managerial teeth at Doncaster Rovers in the late
'70s, where two future Leeds stars played: Glynn and Ian Snodin.
Glynn told me:

> Billy was a hero to the Donny players, a true hero. I considered
> him to be my second dad. He always had time to talk out any
> problems and was definitely a 'hands on' man-manager. He was
> constantly talking of Leeds United and Don Revie's 'never say
> die' attitude. Billy's competitive edge ran throughout the whole
> team.
>
> Every Friday, we would play six-a-side and Billy would bring
> half a dozen or so boxes of Milk Tray for the winners of each
> game. It was only a box of chocolates, but we would kick fuck out
> of each other to win it. In an unlikely kind of way, it instilled a
> will-to-win-at-all-costs mentality that was transferred to the
> pitch the next day. Don't get me wrong, we wouldn't go out and
> break an opposing player's leg, but we would look after each other.
> Bremner had told us that's what Don Revie demanded, and that's
> what Billy demanded from us.

This fighting spirit of Bremner's is confirmed by Brendan Ormsby,
who was his captain at Leeds United:

I was at Aston Villa and soon after winning the European Cup in 1982 I found myself in the reserves. Mervyn Day had arrived at Aston Villa from West Ham and later left us to go to Leeds United. He told me from there that Billy Bremner, then the manager at Leeds, wanted to sign me. I couldn't wait to sign for what I still considered to be a great club. But I then heard that Leeds had signed another defender, David Rennie, and I thought my chance had gone. But Mervyn assured me that I was wanted too to play alongside Rennie.

During my medical at Leeds, in which I must have visited every hospital in Yorkshire, I stayed at Mervyn's home in Bramhope, on the outskirts of Leeds. It seemed to take absolutely ages for my transfer to go through and when it did I drove home to the wife in Birmingham to tell her the good news. The thing is, us footballers are used to just getting on a coach and getting off when we get to wherever we are going. I had no idea where I was going as I was driving. I ended up in Leicester and had to ring the wife to get me home.

I was absolutely chuffed to bits at signing for a great club like Leeds United, and I have to say that Billy Bremner turned out to be everything that I had heard. He was a legend. He would talk to the players and we would hang on every word he said. After almost every game we would have half an hour in the dressing-room and he would tell us about his playing days at Leeds and in particular Don Revie, and you could have heard a pin drop. He said that Revie had instilled a never-say-die attitude, which he then passed on to us.

Whenever I was injured, Billy would get me to have a cortisone injection. He would say, 'I would sooner have you with one leg than someone who isn't as good as you.' For a man such as Billy Bremner to have that much faith in you was unbelievable. Billy, even when he was manager at Leeds, was by far the best player at the club. We would play five-a-side and Billy would play – and never gave quarter. Ian Baird always fancied his chances against Billy, but always came out second.

Billy was a true gentleman. He inherited Don Revie's perfectionism, and, just like Revie, he hated to lose. You hear stories about Alex Ferguson throwing tea cups in anger, but that was nothing compared to Bremner when he was angry. Whenever we lost, he would not speak to the press until the Monday because he was so angry.

Peter Haddock was one of the nicest guys you could wish to meet. He hardly ever said a word and he was a terrific player, but he always played with one eye shut. I always said that if he played with both eyes open, he would have played for England. Anyway, one afternoon we were losing at Elland Road and Billy wasn't happy. We all sat there in silence as he came into the dressing-room and slammed the door behind him. There was a table full of cups of boiling hot tea. Billy just came in, put his arm on the table and swiped away every cup that was there. Every drop of hot tea landed on Peter Haddock, and he never said a word.

Centre-half Jack Charlton has said:

I remained a one-club man throughout my career and learned so much from Don Revie, which I also carried with me into my own days as a manager many years later.

One thing he did insist on was that everything we did, we did first class. When we travelled round the world, or whatever, and when we came back, we'd be on the best buses and we'd be on the best trains. If the directors had the best seats on the train then we had them as well. And if we stayed in hotels, we stayed in good hotels. Don was extremely good at that. And if he made you a promise, he would always keep it. He never broke a promise. He would always fulfil it.

Relating to the chronic lack of credit given to Don Revie, even these days, Charlton has commented:

I don't care about public acclaim or perceptions of Revie. His achievements on the pitch were the proof of the pudding. We knew what we were doing when we were winning games and that was all that mattered. He was terrific.

When I finished playing and went for the manager's job at Middlesbrough, Don gave me a list. When I got to meet the board at Ayresome Park, I handed them the list, which contained all the things that I would be responsible for. I told them that if they didn't agree with all of it, I wouldn't become their manager. I had to leave the room for 20 minutes whilst they discussed it. When they called me back in they told me that I would have total control of the football side of things and gave me the job there and then.

Despite his obvious loyalty to Don Revie, Jack Charlton has always remained his own man with his own opinions. Hours after the historic World Cup final victory over West Germany in 1966, Charlton left the celebration banquet in Kensington and dragged a journalist, Jim Mossop from the *Sunday Express*, with him. 'I've only got 15 quid,' protested Mossop. 'It's OK, I've got 100,' replied Big Jack. Not that he needed it. He was recognised everywhere he went and wasn't allowed to buy a single drink all evening. When Charlton woke up the next morning, he was sat in someone's garden in Walthamstow with the sun blazing down on him. He arrived back at the hotel at noon. His manager, Alf Ramsey, and his mother, Cissie, had been worried sick as his bed hadn't been slept in. 'No need to worry,' said Jack, and produced a card from his top pocket that read, 'This body is to be returned to Room 508, Royal Garden Hotel.'

Moments after Chelsea had miraculously managed to draw 2–2 with Leeds in the FA Cup final at Wembley, Big Jack was inconsolable. Chelsea had been murdered by a rampant Leeds side, yet they only scraped a draw. When Big Jack was told to go and get his medal, he said, 'Tell them to stick it,' and went down the tunnel. As he sat in the dressing-room with Don Revie, who simply said, 'We go again next year,' the Chelsea players could be heard in the adjoining dressing-room, singing, 'We won the Cup!' Charlton slammed his fists on the wall, screaming, 'You lucky set of bastards!'

After such disappointments as the Chelsea final, Don Revie would always rally his troops, with a 'We'll show them next season' or 'There's always next year'. Peter Lorimer confirms this:

When we went for the treble of the league, FA Cup and European Cup in 1970, we came agonisingly close, but lost the lot. Revie simply said afterwards, 'OK, we go again next season.' Which we did.

The remarkable aspect of Revie's time at Elland Road was not simply the empire he left behind, but the mess he started out with. In 14 years, Revie created a dynasty in the truest sense of the word. Without that era, Leeds United would not be the club they are today. No manager has replicated his success and many barren years followed his tenure, but the one unwavering constant is reputation – since he laid the foundations with such brilliance, Leeds United have commanded attention and respect. Many people hate us, of that I'm well aware, but it's better to be hated than insignificant. That was one of the many lessons I learned from Revie. This, after all, is the naked truth – many people hated Revie, just as they hated me and all my teammates at Elland Road. 'Dirty Leeds', as we were charitably known. Even now, half a century after his revolution began, there's a reluctance in many quarters of football to acknowledge Revie as the genius he was in the field of coaching and management.

It's quite pathetic, but not at all surprising. That attitude was born and bred many years ago. In my view, the basic problem was jealousy. Our critics were jealous of our success and our refusal to buckle. Whether they care to admit it, the sports editors who ran the national newspapers in London despised Don. They wanted him to fall flat on his face. As far as I could tell, they saw Leeds United as a jumped-up club from the North who were walking all over teams from the capital. Leeds were the dog's bollocks and for several years no one could touch us. We made it perfectly clear to the men who attacked us in print that we didn't give a damn what they thought.

I've always found that there is a clear distinction between the public's perception of the Revie era and the feelings of the professionals who played the game at the time. The vast majority had total respect for us, just as we did them. We gave a game to teams who wanted a game and we fought with those who wanted a fight, but there was usually a sense of mutual appreciation. The sniping came from the stands and, more often than not, the press-box.

I was a young kid when Revie signed me and I wouldn't have gone to Leeds from Scotland without his persistence, his charm and his personality. Don't forget, at the time he was asking my parents to send me down to a yo-yo club, a club who'd won nothing of any significance. At the same time, as a 14 year old I was wanted by 26 of the top clubs in England and Scotland, from Old Trafford to Ibrox.

My move to Leeds was nothing to do with money and everything to do with persuasion. Revie sold the club to my mum and dad in a way that made them believe I'd be in the best possible hands. To be fair, it was quite an achievement. You might have looked at me joining Leeds United as a strange decision.

Don invested time and energy in you and he filled the role of father figure. I think he accepted that, having brought you to England, the responsibility for looking after you ultimately fell to him. You see a lot of kids drift into the wilderness these days, but Don would never have allowed that to happen. In his eyes, he'd have done a disservice to you, your family and his club by allowing you to rot. I often wonder if people fully grasp the excellence of what Revie did at Elland Road – pulling together a small group of kids and moulding them over time into one of the best sides this country and Europe has ever seen.

Don's strategy wasn't down to spending big bucks; it came down to picking up the best youngsters from far and wide and trusting them to the end. I think I can say that good enough was old enough when it came to our gaffer. I'm biased, of course, but I don't understand how anyone could look at Don's reign with anything other than admiration. Praise for him outside our city is always so grudging. Yet again, in the week of the 50th anniversary of his appointment, we saw slander and insinuations about bribery and match-fixing – allegations thrown at Revie time and time again but never once proven by anyone.

I'll make two points about this. Firstly, if match-fixing had been part of the strategy at Leeds, don't you think players like me would have known or at the very least had serious suspicions? I never once saw anything to suggest that it went on, except when it was at our expense. It's pretty much accepted that in both the European Cup-Winners' Cup final 1973 and the European Cup final 1975 we were the victims of bent referees. On two of the biggest nights of our careers, we suffered from match-fixing, and yet Revie's the one with the finger pointed at him? It's a smear on his reputation and totally outrageous. I don't pay much attention to some of the nonsense talked about him, but these accusations step way beyond the mark. Would Revie care? To be honest, I'm not sure that he would. I mean this genuinely when I say that everything we achieved in that era was driven by a desire to bring honour to the club and pride to the city. We succeeded on both fronts, and the long-standing loyalty of the people of Leeds to its only football club was born in the days of Revie.

That relationship still exists and was never more obvious than during our years in League One. Yes, the travelling thousands went to watch football; but first and foremost, they went to follow Leeds. To me, Revie's greatest legacy was not the trophies but the soul he gave our unique club. It wouldn't matter to him that people in other parts of the country denigrate him. It wouldn't upset him in the slightest. The only thing that would grieve him deeply would be hearing that the city of Leeds felt the same. It was his heartland and this is where opinions matter. The only place he wanted to be revered was in his own back yard.

I'm delighted to say that 50 years on from his first day as manager, his legend is stronger than ever.

Eddie Gray was another young Scot in whom Don Revie and his scouts saw great potential:

My parents were very impressed by what the Gaffer had to say and how he sold the club to them, guaranteeing the best for their son. Remember, in those days no one had heard of Leeds United. I was wanted by a host of top clubs at the time and I had even been for a successful trial at Arsenal, but I didn't like it there – it was Don Revie's whole manner that was influential in my coming to Elland Road. Everyone now knows how he built the club from virtually nothing to one of the most feared sides in Europe for a decade.

Revie was famous for looking after his squad players just as much as his first-teamers. Rod Johnson made his Leeds United debut on the same day as Norman Hunter and Paul Reaney and scored in a 2–0 win in September 1962. Johnson says:

The one thing that always made an impression on me about the Gaffer was his meticulous attention to detail and how he treated everyone at the club as equal. While I was an apprentice, he walked past me one day and looked at me as I was sweeping the home dressing-room. 'See me in my office at twelve,' he said, looking at me really closely. 'I'm a goner,' I thought as I walked into his office later, fully expecting him to terminate my contract for whatever reason. The Gaffer told me to sit down and once again started looking at me real close. 'You feeling OK?' he said to me. 'Do you feel all right?' I told him that I felt OK, but he thought I looked off colour.

He told me to go see Cyril Williamson, who was in charge of the youngsters, and get an egg mixed with sherry from him. I was then ordered to take a steak home from the club every night for two weeks. In those days, big juicy steaks were scarce, and my dad loved it. After a fortnight, when the steaks stopped coming, he told me, 'Make yourself look ill again – those steaks are bloody lovely!'

Apprentices used to have to sweep everything from the terraces to the dressing-rooms in those days. One day I was sweeping under the seats in the West Stand when I reached under one of the seats with my brush and I pulled towards me a wallet. It was absolutely stuffed with money. I took it to Mr Williamson, who then handed it to Don Revie.

This was in the early '60s and that amount of money was an absolute fortune. It turned out to belong to a Leeds butcher. The money in the wallet was his week's takings. Unfortunately, the butcher wasn't as charitable as young Rod Johnson and never even acknowledged the return of his wallet, let alone rewarded him. 'I didn't expect a reward,' Johnson said. 'It just seemed the right thing to do for the club.' But Don Revie found out that the butcher hadn't thanked his young apprentice for his honesty and was disappointed. He once again called Johnson to his office, where he gave him ten pounds from his own pocket. 'Ten pounds in those days,' says Johnson, 'was worth at least two weeks' wages to an apprentice. For me, it was just a demonstration of how the Gaffer rewarded people for acts of loyalty.'

Mike O'Grady agrees:

Don Revie was by far the best manager I ever played for. And that includes the great Bill Shankly, who I played under at Huddersfield Town. Revie was meticulous on detail, right throughout the club, from the players, coaches and staff to the wives or girlfriends.

Nigel Davey was a member of Don Revie's squad for ten years. Although a reserve full-back at Leeds, he could have gone to almost any other club in the country and straight into their first team, but he stayed loyal to Revie before moving to Rotherham in 1974. When left-back Terry Cooper broke his leg at Stoke City in April 1972, it would have seemed to pave the way to a first-team introduction for Davey, but fate conspired against him as he too broke his leg on the very same day, towards the end of a reserve game against West Brom. However, the first person to visit Davey in hospital was Don Revie. Davey remembered:

> I was chatting on the ward with various other injured footballers from local games when the Boss walked in to see how I was doing. He looked around and said, 'I'll get you into a private ward, you'll be much more comfortable.' I told him I was perfectly happy staying on that ward with the other lads and not to bother. The next time the Boss came to see me, he handed me an envelope with a good few hundred pounds in it and said, 'Here you go, Nigel, this is what it would have cost for a private ward. As soon as you're right, you and the missus get yourselves off on a holiday.' He was such a top man and cared deeply about everyone connected with the club from top to bottom.

Don Revie was aware of every single aspect of running a successful football club and knew the importance of a good playing surface. To that end, he enlisted Ray Hardy to become his head groundsman in 1966. Hardy says, 'Mr Revie rang me and told me that to have a world-class team he had to have a world-class pitch. Would I join them as their groundsman? There was never any hesitation.'

Hardy, who had been on York City's playing staff, was an expert in everything connected with turf. He was the secretary of the West Yorkshire National Association of Groundsmen and also won the Brain of the Year award for the theory and practice of groundsman's craft in 1968. Hardy's duties, however, didn't just consist of looking after the grass. In 1967, he wrote, 'The ground is ready for the Sunderland match. The new concrete has set in the Lowfields Road side. The barriers have been painted. A total of 3,300 extra seats are now available. New bulbs that will shed 59,600 watts have been placed on the four floodlighting pylons.'

Hardy recalls:

> Don Revie planned everything to perfection. On more than one occasion, I slept at Elland Road, having worked on the pitch all evening and needing to be there first thing on match day. One night, I had to enlist an army of volunteers, and I bought 110 portions of fish and chips. That was for a game where we had to lay straw on the pitch because of the threat of snow.

Hardy was assisted by his team of groundsmen, Cecil Burrows and John Reynolds. It was John Reynolds who took over as head groundsman in 1974 when Hardy retired to Cleethorpes. Reynolds was on the playing staff at Leeds United after arriving from south Wales with John Charles in 1952. He converted from a full-back to a striker and many have said he was a very gifted young footballer. But when he was only 19 years old, in 1955, Reynolds suffered a cruciate ligament injury against West Brom and never played again. Reynolds says of Don Revie:

> He was unbelievable. He made everyone, and I mean everyone, at the club feel special. He would arrive at the ground early in the morning and his first port of call would be us groundsmen. He would then go and have a chat with the laundry staff before he went to the players. He was a shrewd man, but what a man.

Kathleen Smith was part of that laundry staff, with Ivy Kaye. Mrs Smith says, 'We washed the all white kit every time it had been used. Even if it was only for a photo call.' Mrs Kaye remembers, 'It wasn't just confined to washing. We had to darn [Gary Sprake's] gloves. And there was more darn than glove come May.'

'Don Revie was such a special man to us,' says Mrs Smith. 'He

looked after us and our family and treated us like royalty, he really did.'
Mrs Kaye adds, 'He was one in a million.'

Cyril Partridge was the assistant trainer to Les Cocker and just one
of his duties was to prepare the boots. He recalls:

> Back then in the late 1960s, the boots were around £9 a pair and
> almost always came from Germany. Slim, light, durable and fitted
> with screw-in studs. The studs were changed according to the
> conditions and it could take as long as two hours to change the
> studs for the entire team. Not all footballers then wanted modern
> boots, though. Don Revie always kept an old pair in his locker,
> and he would not have them thrown away under any
> circumstances.
>
> Bobby Collins always insisted on boots with hammer-in studs.
> We used to have to file them according to his taste and the
> conditions. He'd like them shorter on one side than the other.
> When we had finished, he would walk round in them and suggest
> alterations. Don Revie always insisted that the players'
> recommendations were met.
>
> Obviously, the boots varied in size, for example Jack Charlton's
> were a size ten and Billy Bremner's were a size six. Peter Lorimer
> had a pair with part of the uppers finished in a nylon cloth that
> wouldn't tear or rip. The players would leave the final choice to
> Les Cocker and Syd Owen. For an away match, the cobbling
> equipment would include a hammer, two files, three pairs of
> pliers, two pairs of cutters, a knife and two or three old biscuit tins
> filled with assorted studs and washers.

It's obvious that one of Don Revie's many admirable attributes was
his attention to detail. 'I don't want to just build a great team,' said
Revie in February 1964. 'I want to build a great squad and a great
club.'

Bibliography

Bagchi, Rob, and Paul Rogerson, *The Unforgiven*, Aurum Press, 2002

Endeacott, Robert, and Graham Carver, *Fanthology*, Relish Books, 2004

Giles, John, *A Football Man*, Hodder & Stoughton, 2010

Glanville, Brian, *Champions of Europe*, Guinness Publishing, 1991

Hardaker, Alan, *Hardaker of the League*, Pelham Books, 1977

Harris Norman, *The Charlton Brothers*, Stanley Paul Books, 1971

Jarred, Martin, and Malcolm Macdonald, *Leeds United: A Complete Record*, Breedon Books, 1996

Lorimer, Peter, and Phil Rostron, *Peter Lorimer: Leeds and Scotland Hero*, Mainstream Publishing, 2002

Moore, Brian, *World of Soccer*, Artus Publishing, 1976

Mourant, Andrew, *Don Revie: Portrait of a Footballing Enigma*, Mainstream Publishing, 1990

O'Leary, David, *Leeds United on Trial*, Little, Brown, 2002

Revie, Don, *Soccer's Happy Wanderer*, Museum Press, 1955

Revie, Don, et al., *The Leeds United Book of Football*, Souvenir Press, 1969

Revie, Don, et al., *The Leeds United Book of Football No. 2*, Souvenir Press, 1970

Ridsdale, Peter, *Boardroom Truths About the Beautiful Game*, Macmillan, 2007

Sprake, Stuart, and Tim Johnson, *Careless Hands: The Forgotten Truth of Gary Sprake*, Tempus, 2006

Starmore, Andy, *We Are Leeds*, Breedon Books, 2009

Sutcliffe, Richard, *Revie: Revered and Reviled*, Great Northern Books, 2010

Thomas, Clive, *By the Book*, Willow Books, 1984

Tomas, Jason, *The Leeds United Story*, Brown Books, 1971

Thornton Eric, *Leeds United and Don Revie*, Hale Books, 1970